T0313078

Endorsements

"Gautam opens our eyes to the significant role played by value, value creation and value destruction in our business and personal lives. You will inevitably do things differently and better after reading this book."

Philip Kotler, S. C. Johnson Distinguished Professor of International Marketing, Kellogg School of Management, Northwestern University

"In order to Create Value for customers, one must first Create Value for the providers, including employees, suppliers, the society at large, etc. 'The goal is to improve the quality of life, such that the well-being of human actors is continuously improved.' These are the credos guiding this book, expressed by Gautam Mahajan for the development and management of Value. In the book, ways of implementing these thoughts are discussed. This is an important and educating book about Value and how to Create Value. I enjoyed reading the book."

Christian Gronroos, Professor Emeritus, Hanken School of Economics, Finland

"Value Dominant Logic certainly clarifies the concept of Value, the need for it to be the dominant thought in all that a good corporation or organisation should be strategising about. [It] was very readable. An excellent new contribution to the whole debate on and the need for Value being predominant."

Arvind Pande, former Chairman and CEO of the Steel Authority of India

"One of the biggest myths today is that technological advances cause disruption. The reality is that the so-called disruptors just find better ways of creating value by making our lives easier and more fulfilling.

This, however, is just one of many aspects of value dealt with in this comprehensive book on the topic.

I have met and worked with Gautam Mahajan and am an avid reader of all his posts on the topic of value, so it was with great joy that I discovered that he had collected together all his knowledge and experience on the topic in this wonderful book.

Gautam is a world authority on every aspect of value and this book is filled with his wisdom. What is remarkable, however, is that unlike so many books, his is an easy and highly enjoyable read to boot."

Professor Malcolm McDonald MA (Oxon)
MSc PhD DLitt DSc, Emeritus Professor,
Cranfield University School of Management

"This book provides and paints a much-needed broad and rich canvas in relation to a vital issue for the 21st Century – value creation. The book will provide thinkers and practitioners with considerable food for thought and is a provocation to debate. It uses a variety of useful layouts and diagrams in order to make its insightful points and managers and directors will glean many valuable ideas for practice in this timely work."

Professor Peter Stokes (PhD MBA PGCertRDS
PGCertTLHE Cert Coach BA (Hons)
Snr FEMRBI (Vice-President/Country Director),
AGRH (UK Ambassador) FHEA FRSA FCMI),
Leicester Castle Business School, De Montfort
University, UK

"If value creation is at the core of your strategy, this book is a must-read. I particularly like the perspective and in-depth discussion of value creation for key stakeholders, including customers, employees, partner, shareholders and society-at-large. It is a beautiful book, I love it!"

Dr Jochen Wirtz, Professor of Marketing and Vice-Dean
Graduate Studies, NUS Business School, National
University of Singapore

Mr Gautam Mahajan is a Value Creator Thought Leader and has written an exciting and informative new book, Value Dominant Logic (VDL):

How do you describe a man who is branded as *Mr. Customer Value* and a maven in his field of expertise that encompasses all that stands for Value Creation? He is definitely not a man you can define in a few words. He is the A-to-Z of Value Creation and the true Custodian of Customers.

I had the pleasure of meeting Gautam Mahajan around 2015 at a Direct Marketing Association India event in Mumbai. We sought each other out after an exciting panel discussion and my first observations was that he is focused, inspiring, motivated, dedicated, quiet but determined and has the knowledge and experience on how to create customer value. The emphasis on *Customer,* who is the centre of our business Universe and our Economy.

I'm an avid reader of his writings, be it books, blogs, articles or white papers and am impressed with the clear and simplistic writing style he uses in sharing his invaluable knowledge on this complex subject.

I have been aware, for many years, that our customers suffer from an affliction called 'Value Starvation'. And his new book *Value Dominant Logic* (VDL) has answered it by explaining with varied industry examples, step-by-step and chapter-by-chapter, how to find value and pay it forward to all those that touches our lives.

Gautam is a man that leans into value and pays attention to when and where it should be created – and how. He believes in *'every touchpoint becomes a potential brand-building activity and potential point of activation and retention'.* In VDL he shows that value is not a once of 'gift', but co-created by all involved in their circle of convenience and accessibility. It forms part of the journey we walk with our customers and the experiences we – or they – create with us.

There is no clear definition of value. Value can be defined in many ways and across many actions and interactions. Value is all about micro-moments that transforms *'companies to focus on creating value for their customers by aligning each person's role in creating the value customers so desperately look for and getting shareholder wealth and value'.*

VDL clarifies many of the uncertainties of what real value represents. It is different for different people and within their different circumstances. Value is directly linked to peoples' experiences throughout their journeys.

Gautam recognises that customers reward companies with their loyalty and time, increased business, market share and share of wallet and profitability. Understanding and implementing Value Programs is a customer value investment that needs to be budgeted for and seeks a handsome return.

With his solutions-driven personality and sharer of knowledge and experiences, I believe VDL will be a disruptor and distractor – with technology to match – to the complacency of many marketers in this 'cross-device' world.

Gautam is an acclaimed author of many books on value creation, VDL is an excellent addition to his already well-read collection of books.

Thanks for sharing your time and knowledge with us, Gautam. I wish you well with converting many new and informed value creators from reading and studying Value Dominant Logic.

May it find a place of prominence in every library – personal or business – around the world. A Value waiting to happen."

Winnifred Knight, Managing Director and
Owner – CUBE [ON THE SQUARE] Pty Ltd
and TheMarketingSite, Trainer/Mentor:
Practical Direct, Data and Digital Marketing
Workshops, Train-the-Trainer Workshops,
Consultant and Professional Speaker,
Email: winn@themarketingsite.com

Value as an Interactive, Reciprocal Organisational System

"This book will revolutionise how you think about, consider and employ value no matter your position or role in commercial or human activities. It is a 'must-read' for any and everyone involved in any type of commercial organisation.

Value has traditionally been defined vary narrowly, i.e., the creation of worth by one person or party for another, often viewed through a financial lens. Mahajan, in this wide-ranging text, shows that Value comes in many forms, impacts and influences for many participants and is a key element in all human interactions related to the firm. Value is not just a marketing term or technique, instead it is a holistic, integrated way of thinking about all human relationships and inter-actions which means it influences and impacts all levels of the organisation. In this example-laden text, Value is not a 'thing' but an interactive system that can be created or destroyed by all participants. It is communication and behaviourally based, reciprocal and ever changing."

Don E. Schultz, PhD
Professor Emeritus (In Service)
Medill School of Journalism-Media-Integrated Marketing Communications
Northwestern University

"Creating Value incorporates many important concepts, including customer service and the thought process of how people can add value to not only customers, but bosses, fellow employees and more."

Shep Hyken, customer service/experience
expert and New York Times bestselling
author of *The Amazement Revolution*

I often say that, in terms of the evolving role of business in society, we are in the decade of value creation – of rethinking what we mean by value, how we measure value and to what extent we are collectively creating or destroying value. Hence, Gautam Mahajan's book, Value Dominant Logic, could not have come at a better time. By building on his long experience with foundation concepts like customer value, Mahajan casts the net broader and finds that value creation is a helpful lens for other spheres of business and life – whether it be Prof. Freeman's concept of stakeholder value or my own notion of integrated value. The book also provides compelling evidence for what I call the 'values dividend', which is the extensive value that is created for society when individuals, communities, companies and governments use self-transcendent (non-selfish) values as their guide for action. At a time when value destruction is still so pervasive in politics and economics, Value Dominant Logic may be the very catalyst we need to turn the tide.

Dr Wayne Visser, Professor of Integrated
Value and Chair in Sustainable Transformation
at Antwerp Management School

Value Dominant Logic

Helping Individuals and Their Companies to Succeed

by Gautam Mahajan

CRC Press
Taylor & Francis Group
Boca Raton London New York

CRC Press is an imprint of the
Taylor & Francis Group, an **informa** business

First edition published in 2019
by Routledge/Productivity Press
52 Vanderbilt Avenue, 11th Floor New York, NY 10017

2 Park Square, Milton Park, Abingdon, Oxon OX14 4RN, UK

Routledge/Productivity Press is an imprint of Taylor & Francis Group, an Informa business

No claim to original U.S. Government works

Printed on acid-free paper

International Standard Book Number-13: 978-0-367-03057-5 (Hardback)

International Standard Book Number-13: 978-0-367-03058-2 (eBook)

Typeset in AGaramond
by Integra Software Services Pvt. Ltd.

Visit the Taylor & Francis Web site at
http://www.taylorandfrancis.com

and the CRC Press Web site at
http://www.crcpress.com

Contents

Preface

Value Dominant Logic is important for all of us, because it tells us how to succeed and do everything better. This book will assist you in creating more Value for yourself as an individual or as an institution.

All of us (including individuals and companies) wish to Create Value for ourselves. But many of us are unable to achieve our real Value potential, because we are not trained to have a Value mindset, and the focus is on the ends (profit, success) instead of the means (Value creation).

This book goes on to the next level to show how Value is basic to human endeavour and life. Most Value creation/destruction is done unconsciously. With this book, Value creation will become a conscious process so that you can create more Value and destroy less Value.

Value Dominant Logic has great appeal for individuals, academics, businesses and social/government institutions. Students at all levels can benefit from this book, because it teaches them how to Create Value and become successful.

The book discusses Value and disruption; Value, dilemmas and decision-making; Value, technology and society; Value and education; Value waiting to happen and the nuances of Value, with real-life examples of Value creation.

Acknowledgement

Many friends and associates, especially at the First Global Conference on Creating Value in May 2018 in the UK, and among others Prof. Peter Stokes of Leicester Castle Business School encouraged me to write this book because they all saw its Value to others. I acknowledge and dedicate this book to Peter, my other friends and my family for their support and encouragement.

About the Author

Gautam Mahajan, President of Customer Value Foundation is the leading global thought leader in Total Customer Value Management and Value Creation. He mentors the global Creating Value Alliance, CreatingValue.co and is Founding Editor of the Journal of Creating Value, jcv.sagepub.com

Mr. Mahajan worked for a Fortune 50 company in the USA for 17 years and has hands-on experience in development of leaders, CEOs and executives; and in consulting for numerous MNCs (such as Alcoa, Continental Can, DuPont, GE, GTE, ITC, Reynolds, Rexham, Schmalbach, Sealed Air, Tatas, Birlas, Godrej, Azelis, Toyo Seikan, Viag, and Solvay).

He is the author of *Customer Value Investment: Formula for Sustained Business Success, Total Customer Value Management: Transforming Business Thinking, Value Creation: The Definitive Guide for Business Leaders, and How Creating Value Makes You a Great Executive.*

Gautam was President of the Indo-American Chamber of Commerce; Chairman of the US India Economic Relations Forum; Chairman, PlastIndia Committee; Vice President, All India Plastics Manufacturers Association; and Trustee, Plastics Institute of America. He was a member of the US India think tank. Among his honors is a Fellowship from Harvard Business School and Illinois Institute of Technology. He also has 18 US patents. Commercial examples of his patents include noise-control kits and plastic beverage bottle bases. He was honored by the Illinois Institute of Technology with its Distinguished Alumni award in 2001. He is a sought-after speaker and has spoken around the world, including to CEOs. He also lectures and conducts workshops on creating value (for yourself, for customers), value and pricing, strategy and business development.

He has started a program to create entrepreneurs at the Bottom of the Pyramid. Mr. Mahajan is a graduate of IIT Madras, where he was an Institute Merit Scholar; has a Master's degree in Mechanics from the Illinois Institute of Technology; and an MBA from Suffolk University. He is happy to discuss value creation with readers at gautam.mahajan@gmail.com.

Value Dominant Logic (VDL): Introduction

This book will make you superstars by contemplating what you really are and want to be; understanding what Value is and how you can Create Value for yourself and others because while creating Value for others, you end up co-creating greater Value for yourself. In this process you become aware of what is happening around you, noticing Value around you and Value waiting to happen; and how you can create more Value. This book will change your thinking and that will make you create greater Value. The central theme of this book is that Value is of importance to you, and your ecosystem, including business. This book is about understanding and creating Value to become more prosperous and successful and become a better executive, manager and leader; a better person and a better human.

> Value Creation is the essence of humankind — Amnon Danzig: From Enigma to Paradigm

By giving examples, it is meant to instil in you a Value creation mindset and think about how you can Create Value. It is meant to make the invisible work of Value creation visible.

Value is inherent in you and responsible for making you noteworthy. Most people are not truly conscious about Value and creating Value. VDL makes you more conscious about creating Value and induces you to create more of it. Successful people Create Value, and those who wish to become successful must create more Value. This book

> Carl Jung stated: "Unless you make the unconscious conscious, it will direct your life, and you will call it fate."

> Fewer business concepts are more prominent than value, a word used imprecisely, and a concept not really practiced as a science.

provides you with ideas on doing this, and how not to unconsciously destroy Value or starve people and customers of Value.

VDL makes Value creation by and for you easy because you need to make a simple change in your thinking and mindset. It builds on what you already know to perform better and become more valuable to others. Our normal concentration is on either the goal (as in the case of a CEO seeking higher returns for his business), or just doing our job, or just being functional, or just working mechanically, without understanding what a powerful notion Value creation is or could be for you and your business and society. (A simple example is an accountant who does his job well and you, as his boss, have no complaints and are happy with him. Another accountant performs similarly but goes beyond his job to tell you what you should do as Brexit becomes a reality. The second accountant is creating Value for you.)

VDL is a way of thinking that makes Value dominant in your daily life and in making a new future for you.

Value Creation[1] is executing proactive, conscious, inspired or imaginative and even normal actions that increase the overall good and well-being and the worth of ideas, goods, services, people or institutions including society, and all stakeholders (like employees, customers, partners, shareholders and society), and ideas and Value waiting to happen. That is why our parents teach us to be good kids and to do good. But this is soon overtaken by the goal of making a living, of being successful.[2]

Value and Value creation are words used by most of you. All of you play in the Value creation/destruction arena, but few understand they are in the game, and even fewer are conscious that they are creating or destroying Value.

The book describes Value Dominant Logic (VDL), a concept that encompasses all aspects of human endeavour and happiness and even touches Value in inanimate objects (such as products you sell). VDL goes beyond just Value

---

[1] Mahajan (2016) Value Creation, Sage.

[2] Other definitions abound such as:

Eric Beinhocker in The Origin of Wealth defines the creation of economic value, based upon the work of the Economist Georgescu-Roegen:

A pattern of matter, energy and/or information has economic value if the following three conditions are jointly met:

1. Irreversibility: All value-creating economic transformations and transactions are thermodynamically irreversible.
2. Entropy: All value-creating economic transformations and transactions reduce entropy locally within the economic system, while increasing entropy globally.
3. Fitness: All value-creating economic transformations and transactions produce artefacts and/or actions that are fit for human purposes.

creation to helping you (and businesses) understand and define the Value potential in you and others and objects around you and understand yourself to become a winner. VDL mirrors the real world and life.

Just stop for a moment. Is your son looking for Value from you or just an inheritance? Is your employee looking for Value or just a salary? Your customer for a price or for Value? Your stakeholder for just short-term wealth or long-term Value? Is the society or your state or your government looking for funds you can provide (i.e. taxes)? Or are they looking for the Value you (or they) can bring to the community? The answer should always be Value! You must read this book to understand why.

Value creation[3] (and I include Value starvation[4] and destruction in this) is a universal phenomenon. In business it is often considered to be the result of what businesses do, and Value creation is profit or wealth creation for shareholders. But the leaders and the company have to Create Value first for other stakeholders (not just owners, but also for employees, partners, customers and society) to create higher Value for themselves and a Value stream (a sequence of Value-adding activities that achieve a specific result that is of Value to a stakeholder). Many Create Value for others so as to create more Value for themselves.

Leaders and businessmen Create Value and are recognised as Value creators as they move upwards in the corporate (and governmental and non-governmental) ladder or in the political system. Sometimes Value is created for one actor (person or institution) by destroying Value for others (just cheating and being corrupt destroys Value in of itself, but also destroys Value for others for whom opportunity is lost, or because they are wrongly treated. An example is poor people, who are not well treated in government offices). Schools and business schools teach us (and businesses expect us) to be good efficient administrators doing a good job (defined by the company or the school), but not to be Value creators, to Create Value as a goal, to Create Value consciously, and to destroy less Value.

Therefore, we have to understand what Value means. Value is doing something that is good or improves well-being; and worthwhile, or more importantly what others consider worthwhile.

Jonathan Wells[5] says adding Value to others is like making a bank deposit, and you get payback in the form of interest with your capital safe.

John Maxwell states:[6]

---

[3] Creation and co-creation are used interchangeably in this book. One can argue everything is co-created.

[4] Value starvation is a word coined by Winn Knight.

[5] Jonathan Wells, 7 Simple Steps.

[6] https://www.success.com/article/john-maxwell-success-or-significance

> I know a lot of people who believe they are successful because they have everything they want. They have added Value to themselves. But I believe significance comes when you add Value to others – and you can't have true success without significance.

Leadership also requires similar traits: The bottom line in leadership isn't how far we advance ourselves, but how far we advance others.

So, I ask why (and you should also ask why) it takes Citibank Cards three months to refund my overpayment, and why I cannot get to a grievance officer or a senior officer? Or in general, why I cannot reach an officer of consequence who can help me, and why I have to listen to high-tech words like chatbots and AI to help customers. Value is far from their thinking. Why are companies asking us to keep away; I can communicate with you, but you cannot with me.

VDL tells you about innate and latent Value, Value that is waiting to happen. How this potential Value is shaped by many to create further Value, and how this Value can be shared or co-created, how this Value has to be perceived for it to become usable Value, and how Value can die over a period of time for some and grow for others. Sometimes Value just dies, and often disruption causes Value to disappear for some while appearing for others. Just think of driverless cars, as an example of Value waiting to happen 10 years ago, and now it is happening.

Apart from helping you create enormous Value, I also want people to know of missed opportunities by ignoring or not seeing Value around them or their opportunities to Create Value, the power of Value creation. As people learn to become aware of Value around them, they will create more Value. I want schools and colleges and innovators to think of themselves as Value creators and incorporate Value creation into their thinking and curriculum, and their students. Let them think of a Bachelor's or Master's in Value Creation degree. We want business and society leaders and government leaders and politicians to think of Value creation not only for themselves but for others and their nations and society.

We want Value creation to be treated as an important topic, and to be taught and practiced to make this a better world.

Wayne Visser, Professor of Integrated Value and Chair in Sustainable Transformation at Antwerp Management School, says about Value[7]:

> Value creation is so fundamental to our human belief systems that we intuitively feel that it is a worthy, if not an imperative goal, whether in our personal and family lives, our careers and institutions, or our communities and societies. It is in fact one of our most powerful

---

[7] https://www.csrjobs.nl/csr/integrated-value/

myths (by which I mean meta-narratives or guiding ideas rather than lies or deceptions). Creating something worthwhile or better – something of Value – is the professed, if not the actual aspiration of almost everyone.

A dominant logic is a fundamental and underlying belief and a common way of thinking about how businesses, society, governments and their components create and can Create Value. VDL builds a Value ecosystem.

Thus, it is strategic to think about Value and the fact that it is a fundamental belief and aspiration of human beings, businesses, institutions, society and governments. The notion of happiness as the ultimate end or highest Value has hardly been disputed (Walker and Kavdzija[8]).

Hence VDL.

In fact, Value creation is the goal of most dominant logics that include Service Logic, Service Dominant Logic,[9] Customer Dominant Logic, Customer Value Dominant Logic and so on.

Value Dominant Logic is used to build a framework for understanding and using Value. This is described in this book.

Lastly Values are different from the Value we discussed earlier, and Values Create Value. Values are the moral and ethical thinking that forms the culture of a company and our own beliefs.

We wish to impact educational institutes and start Value Creation Centres. These will help the constituents research and build Value. We have also started a Creating Value Alliance (creatingvalue.co). It might lead to more Chief Value Creation Officers to encompass Chief Happiness officers, Chief Customer Officers and the like.

Join me in this interesting journey about yourself. Discover yourself and your Value potential, create more Value for yourself and others and find out how this creates greater Value for you (when others recognize you as a Value creator and valuable). See how it changes your life and businesses positively and leads to higher success.

This Book

The book covers different aspects of Value, and how they impact you, business, society, technology, innovation and creativity, education; and when and where it exists, how it can be increased, how it is destroyed and dissipated, and how it can

---

[8] https://www.haujournal.org/index.php/hau/article/view/hau3.002/2096
[9] We recognise the importance and primacy of Service Dominant Logic (SDL). This book supplements SDL teachings.

re-emerge. Thus, we discuss these topics to explain what they are and how VDL impacts them. We have given enough references for readers who wish to learn more about the details. Practicing the principles of VDL can help you create more Value.

The book includes the Principles of Value Creation, and as a subset, the Principles of Customer Value Creation. It also has the Principles of Flexible Management required in today's fast-moving world. The book also describes the 6As that make executives and people successful.

Covered in this book are sections on Value and Business, Value and disruption, Value and dilemmas, technology, innovation and sustainability, the nuances of Value, Value waiting to happen and Value emerging.

The reader will observe how Value Creation is of prime importance and is encouraged to think of how they could Create Value in their sphere of influence.

Some sections in this book are taken from my previous writings because they are effective in understanding Value and Value Creation.[10]

---

[10] Some portions of this work have been drawn from the books, The Value Imperative © 2019 and How Creating Customer Value Can Make you a Great Executive, by Gautam Mahajan, published by Business Expert Press. EISBN 9781948976855; Print ISBN: 9781948976848. Per the author's contract with Business Expert Press, the author has permission from Business Expert Press to repurpose this material in this Work.

Some sections in this book are being reproduced with permission from my earlier books, titled Value Creation (ISBN: 9789351508977, 2016) and Total Customer Value Management (ISBN: 9788132103127, 2010) both published by SAGE Publications Pvt Ltd under the imprint SAGE Response. For more information on these topics, please look up the SAGE website and refer to these books.

Chapter 1

Value Dominant Logic

We start this chapter, by looking at what Value Dominant Logic is, and the eight principles of VDL. We follow these with a commentary on VDL. We want the reader to not only understand Value but to ask how they could Create Value using the ideas and examples in this book.[1] VDL thinking runs through the entire book.

Value Dominant Logic is the fundamental thinking on Value, why and how it is created. Value is a dominant logic because it is basic to humans, and all their actions and endeavours. All dominant logics such as SDL (Service Dominant Logic), Service Logic (SL), CDL (Customer Dominant Logic) and CVDL (Customer Value Dominant Logic) want the creation of Value as their ultimate goal. Mostly, they focus on the process of creating (or co-creating) Value, be it through service, customers, goods or the like, and less on the end result, that is Value itself.

Value goes beyond the business world into creating happiness and good for, and improving the well-being of people.

Jim Spohrer, in his preface to Service-Dominant Logic,[2] comments that the market is a quest of human actors for well-being in an ever-changing context (I might add that companies are human actors though they pretend not to be). In other words, people seek Value (good, well-being). The quest to improve the quality of life is fundamental.

This book talks about Value and its creation.

---

[1] Mahajan, G., Value Imperative: Business Expert Press, 2018; parts of this section are used as author has the rights to do so.

[2] Lusch, R. F., & Vargo, S. L. (2014). Service-Dominant Logic. Cambridge University Press.

The Principles of Value Dominant Logic

These principles were first enunciated in my book, *Value Creation: the Definitive Guide for Business Leaders.*

The Eight Principles of VDL

VDL is in sync with most dominant logics and the VDL principles show how.

Value Creation is executing proactive, conscious, inspired or imaginative and even normal actions that increase the overall good and well-being, and the worth of ideas, goods, services, people or institutions including society, and all stakeholders (like employees, customers, partners, shareholders and society), and ideas and Value waiting to happen.

The First Principle: Value and its creation are a basic requirement or a necessity for sustained human flourishing and the advancement of human activity, behaviour, of caring, of well-being, and progress and creativity. Value and its creation are important in all fields, education and academics, society and government, and social work, innovation, entrepreneurship and business. It impacts humanity and society. It is an essential trait for executives and leaders. It goes beyond the classic business/social ecosystem. It can be latent Value or Value waiting to happen, which when perceived could provide the basis for greater Value. Value can also be enhanced, dissipated or re-emerge over time.

The Second Principle: Value is proactively or naturally exceeding what is basically expected of you or your job. It is going beyond your functional and routine roles to adding and creating Value in your ecosystem. Value creation can be planned or spontaneous, and in both functional and emotional thinking and should be consciously created (today most Value creation is unconscious).

The Third Principle: Just creating Value for yourself is not enough. True Value comes from creating Value for others who turn around and say you are valuable. Value is created for you by others using your potential Value or your potential to see Value (this, in a sense, is the real reason why companies are in the marketplace, because creating Value for customers creates Value for their stakeholders). What is interesting is that such Value is not just the realm of the producer; it is also the realm of the user. Co-creation is where mutual Value is expanded together.

The Fourth Principle: Value and its creation impacts all stakeholders, that is, you, your colleagues, your employees, your partners (supply chain, delivery chain, unions), your company and government and society to create resounding Value for the customer and thereby for the shareholder. Customers tend to buy or use those products or services that they perceive creates greater relative Value (or worth, which is loosely Benefits minus Cost) for them than competitive offers. It is essential for executives and leaders to create and deliver higher Value for their customers than competition can, or does, create.

The Fifth Principle: Value and its creation leverage a person's, or an organization's or an actor's potential, learning, knowledge and creativity while making it meaningful and worthwhile for people and actors to belong and perform, both physically and emotionally.

The Sixth Principle: Value and its creation presents a very powerful decision-making tool for companies to select actions, programmes, strategies and resolutions of dilemmas and choices for individuals and the actors that can increase the actor's longevity (prevention of destruction/disruption) and profitability. An example is how much value to create, and how, and how much value to extract for the company.

The Seventh Principle: Value and its creation must exceed Value destruction or reduce negative Value and be done consciously (not just done unconsciously as is often the case today). You must create more Value than you consume, or else the process will become destructive. The sharing of Value has to be equitable, otherwise Value will be

Important for CEOs and executives:

1. Value thinking is basic to your business.
2. Value goes beyond functional thinking.
3. You have to Create Value for others.
4. Customers buy those products with higher relative Value than competitive ones,
5. Value is important for creativity, decision-making and for disruptive thinking.
6. Therefore have a Value creation culture and mindset.
7. Value creation has to be greater than Value extraction for longevity.
8. Values are essential for success.

destroyed for one or more actors. Often by not being caring, governments and people negate the impact of the Value they are trying to create. Non-Value-adding tasks[3] such as wasted time are Value destroyers. Value starvation, where companies ignore customers, or just do not do enough for them, or make it difficult for them to do business or get solutions to their problems has to be avoided.

Sometimes companies try to extract more Value than they create (for employees, partners, customers and society), and this is destructive.

---

[3] Adam Smith differentiated between productive and non-productive work.

The Eighth Principle: Values (what you stand for, integrity, honesty, fairness, etc.) Create Value. This holds for all actor-to-actor interactions.

Having Values prevents destruction of the type witnessed at Enron by a few people in Enron who flouted Values. Creating a culture of Values is essential for companies to succeed.

What Is Value?

From a practitioner and common-sense point of view, Value is the good, well-being and worth we create for ourselves and others through our actions, beliefs, circumstances and thoughts.

Value creation is a process that is easier to define than Value which is generally intangible, though we try to define and label it as a tangible. Our definition of Value creation is executing normal, proactive, conscious, inspired and imaginative performance of actions that increase the overall good or well-being and the worth of goods, ideas, services or institutions including society, and all stakeholders (like employees, customers, partners, shareholders and society, and ideas waiting to happen). In fact, Value creation is a basic requirement for sustained human flourishing. Value is the balance between the effort (or the sacrifice) and the result (or the benefit), and if Value is positive (that is the perceived effort is less than the perceived result), it is said to be created. If the reverse happens, Value is destroyed. Value is also the benefit one gets versus the cost and is generally seen[4] in a competitive situation, since actors have alternatives. Value being intangible depends on the various actors in the Value ecosystem and their perception of Value. Ralph Badinelli states that Value is transitory, stochastic and multidimensional.

In the non-business sense, if you visit a friend at his house, the interaction creates Value, (either in the form of benefits or the good offset by the effort). For the friend whom you are visiting the Value may be different. Value depends on what is being done

> Think how you can Create Value for a friend, and the Value he adds to you.

or offered and for whom. Value is dynamic and not static and could be ever-changing depending on the context and the circumstances (which includes emotions). Hence concepts like loyalty that are directly linked to Value and Customer Value Added are dynamic. Unfortunately, businesses do not fully understand its dynamic nature.

---

[4] Mahajan, G. (2016). Value Creation. Sage.

Value is fundamental. It is what we are seeking for ourselves and for our ecosystem. Value exists in what we see and in what we do not see. It implies something is good and worthy (or meritorious). Value leads to outcomes, and there is a Value related to the outcome (was it worthwhile, useful, good?) VDL works in spite of the varying nuances of its definition. Value creation is a goal of all the dominant logics we have discussed, and some describe processes for Value creation.

Scott Sampson[5] suggests that Value, or the well-being of a population, or citizens of a country is not related to GDP (the GDP Paradox), nor is it related to income (the Income Paradox). Another paradox is the Labour Paradox that states that unemployed people and employed people with the same incomes have different subjective well-being (SWB) (the unemployed have lower SWB even with the same income). This could be related to lower self-esteem of the unemployed. Related to this is the work paradox, where leisure is pleasure, work is pain. However, SWB is higher for work than leisure.

> You can add value to someone by improving their self-esteem, and making them belong, feel useful and have a sense of ownership.

The Preference Paradox is even more interesting, quoting from Sampson's paper: The Preference Paradox is particularly poignant for individuals who place high value on material goods. Frey and Stutzer suggest that "individuals who prize material goods more highly than other values in life tend to be substantially less happy." They cite research that argues that the production of some luxury goods, such as expensive watches or yachts, is a waste of productive resources, because their net impact on overall happiness is negative. Easterlin goes so far as to suggest that the Preference Paradox may actually explain the Income Paradox:

> Happiness does not depend on wealth. Value can be created in many other ways. Can you think of some ways to Create Value for people?

> Income growth does not, however, cause well-being to rise, either for higher or lower income persons, because it generates equivalent growth in material aspirations, and the negative effect of the latter on subjective well-being undercuts the positive effect of the former.

5 Sampson, S. (2015). Value paradoxes and the time value of value. *Service Science*, 7(3), 149–162.

The Elements of Value

Eric Almquist[6] and others from Bain built the Elements of Value shown in Figure 1.1 (which is reproduced here with permission of Bain and Company). Most businesses play at the bottom of this pyramid. Value mindsets help companies thinking of working towards the top of the pyramid.

> Can we see how greater Value is created as we go towards the top of the Elements of Value pyramid? Create more Value by focusing on the higher needs of people, and less on their lower needs.

Value and Satisfaction

It is surprising that in today's day and age Customer satisfaction is more used than Customer Value. Satisfaction and Customer experience is based on the here and now, and therefore the focus on improving the transactional experience. However, Customer Value is based on the experience and the memory of the experience. Value is based on embedded feelings, and therefore is a better predictor of what customers feel and why they buy. Hence Value measurements should be used. Remember, Value is based on the well-being or subjective well-being of people.

Paraphrasing Sampson,[7] there is direct utility (instantaneous pleasure and pain) and remembered utility (a retrospective collection of pleasure and pain). Direct utility is typically measured by asking about an experience immediately after it,

> Value creators know that remembered utility creates more Value than direct experience.

whereas remembered utility is the SWB (subjective well-being) measured by life satisfaction or value surveys. Remembered utility depends on a sequence of interactions over an extended period of time. Direct utility is therefore transitory, whereas remembered utility tends to be persistent. Customer Value states that the memory of the experience is more lasting than the experience itself (what you remember is more important).

Measuring Value

Value can be measured.

Measurements of Value were proposed by Kordupleski (2004) and called Customer Value Added, (and if focused on employees as Employee Value Added).

---

[6] http://www.bain.com/publications/articles/elements-of-Value-interactive.aspx
[7] Sampson. Sampson: Value Paradoxes, pp. 149–162, ©2015 INFORMS.

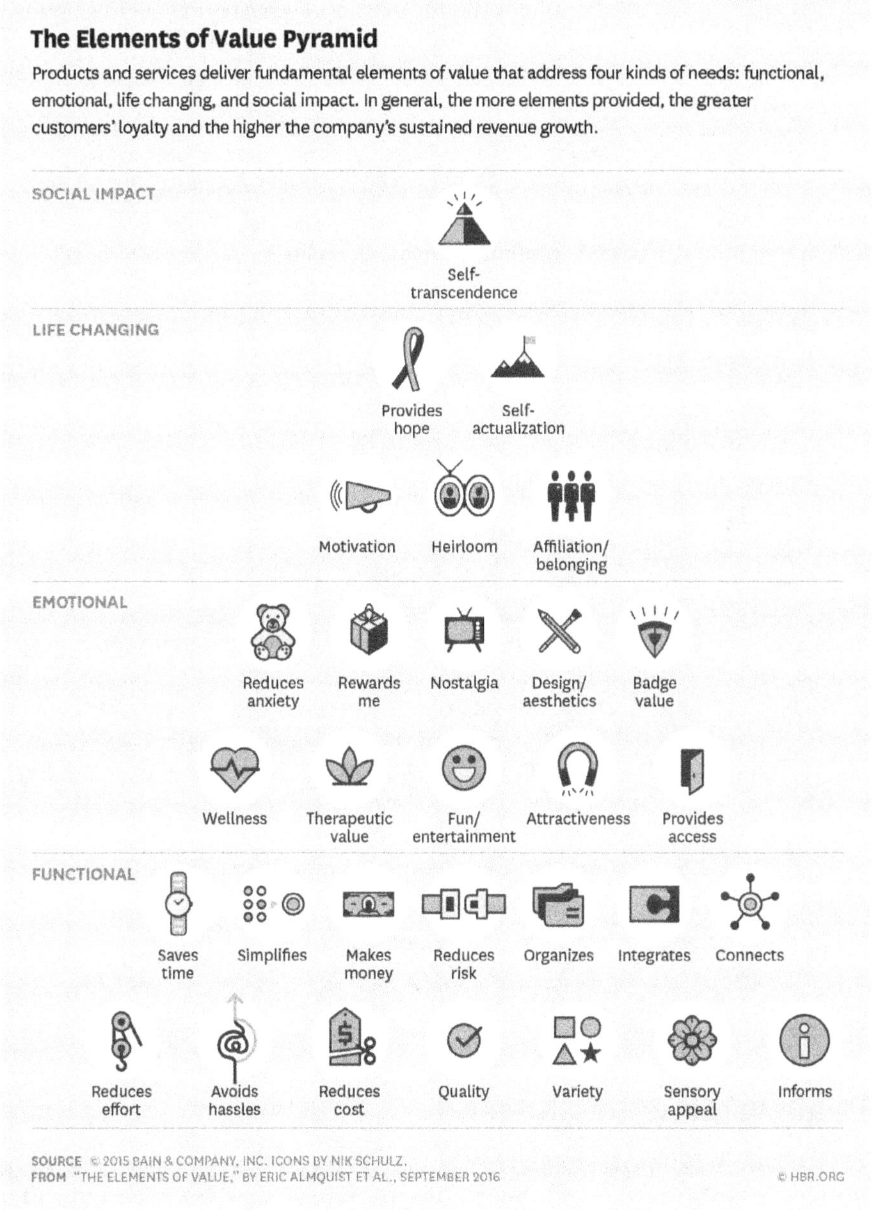

The Elements of Value Pyramid

Products and services deliver fundamental elements of value that address four kinds of needs: functional, emotional, life changing, and social impact. In general, the more elements provided, the greater customers' loyalty and the higher the company's sustained revenue growth.

SOCIAL IMPACT

Self-
transcendence

LIFE CHANGING

Provides   Self-
hope   actualization

Motivation   Heirloom   Affiliation/
belonging

EMOTIONAL

Reduces   Rewards   Nostalgia   Design/   Badge
anxiety   me   aesthetics   value

Wellness   Therapeutic   Fun/   Attractiveness   Provides
value   entertainment   access

FUNCTIONAL

Saves   Simplifies   Makes   Reduces   Organizes   Integrates   Connects
time   money   risk

Reduces   Avoids   Reduces   Quality   Variety   Sensory   Informs
effort   hassles   cost   appeal

Figure 1.1   The Elements of Value

Customer Value Added

$$CVA = \frac{\text{Perceived worth of your offer}}{\text{Perceived worth of competitive offer}}$$

> Avoid Value Deduct and Value Starvation.

Customer Value, and Customer Lifetime Value (the profit motive, and what a firm gains from a customer) are outlined in detail by Kumar and Reinartz (2016). Harish Pant suggested that in many companies we have Customer Value Deduct. Winn Knight states there is Value Starvation.

VDL and Value

We define VDL to encompass nuances of Value as shown below:

Value exists, and can be seen, used by a person (actor) or enhanced by him, it can be shared, it can be exchanged; it can be created (increased) or co-created, and it can be destroyed.

Creation of Value for oneself is self-limiting, unless shared and further created or co-created with others which increases the Value to the original creator of the Value, particularly when the receiver or sharer of Value notices or perceives the Value being provided. This is an important concept, as companies believe that they can create great Value by themselves for customers, without having the customers perceive the Value and grow it either by co-creation or by use or further creation or by communication to others about the Value the firm has created (which is of course modified by the communicator based on the Value he receives and creates or co-creates).

Value in an ecosystem is allocated to various actors, and if unfairly, then Value can be destroyed.

Value can be built for someone while simultaneously being destroyed for others.

Graphically we see how Value is interrelated and there is a Circle of Value, Figure 1.2.

Value Waiting to Happen

We have all heard of the phrase "a disaster waiting to happen". Just as much is the phrase "Value waiting to happen". We just have to look for it, be aware of it and Create Value from Value waiting to happen.

A simple example is the new dating app for businesses. Instead of individuals finding each other on the app, businesses do so. Bumble added this business feature to a more common dating app. The business feature was Value waiting to happen.

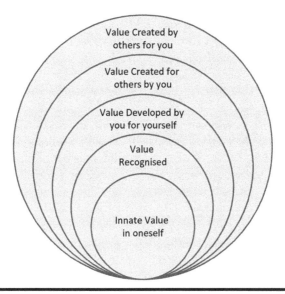

Figure 1.2 Circle of Value Showing How Value Is Interrelated (Copyright Author)

Plant microbial fuel cells that generate electricity by using the electricity found between plants and microorganisms in the soil is an example of Value waiting to happen.

The ability to make plants glow (and be used as a table lamp) by using the plant itself to create electricity is another idea waiting to happen.

> Become aware of Value around you. Can you add value by improving things or helping people Create Value? Learn from Value waiting to happen

Jeff Karp,[8] a bioinspirationalist is someone who is making Value and ideas waiting to happen really happen. He learns from nature (plants, animals, birds etc.) to create products of Value, from porcupine quills inspired surgical staples, using gecko feet adhesive-based bandages for sealing surgical cuts and for developing methods for sealing intestines cut during surgery with an animal-inspired tape.

While research labs dedicated entirely to bioinspiration are rare, Karp's is not the only one. Don Ingber's Wyss Institute at Harvard University, which has been running since 2009, is a bioinspiration factory. There are some 375 full-time staff.

---

[8] https://www.theguardian.com/science/2016/oct/25/bioinspiration-thrilling-new-science-could-transform-medicine

At IIT Guwahati, scientists have created a polymer superhydrophobic coating that mimics lotus leaves and rose petals. Water just runs off, and forms drops. The coating can be modified in situ.

Thus, Value also exists in a larger ecosystem than a classic business/social ecosystem. And it runs the risk of being destroyed by being overtaken by a better product, idea or system. This is shown in Figure 1.3.

> Are you willing to look outside your traditional circle of influence, and see things you were not aware of earlier and instead of thinking out of the box, create a new box? This will help you with a Value-creating mindset.

This thought process is valid for society, for people, for institutions and outside these circles or boundaries.

Take a student, he may have Value potential. He creates some Value for himself by studying alone. His school adds further Value to him. His Value is perceived by an employer, and with him further Value is co-created. If the person gets outdated, or the need for his service is reduced (such as professional drivers who become redundant in a driverless car system), he loses his job and Value is destroyed for him. Later we will examine the Value destruction/creation outside the classic business boundary.

There are times, when the Value remains potential, such as in a painting. When the artist goes to sell it, then it has potential Value in his mind. If Value is recognised and someone buys it, then the potential Value is converted to Value-in-exchange for the artist. Then we have to think of increasing the Value potential, and how is that done? Just by facilitation and Value creation, to improve the potential, (such as showing in an exhibition or adding a frame to the picture and then to make it saleable). If he does not want to sell it, he has still

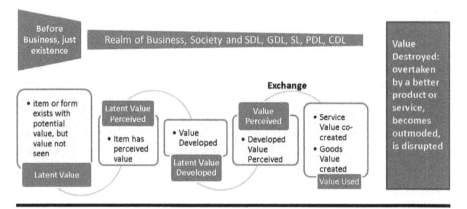

Figure 1.3 The Expanded Value Ecosystem (from the Author). (Latent Value Is Potential Value or Value waiting to happen. Service includes Services and Goods.)

created/destroyed Value for himself, and the exchange has no meaning. The Value potential may still exist in the future.

VDL suggests you must also look outside your ecosystem to prevent the impact of obsolescence and disruption.

An example is desolate-looking land having innate Value to become an orchard or become more valuable if a road goes by it.

The 2006 movie, *Invincible* is the story of Vince Papale, a 30-year-old bartender from South Philadelphia who overcame long odds to play for the NFL's Philadelphia Eagles in 1976. He was Value waiting to happen.

Million Dollar Arm is based on the true story of how sports agent J. B. Bernstein discovered professional pitchers Rinku Singh and Dinesh Patel through a reality show he staged in India with cricket players. Bernstein noticed how similar the game's throwing motion was to that of baseball pitchers and created the reality show *Million Dollar Arm* to audition 40,000 cricket players. Not only did he have to teach Singh and Patel the rules of baseball, but he also had to teach them about American culture and how to speak English. Bernstein's work paid off when the duo became the first Indian players to sign with pro baseball teams when they got contracts with the Pittsburgh Pirates.

In India, the once helpless service people like independent plumbers and electricians who could not afford to own land-line phones can now stay in touch with their customers with mobile phones, do more with their lives and be reached by the customer (sharing their time effectively). This is an example of Value waiting to happen, and did not happen by design, but happened as these people acquired cell phones and became connected.

Audhesh Paswan, Associate Dean of the University of North Texas, talked about the Value creation of Bollywood culture. It exposes India and Indian culture to countries in Asia, Europe, the Middle East and the Americas. People are now learning Bollywood dance.

Had the Indian Foreign Service/Indian Government looked at this as a way of making India known and Indian culture popular, they would have promoted Bollywood into these countries and converted latent Value into real Value years ago, rather than latent Value evolving as a matter of course.

A similar example is the Indian brain drain, which was bemoaned by everyone including the Government, because educated Indians were leaving India (also many of the brain drainers had studied in subsidised government colleges like the Indian Institutes of Technology and the Indian Institutes of Management). I was part of the brain drain. Today, everyone says "wow!" how smart, to allow brain drain. We have Indians around the world contributing in so many different spheres, and becoming recognised. Most send money back to India. Some have become leaders in business, in technology, in entrepreneurship and its funding, in education around the world. Others come back and contribute to India. The latent Value of brain drain was not developed and not harnessed. It just happened.

Getting more out of data is an example of Value waiting to happen. There is oodles and oodles of data and information and knowledge tucked away from years of research, development, unfructified projects, clinical trials and nuggets of information on what to do and what not to do for a particular project or research area. Billions of research dollars have gone into this. As a society we have generated more information and data bases than we could use. Such information is huge compared to our ability to utilise this information into worthwhile action.

An entrepreneur could start to codify and then extract cogent and pertinent information and scientific and technical knowledge for use by others going into the field or requiring this information. That group requiring this information may not have an adequate idea about past work in the field, or the intelligence they can get from such data. A great task for big data experts. Capturing such information can help all fields including medicine, design, technology and manufacturing. The entrepreneur will have to spend energy to find this knowledge and gain Value for himself and clients by utilising the huge sums of money spent in the past, to save research dollars and unnecessary expense.

Randy Guard, Executive Vice President and Chief Marketing Officer for SAS Data Management states that the not-for-profit Project Data Sphere, LLC, an initiative of the CEO Roundtable on Cancer's Life Sciences Consortium is a "free digital library and laboratory that provides a single place for researchers to share, integrate and analyse historical, de-identified patient-level data from academic and industry clinical trials." In fact, anyone interested in cancer research can apply to become an authorised user.

The Project Data Sphere initiative aims to spark innovation and enable the cancer community to unlock the potential of valuable data by generating new insights through analytics and expanding research possibilities.

Project Data Sphere enabled the first-ever crowd-sourced prostate cancer data mining competition. This effort identified new models to predict patient outcomes and has provided doctors with treatment options that help to positively impact patient results.

Project Data Sphere demonstrates the analytics economy in action. Through data sharing and collaboration, insights are compounded to discover more effective treatments.

Value Dominant Logic is all about creating good and improving the well-being of each other as in the Project Data Sphere example.

The first cell-based gene therapy drug (from Novartis) for leukaemia has estimated cost: $475,000, a "whopping price tag" according to Dr Kenneth Thorpe. Based on the benefits, price is not high for the patient given potential remission, and reduced long-term health care costs, an improvement in lifestyle and rewards the manufacturer at the same time.

Dr Thorpe continues, fortunately the drive to create a Value assessment framework has started at Duke University where Director Mark B. McClellan is creating an "Evidence Hub" that will bring together "expertise, best practices, and multiple data sources" to "address key policy questions related to health care delivery, with particular attention to payment reform. Such information will allow patients to understand the cost benefit of high cost drugs and will form a cost-benefit Value assessment."

A new start-up is transferring money from one bank from one country on behalf of their client to his payee in another country's bank at a 0.5% commission. They have removed intermediaries that traditional transfer systems used and therefore demanded higher commissions.

Silicon Valley and venture investors made many ideas waiting to happen really happen. Just the venture capital and entrepreneurial thinking made many Value waiting to happen projects to become productive.

And security systems, to add Value for those seeking security or those seeking to penetrate security. From invisibility solutions to overwritten videos, from molecular keys for locks to... (Let your imagination run wild. See what you'd like to see and ask why it isn't there).

Thus, Value is being created on all fronts.

Disruption and Value Waiting to Happen

Disruption is the waking up of people, becoming aware of latent Value and Value waiting to happen. And when this latent or potential Value is noticed, we call it disruptive technology or innovation.

> Slow death or deep change?
> What will be your choice?
> (Experience Accelerator)

Be aware of potential Value (learn to become aware, because Value exists but it has to be seen, it has to be noticed and appreciated, like beauty). Latent Value has to be nurtured and built into real

> Look for Value around you and start the disruption process.

Value by you. It then has to be shared (or co-created with customers).

You can be a disruptor, too. Look for potential Value. Value is everywhere around you and waiting to happen. You have to notice it and build the latent Value to real Value. You can use any of the techniques above.

Here are examples:

A seed is a plant waiting to happen. Can we learn from the seed system and come up with products that just erupt like seeds or how seeds absorb a large amount of water?

Learning from nature can show us Value waiting to happen, like root systems of trees. A Danish scientist has used technology of roots' ability to detect content in soil to detect mines.

Disasters waiting to happen is another aspect of Value destruction. You just have to look at climate/weather change; or lack of safety (accidents waiting to happen).

Waiting...To Happen! is a book on the tragedy of Air India Express Flight IX812 by Captain Samir (Sam) Kohli[9] provides information on how to detect a carrier's lack of Safety Risk Management and how civil servants and bureaucrats let it happen.

S&P's biggest drop was a selloff waiting to happen[10]

Service waiting to happen is an example of Value waiting to happen:

Every product is a service waiting to happen. Rolls-Royce engines being installed as a service on planes, rather than being sold is an example. Rolls-Royce owns the engines, services and maintains them, and has a revenue model for a fixed fee and a per mile usage charge. The entire worry and risk of the airline on the engine is transferred back to the engine manufacturer.

Another example is FlixBus where Flix has aggregated different buses and drivers, and bus companies by standardising operations, and selling the service on the internet.

Another example of products is service waiting to happen: Instead of owning a car (product) you can use a service like Uber or Zip Car.

Philip Frenzel, an engineering student in Germany designed a phone "air bag" which works when the phone is falling. Value waiting to happen. Almost as good as the flying phone which is now capable of being a drone, which you can get to take your picture, light your path when walking in the night, come to you on demand. These are things people saw as needs and discovered solutions. This is what Value Dominant Logic teaches you and how to tune your thinking to make things happen.

Disruptive ideas, products and services such as driverless or autonomous cars can spur further disruptive thinking. Why cannot these mobile cars become mobile towers for telephone and Wi-Fi systems? Why do we have to rely on stationary towers with high asset costs. With the density of cars, we can have a super mobile system. This is an example of disruption and Value waiting to happen.

VDL and Value Waiting to Happen

Most people think of Value as happening during the course of a business or an activity.

We wish to also look at Value waiting to happen.

1. This can happen when there is a Value potential in goods, services and objects but is not noticed.
2. Or when we start to work on something, Value is potentially waiting to happen.

---

[9] https://www.amazon.in/Waiting-happen-Tragedy-Express-Flight-ebook/dp/B00HGRNN1I
[10] www.bloomberg.com/...rticles/2017-08-17/dip-buyers...

It is important to note that Value has to be noticed, and that we have to become aware of it.

Thus, you could own a property, not knowing there is oil under the property. The Value of the property is not enhanced in your mind. On the other hand, if you are aware of the oil, the Value increases.

The Value of a family heirloom may be high in your mind but not in the mind of others. But if you did not know it was an heirloom, you could have little Value for it.

Two important ideas come out of this:

1. You have to be aware of the Value;
2. Your perception of the Value is what the item is worth to you.

Chasing stars or thinking blue oceans is good, but not good enough. Because in the process we ignore even greater ideas that are all around us, just waiting to happen.

Value is all around us. It is happening, it is being created. It is waiting to happen. We become Value blue oceaners by looking around us and finding Value waiting to happen.

An example is the discovery that ulcers were treatable by antibiotics by the Australian doctor Gerry Marshall who started work in 1981 and discovered gut infections led to peptic ulcers. He was ignored and heckled by gastroenterologists who thought ulcers came from stress, spicy foods and acid. Marshall got a Nobel Prize in 2005 for this. Why did the other doctors not see this?

> Think of how you could Create Value for yourself with driverless cars. Or avionic cars. Will you still have to pick up your kids from school. Would you want your kids traveling alone in an empty car? What control would you like?

He was able to see or became aware of something that existed, but others could not see it. This was Value waiting to happen.

So, we come up with two more thoughts apart from being aware and having a perception, you have to ask why it is not this way or why is it this way? If you want to develop the Value or the idea you have to ask how (be aware and be curious).

An example we can all relate to is driverless cars. Today, we can all imagine or see these cars in our mind, but some years ago, we (or our minds) refused to see them, and so they did not exist. Some who thought of such cars discarded them as impractical. Value was waiting to happen till someone picked up the concept of driverless cars, and why they were important and how to make them happen. Elon Musk asking why cars need drivers and "seeing" driverless cars. Such an obvious Value waiting to happen but none of us saw it. A Value stream then follows, which is a sequence of Value-adding activities that achieve a specific result that is of Value to a stakeholder: New Value, more Value, better Value. Some think Elon Musk wins because of deep-rooted passion, first principles and transformative thought. That too, but also the ability to see Value waiting to happen.

Michelangelo looking at a huge piece of marble and seeing David in it is an example of Value waiting to happen:

Amazon noticing it could sell and put stores on the internet.

Tony Hsieh noticing doing good for customers was good business.

The discoverer of a precious stone called diamond, or gold and discovering its Value.

A teacher discovering the Value and talent in a student.

Selling service rather than selling goods. We have already given you the Rolls Royce engine example.

Sharing cars in the form of rentals was there for long but converting that further into Uber. Now people are getting personal cars to pick up friends and neighbours, if close by (24/7) through an app.

Robert Clive in India trying to Create Value for himself (survival, first and becoming rich later). Instead, he created Value for the East India Company and inordinate wealth and power (Value) for himself.

3D printing, now a $33 billion market, has created Value by de-centralising and re-positioning manufacturing.

A disruption in the medical profession, teledocs, docs on call, telemedicine, teleclinics and the like is happening. Long waiting lines at doctors' offices will be reduced. More time will be available to the patient for useful work.

So, look for Value around you and become aware of Value and its potential, and your potential as a Value creator.

You could Create Value for yourself. You could use your potential Value for your kids and family, for your business and colleagues or for yourself in business.

What Value can you create for your kid? What is he good at, how can you develop that, how can you drop your preconceived notions of what is good or right for him. Can he be a drummer or a tennis star? Are you willing to Create Value for him?

Or at business, you think of a company which you could do business with, but your colleagues don't see it. You grab this Value waiting to happen and run with it.

Or you are a cricketer and discover an unconventional shot that is Value waiting to happen, like the helicopter shot.

Or you are a housewife and start baking and become famous like Cheryl Kumar of Chocolate Log Hut in Dharamsala, India.

Value and You

We have a program to create entrepreneurs at the bottom of the pyramid (BOP), people who don't even know they can be entrepreneurs or even be special, till someone comes along and shows them how. They learn nothing is impossible, and they too can be somebody significant.

Impossible is a word which you use when you aren't able to do something, or when you do not perceive the Value that could ensue, or you do not consider it necessary or do not want to do it..[11] It is a case of the impossible being necessary; and the necessary being impossible! Impossible is something we haven't been able to do before, until it becomes necessary. The fall of the Berlin Wall and Soviet Russia eradicated impossible from my dictionary, because till then I felt it was impossible that those things could happen.

> The necessary is impossible. The impossible is necessary.

The message is to imagine the Value that could happen, and then how you could create some of or all of that Value even if it is seems impossible. Tell yourself it is necessary, and therefore must be done. So many impossible-looking things can happen or should happen: eradication of poverty, equitable education for all, education that is meaningful, providing opportunities for people, driverless cars, the eradication of cancer, of child trafficking, of society before profits, making the human race multi-planetary like Elon Musk is trying to do.

Next time you see Value waiting to happen, think of how it can become possible. Make people's lives easier. Make a difference in people's lives.

"And I'd also say fall in love with the notion that each and every day can be a day filled with personal and professional flourishing. The world needs more people on fire with human flourishing."[12]

Creating Value for Yourself

Value apart from being all around you is also resident in you (this is different from the Values in you that you hold to be important). You first have to recognise the Value in you, latent, inherent or otherwise and figure out your potential. You have to grow this Value and learn to Create Value for yourself. You must first understand how to Create Value for yourself, and proactively want to do so.

To do this you must view Value as a resource, and to look at potential resources you can use. One of these resources is knowledge. Resources can be tangible or intangible.

---

[11] http://fiercegentleman.com/necessity-impossible/
[12] http://fiercegentleman.com/necessity-impossible/

When you start creating Value for yourself, you will soon realise that you can create only so much Value for yourself. To create greater Value for yourself you have to interact with others and Create Value for others. You will learn that this process will co-create greater Value for you through awareness and others (for whom you have created Value) who will Create Value for you.

> Your Value creating mindset will make you think about creating Value for yourself by creating Value for others. Think how?

A great investment for your success is adding Value for others, who will help you later. By adding Value, gain more experience and learn more and become more effective. You learn to seek Value, to recognise it, add and Create Value

Hugh Blaine[13] talks about transformational leaders. Most of us do not have a strategy for ourselves. We need to ask ourselves what we want out of life, out of work and what we Value at work. Is it learning, is it getting recognised, is it being given responsibility, is it a sense of belonging and being part of a group of people, is it the Values of the company, the growth of the company, the reputation of the company, the challenge, the opportunity to achieve, the management, the colleagues, the prospects for advancement and the money? Which are more important? Monetary gains or other monetary advantages such as free courses, travel and an expense report, etc. or is it the other benefits? Are integrity, heart-to-heart connection, and telling the truth important?

What helps you Create Value or destroy Value? It is your thoughts, feelings, beliefs and behaviours. Traits like keeping promises, being nice, praising others, making Value creation a priority for whom and how. Get a Value creation mindset.

We know that from birth as babies we have our self-worth or Value.[14] As babies our interaction with and being exposed to people's comments, attitudes, expectations start changing our notion of our own Value. Our concept of our own Value makes us believe in ourselves and gives us a sense of our capabilities and what we can do with them. We need to grow this sense of Value. It is a natural phenomenon and helps us develop and contribute in society. Building it up again is therefore natural, essential and healthy.

Build up your attitude towards yourself and understand how important this is for you. Have healthy self-love, trust yourself and analyse yourself. This will build your self-image and tell yourself you matter. Learn to forgive others and forgive

---

[13] https://books.google.co.in/books/about/7_Principles_of_Transformational_Leaders.html?id=w0kOvgAACAAJ&source=kp_cover&redir_esc=y

[14] https://centerforparentingeducation.org/library-of-articles/indulgence-Values/Values-matter-using-your-Values-to-raise-caring-responsible-resilient-children-what-are-Values/

yourself. Value yourself, your time, and live in the present. In essence, be positive to yourself and others.

Your perception of your own Value, and the attitude towards this perception (whether realistic or unrealistic) helps you create more or less Value. This is also true of self-belief and self-love, your attitude towards yourself, and whether you can realistically analyse yourself, your development, your future and the Value you can create.

Service Dominant Logic suggests that an actor-centric approach is a Value-centric perspective. In addition, entrepreneurial activities are fundamental to Value creation. Thus, thinking like entrepreneurs helps in Value creation.

Creating Value for yourself is also dependent on the expectations of others and their perception of you and the Value you have in you. Learning to forgive others and yourself helps you also create your self-esteem and self-worth, and a positive self-image of your own Value. In this process, you will notice what creates self-worth and Value of others, your respect for them, their time, their energy, their psychic needs and their self-image can all create or destroy Value for them.[15]

To Create Value for yourself, you can also look at yourself as a brand and how you can improve your brand equity; it could be grooming, it could be your interaction with others. And it depends on the perception of others. When you Create Value for others your brand equity and Value goes up.

Moreover, you have to differentiate yourself. Learn the 6As of Value creation, awareness (including curiosity) ability, attitude, agility, anticipation and ambidextrousness (read multidextrousness). This requires a mindset change.

You need to be genuine (not fake), be consistent, be committed, be a learner and be adaptive. Learn to be generous and gracious, be comfortable with uncertainty (reduce anxiety).

> **Difference between Values and Attitudes**
>
> Our likes and dislikes towards people and things are our attitudes. It may show up in our behaviour and thinking. Attitudes include our likes and dislikes. Attitudes can depend on the circumstances.
>
> Values include our beliefs and morals and are like our guiding principles. Some common values are honesty, integrity, love, compassion, fairness, justice, liberty and freedom.
>
> Values and attitudes vary by culture and religion.

Some people will say think of yourself as a product whose Value you wish to increase. I would say think of yourself as a service (which includes product) and co-create Value for this service. Do you need to get coaching, increase

---

[15] http://advancedlifeskills.com/blog/create-success-by-creating-Value/

skills such as communications, oratory/speaking skills, listening or knowledge? Eventually, as you understand your Value, you will be able to price yourself, always remembering Value is always relative to others (or your competitors). Keep learning and increase your knowledge and 6 A's, attitude, awareness, ability, agility, ambidextrousness, anticipation; and other skills. You will then differentiate yourself and be seen by others as a Value Creator and, as a result, will become successful.

Creating Value for Yourself Means Creating Value for Others

Look at successful people, and people of Value. You will see they are adding Value to others, doing good for others, increasing the well-being or worth of others, giving unto others. These people sometimes do it unintentionally, but the truly successful ones do this consciously. One of the greatest success strategies is creating Value for others. Think of someone who recommends you, or introduces you to an important person, or gives you tickets to a show you love. They are creating Value for you.

Create Value for others, don't worry whether it will Create Value for you or come back to you.

The reverse is also true; many people are adding Value to you and to your life.

Jonathan Wells[16] says when you Create Value for others you become more valuable to them. It is like putting a deposit in a bank and getting returns from it. It also enhances your Value creation as you do it consciously. Creating Value for others is the best investment you can make for yourself. Note the following:

People with high self-Value necessarily Value others.

Valuing others makes our Value increase.

Ask yourself how you can understand and Create Value for others including your clients, make them achieve more and become happier, and help your partners and others in whatever way you can to Create Value for them (doing good, improving their well-being or improving their worth including self-worth).

You can increase your Value to yourself and others through physical and emotional well-being, being good and having Values.

Let me give you some examples. I learnt a lesson when I came back to India after living in the US. I went to a lawyer to discuss a case. I asked him his fees. His response was, I know your family, I cannot charge you. I learnt a lesson because he created Value for me, and I have followed this, by giving to people as much as I can, help, advice etc. free of cost. In return people have come back and helped me when I least expected it, by introducing me to

---

[16] Jonathan Wells, 7 Simple Steps.

others, by promoting me, by helping in my endeavours, both social and business.

Ask yourself, are there people who have helped you unexpectedly? Did you feel good? Can you help or Create Value for others?

Value Starvation

A wonderful concept, introduced by Winn Knight of Marketing Insight, South Africa. Something we do not think about. How starved people are for Value. Your daughter may have a luxurious lifestyle thanks to you but cannot relate to you and does not get the love, regard and recognition she is looking for: She is Value starved.

> Do not starve your customer of Value.

Or your Customers, who cannot reach you when they have a problem or who you keep in a state of anxiety; or do not give them their due.

Here are examples:

- HP sent me an ink cartridge which was leaking (an internet purchase). I wrote to them. They asked me to bring this to their store. Why should I? If I had wanted to go to a store, I would not have bought it on the net. I wrote this to them but got no response. Why are you starving me of Value, HP?
- I overpaid to Citibank by a substantial amount. I just could not get my money back without many steps (no automatic refund; I had to tell them how I had paid, which bank, account number etc., and yet they did not refund it. It took three months to get my money back, and with no interest. Imagine if I owed them money, how much interest they would have charged). They starved me of Value.
- A friend told me about an Uber ride in Delhi for his sister. She had to go to a local railway station and the driver said it was 200 km away. She finally called her brother, who talked to the driver but to no avail. He tried calling Uber, but you cannot call Uber. So, he called the police, and when the driver was told the police had been contacted, he turned around, dropped off my friend's sister and drove away without any payment (in India you can pay with cash). Uber is starving the customer of Value.
- Loic Ple's example of Amazon who would not replace an item till the provider was given a good rating is discussed in Value destruction on page 82.
- The example from Jack Cunningham about Airbnb[17] where he is blacklisted by a host because he complained that the host had walked in on him is a case of Value starvation and destruction.

---

[17] https://medium.com/@jacksoncunningham/digital-exile-how-i-got-banned-for-life-from-airbnb-615434c6eeba

■ Bank of America deducted an amount from my account, but when I finally reached them by phone (it is not possible to reach them by email, and very difficult to find an address to write to) they asked me to call another number. Their reply to my mail was to call the first number that gave me no details. Who cares if a customer is Value starved?

Value, Values and Happiness

Doing good and improving the well-being of people should really be the pursuit of politicians and governments, a goal not always met. Creating Value is a way of creating happiness. The US Constitution talks about the Pursuit of Happiness. Isn't Creating Value a way to build happiness?

> Happiness is not having what you want. It is appreciating what you have.

You do not get happiness by pursuing it. It is a result. You do not gain profits by pursuing it. It is a result of the Value you create.

What is the Value of happiness? Priceless!

Happiness economics define Value as subjective well-being (SWB), and this is measured by surveying people[18] and is the ability to improve SWB or one of its synonyms – happiness, quality of life and life satisfaction.

Jeremy Bentham's utilitarian "science of happiness"[19] was intended to be a means by which governments could measure the expected pleasures and pains (Value) resulting from policy proposals and select those that would produce the greatest net happiness.

Contentment is what makes us happy. Happiness is related to Value and Values or what matters to people. Happiness is a perception and depends on culture, context and circumstances, and of course, the people involved. Is happiness the most important good in every circumstance? In fact, happiness may not be the ultimate good.

> Happiness is when what you think, what you say, and what you do are in harmony.
>
> - Mahatma Gandhi

Is happiness the ultimate need of a person, or does it depend on the many goals a person may have. Different Value we create could create happiness (peacefulness, money stability, good feelings and family).

---

[18] Happiness economics is a subset of economics and positive psychology.

[19] "Bentham's Utilitarianism: A Differential Interpretation". David Lyons, In the interest of the governed: A study in Bentham's philosophy of utility and law, Clarendon Press, 1973, pp. 19–34.

Many items Create Value, and therefore to say one item creates the right Value is not true. Should these different Value and Values be in harmony? This means

> Happiness lies in control of oneself. . .Aristotle

there is no one Value which is the superior Value. Some of these Values[20] may be in conflict, as seen in the Bhagavad Gita. Arjun is told by Krishna to fight and kill his enemies, whom he valued as his family and teachers. Fighting against the enemy was fighting against evil, and to do so he had to kill people he revered or respected. This is a conflict of Values.

Being happy is a great goal, but can we do this by ignoring the lack of sustenance for poor people, which we might ignore to keep our happiness secure? Do Value spheres have to intersect?[21] Should they be independent?

In a crude sense, Value spheres can be drawn for ourselves and our interactions as shown in Figure 1.4.

There are ethical Values which daily may conflict with others, and we are forced to make judgments and prioritise.

Virtues are innate good qualities or morals within people. To get to great Values, virtue is a prerequisite.

John Stuart Mill, a stalwart believer in free markets and liberty, said, "Those only are happy who have their mind fixed on some object other than their own happiness. . .not as a means, but as itself an ideal end. Aiming thus at something else they find happiness by the way."[22]

Deborah Mills-Scofield[23] says happiness is not the same as Value. While it is important to find happiness in life, she says, business is all about Value, not emotion. Business must first and foremost create and deliver real Value to customers (and then to other stakeholders, like shareholders). The way Tony Hsieh has run Zappos is a great example of a "happy" culture. . .which delivers significant Value.

What if that meant creating something truly good, truly valuable, consistently, for someone else? Isn't that what companies should be doing? If they don't, we won't need to worry about happy employees and customers. So, in this 21st century, let's focus our energies, time and resources on providing real and substantial Value.

That is why companies are now employing Chief Happiness Officers.

---

[20] Values are not the plural of Value, but what we stand for.

[21] Each sphere has an orbit of influence and could intersect with, react with or destroy Value in some other sphere. They can be rationalised also where Value evaporates and remains; it could be the conflicting possibilities in religion and business.

[22] https://www.forbes.com/sites/work-in-progress/2011/05/01/happiness-or-Value/#23550b35237e

[23] https://www.forbes.com/sites/work-in-progress/2011/05/01/happiness-or-Value/#23550b35237e

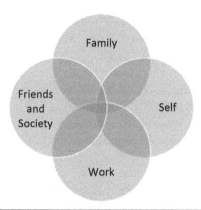

Figure 1.4   Intersecting Spheres in Our Lives (Author's Own)

You can only create so much Value by yourself, but the true Value comes from creating Value for someone who turns around and says you have created Value. Value is created for you by others using your potential Value.

Values

So, what are Values. Notice Values are plural and Value is singular; both are distinct, and Values Create Value. Values are such a broad topic and can't really be summed up in a single sentence, but put simply, your Values represent what is important to you, and of moral and ethical consequence. Values may be the driving force behind why you get up in

> Think of the Values you must have that will Create Value for you.

the morning, the choices you make and why you behave the way you do. Examples of Values are honesty, integrity, ethics, morals, what is right and wrong. Values includes belonging, health and success (and these could be of Value to you). Some people suggest that other activities such as reading, swimming or socialising are Values, however these would be symptoms of what you Value. For example, if you feel reading is a Value, it is probably more accurate to assume that your actual Value is learning, or relaxing or something of a similar nature. Think about the actual reason as to what it that led you to read? Similar to swimming, is this truly your Value or is it that you Value health, well-being or success? Perhaps you socialise while swimming and your true Value is friendship. These are the reasons that made you choose to go swimming. Understanding exactly what it is that you Value is the perfect starting point for understanding yourself and understanding your motivators.

You notice we differentiate between what you consider Values and what creates Value for you.

Understanding What You Find of Value to You

It becomes important to understand what you Value and what Values you stand for. While searching for these, one finds that most people consider Value and Values in one list without differentiating between them. One has also to differentiate between Value and Values. One has to see if those considered Value are motivators and happiness creators. Aristotle felt that one's well-being is linked to others. This is our view: when creating Value for others it creates Value for you.

Well-being is also called prudential Value to differentiate from Values of a person. Well-being is eventually what is good for you and goes beyond happiness.

Thus, you may think things important to you are wealth, career, learning, determination, fitness, honesty, individuality, fun, friendship and family. These are as much traits as things that can Create Value for you.

The Principles of VDL and This Chapter

All the eight principles of VDL are applicable, as shown in the beginning of the chapter. Any CEO or executive incorporating these will become a great Value Creator.

We have discussed Value and what it means, and the eight principles of VDL. You can use these to see how they apply in a given situation. Value can be measured. This is important for executives and leaders. Value waiting to happen is analysed with examples to build the thought process of looking around you. Also, how to Create Value for yourself is important. Value starvation and happiness and Value are analysed, keeping in mind Values.

Chapter 2

Value and Disruption, Dilemmas and Decision-Making

Value Dominant Logic comes into its own when we have to view Value creation for some versus Value destruction for others, which are aspects of disruption and dilemmas. VDL helps resolve dilemmas, some of which are destruction/creation payoffs and others where the leader has to distinguish between one option or the other, or competing options, or abandon or modify past traditions, products and markets.

Stark states,

> Each of us confronts this question on a daily basis. Faced with decisions involving incommensurable frameworks – work versus family life, career opportunities versus loyalty to friends or attachment to a locality, vacations versus investments for retirement, and so on – we ask ourselves what really counts. What is valuable, and by what measures?[1]

[1] Stark, D. (2011). The sense of dissonance: Accounts of worth in economic life. Princeton, NJ, Princeton University Press.

Business Dilemmas

One important business dilemma is suggested by Cesar Hidalgo,[2] where he says:

"New start-ups tend to create more Value than they appropriate. The dilemma they face is one of staying afloat, yet growing aggressively, of consolidating versus speed of growth."

In uncertainty, Value can be impacted but not actually forecasted. And companies are always adapting.

> Cesar says: I see a big difference between the generation of Value and the appropriation of Value. What I see about the generation of Value is that usually it's more about reducing the cost to a very small amount, to reducing the cost sometimes even to zero. When you reduce the cost to zero, and you make something accessible, you have generated a lot of Value. But when you reduce the cost to zero and you make something universally available, you cannot appropriate any of it. There's a big contradiction between these two dimensions.

> As a Value creator, think about Value giving first and Value extraction next. Could you do this in your business or life? How?

Thus, there is the dilemma of pricing, of giving away to secure a larger business base, or to spend on advertising to make your product known while you are suffering losses and cannot afford the ads.

However, in start-ups, investors are often willing to look at the number of clicks or the number of users vs. profits. Investors, too have their own set of dilemmas. These include hold or redeem decisions.

Start-up leaders have to think of the Value each of the options creates.

Alan Cornford was working on an app for this. He uses Value to decide what do you pay partners, what portion should you give up to a specific investor? By understanding the Value created by each, you can make decisions in these dilemmas.

Value and Disruption

We can look at the impact of disruption.

De-institutionalization is a phenomenon happening everywhere in the west and India. Institutions that powered nation-states, the constitutions and laws and courts, bureaucracies, corporations, civil society organizations, schools and universities, the

---

[2] Cesar Hidalgo interview: WHAT IS VALUE? WHAT IS MONEY? A Conversation with Cesar Hidalgo [8.28.12], Edge.

United Nations, a multitude of international treaties, and are under threat. President Trump is anti-institution.

> Institutions will be disrupted, by greater Value creation ideas.

Other disruptors are the old age of institutions. Another disruption driver is technology, including social media. Social media platforms discuss institutional reforms. A real reason is that the Value these institutions are delivering is not good enough or always relevant.

It is difficult to separate disruption from evolving technology. Evolving technology such as driverless cars or even electric cars will cause disruption in the marketplace, for the manufacturer or for the user. Only through a slower evolution, is there time for companies and people to re-adjust. Disruption can also be abrupt. Death is an example.

What about externality?[3] Will it impact people who are not involved directly with the decision-making? Thus, taxes get impacted with the introduction of driverless cars but may not have been anticipated.

These are not easy questions but need to be answered.

People are starting to understand the logic of Value creation in disruption. Thrive[4] states:

> This (disruptive) environment leaves a credit union with no option but to disrupt itself before someone else does. At the core of the disruption battle is Value creation. How the credit union define, create, and deliver Value to the members they serve is critical to understanding how to improve their offerings and delivery channels. Fellner in 2017 suggested that Value creation is more important than job creation for the economy.

Moving on, it is not a matter of just knowledge and awareness. It is a mindset, a VDL mindset that looks at the new ideas. Will the Value of the new idea increase over time? Will it overtake the Value we are providing or can provide? What should we do to embrace the better Value potential?

Does Disruption Create Value or Destroy It?

Let us look at driverless cars. Disruption impacts customers, companies and society by reallocation of resources. One can look at the Value impact through a Value tree in Figure 2.1. We see many areas of Value destruction as companies

---

[3] https://en.wikipedia.org/wiki/Externality
[4] https://www.cutoday.info/THE-market/THRIVE-Releases-White-Paper-on-Disruptive-Environment

and their ecosystem have to abandon some or a large part of their past thinking and re-invent themselves. At maturity the Value tree will have more light greys and fewer dark greys.

> It is only your Value creation ideas over competition that causes disruption.

An example is Mercedes Benz stating they are not in the electric car race because the hydrogen car they are working on will be a winner. In this case they will cause more disruption.

Driverless cars can reduce the number of cars on the road. The number of parked, unused cars during a day may reduce. The sharing economy may force cars to be shared rather than be owned. There could be a great change in the thinking of self-owned transportation.

Will this reduce the number of cars sold, and impact the economy? Will there be a negative net Value impact?

So, a serious question is whether there will be an overall Value reduction or increase in the future. For people, there might be a great Value increase, not having to worry about buying and taking care of cars, and getting transportation without having to drive, and getting more safety all around, for cars, occupants,

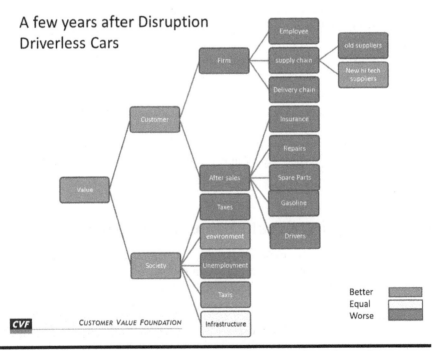

Figure 2.1   A disruption Value Tree for Driverless Cars (from the Author)

pedestrians, other infrastructure. This will spawn an in-car service industry like videos, audio books, massaging, manicures etc.

Value increase for others such as for insurance, governments and society can be estimated. The overall Value increase is positive.

While $150 billion to $200 billion of traditional automotive supplier revenues are at risk over the next decade, more than $700 billion of opportunities exist for Value chain players to capture, according to Deloitte's third annual "2018 Global Automotive Supplier Study." The study analysed shareholder Value performance.

More and more transportation could be owned by software companies like Google and Microsoft!

Uber would not have drivers, but may be forced to own car fleets that might disrupt its model. What about bus fleets if cars are so easy to find? Will there be a more seamless multi-modal transportation system?

Parking garages would be less used. Drive through sales of McDonald's (now 70% of their business) might decrease. Amazon with its new transportation system may disrupt FedEx and UPS. What about roads? Will we need less or more? And how will real estate be impacted?

> What do you do to prepare for disruption from autonomous cars? What will create the least destruction and Value for you? Use your VDL mindset to be more aware of the disruption.

Your driverless car could pick up a pizza and impact the current delivery system.

Some say that disruption is connotatively and denotatively negative. I do not agree. We will show disruption can be positive for some and negative for others.

Entrepreneurship is the creation and capture of extraordinary Value. Placing Value creation (usually economic) at the heart of entrepreneurship helps us recognise (and therefore engage in) disruption where it is often ignored. Dan Isenberg says:[5] "Creation and disruption are virtual opposites. This distinction is both practical and important; because people can create a lot of disruptive innovation while destroying Value rather than creating it."

An extreme (and painful) example to make the point: On September 11, 2001, a group of 19 men disrupted life as many of us knew it, killing thousands, shaking our feelings of safety, and disrupting the normal course of events in the world's most powerful cultural and commercial centre while negatively impacting the lives of many millions. The masterminds of this terrorism used totally unanticipated and novel methods that defied detection by the best trained intelligence apparatus in the world.

---

[5] https://www.virgin.com/disruptors/entrepreneurs-dont-disrupt-they-Create-Value

The 9/11 terrorists were disruptive innovators. Isenberg continues:

> Don't try to escape your (and my own) discomfort with this by forcing the definition of innovation as intrinsically good, it won't hold much water. This tragic example warns us not to treat disruption as a good in and of itself and suggests that entrepreneurs recognize that disruption is neither an objective of, nor a strategy for entrepreneurship; sometimes it is a by-product.

Liam Colley in his "Insight: Value Creation discusses Creatively Overcoming Disruption" asks how to innovate to create and protect Value?[6] The answer may lie in our ability to foster and harness creativity.

A group of CEOs suggested work with what you have, expose people to new experiences, and take calculated risks, develop the right environment and enable creative courage. Unleashing creative forces will help you face disruption and create sustainable Value. The pharmaceutical industry suggests being disruptive or face disruption. Their thesis is to move from molecule-type thinking to patient-centric thinking. New products will not prevent disruption. You need new business models. These include convenience, cost, integration, empowerment and satisfaction and crafting disruptive solutions including user-friendly formularies, mobile and personal devices, actionable information and customer relationship building. It's a radical change from a long-held strategy: Pharma's next generation innovation is streamlined towards long-term, replicable customer engagement.[7] This includes wearables, body sensors, visible and invisible, AI, augmented reality, virtual medicine.

Disruption can come from Google or Amazon, outside their business. The suggestion is to put people and culture first, look for partnerships, architect innovation. Remember, Rick Krohn,

> As a business Leader how do you prevent disruption? By thinking of how to Create Value and making it happen. What could you do in your business to Create Value?

> These disruptive business model ideas are important for you to get a VDL mindset and create Value. Think how you can use these ideas for creating Value for yourself and your business.

---

[6] https://legacy.alixpartners.com/en/Publications/AllArticles/tabid/635/articleType/ArticleView/articleId/1543/Creatively-Overcoming-Disruption.aspx

[7] http://www.pharmatimes.com/magazine/2018/march_2018/be_disruptive_or_be_disrupted

President of HealthSense, says deliver Value to the physician, the payer and the health care consumer.

Universities such as University of Helsinki are crafting programs and research along these lines. Their studies in innovation, market disruption and Value creation look at consumption and consumer behaviour as challengers of established market practices. Drivers for change frequently include technological change and digitalization, which have first created new markets (online and mobile services, for instance) and then changed market structures and practices (in energy, electric traffic and shopping). Ecological and economic sustainability are highlighted in their studies, which are typically multidisciplinary in their character.

Accenture[8] suggests that M&A is changing from the classic methodology to focus on the ability to disrupt business models, long-term Value creation, resulting in new practices and organisations. Their target screening focus is on disruption potential, adjacent and unrelated industries, smaller bets (with a bigger impact).

Failure of an M&A should lead to greater learning/experience and lower Value destruction.

The first reason for failure is simply the inability to understand the environment in which you operate.

The second, the inability to adapt to that environment.

> VDL suggests you look at creating Value through consumption and consumerism. Relate this to your business to Create Value.

Consumption is approached through a number of parallel concepts such as collaborative consumption and access (Belk 2014), co-creation (Prahalad & Venkatesh 2006), lead users (von Hippel 2005) and prosumerism (Toffler 1980). Value creation is viewed from the vantage points of consumption and consumerism.

Disruption hits legacy companies the most. Only a third can navigate through to success and two thirds go out of business or are acquired. An example of a successful transformation is Monsanto who changed from a chemical producer with expensive feedstock (high oil prices in the 1980s) to genetically modified organisms – which it paid for by spinning off legacy businesses. They spent 3–5% of their profits for over a decade to change over.

Ten percent of their market capitalization may be needed to cover these disruption bets. Those with less than this seldom make the grade.

Old beliefs and not looking at Value waiting to happen prevent companies from changing. They have to engage with the threat and the disruption model. Adobe for example, moved to paid subscription cloud-based software as a service

---

[8] https://www.accenture.com/in-en/insight-outlook-m-and-a-Value-creation

model. They went from service giving 12% of its revenues in 2012 to 85% today and a 33% increase in revenues by taking share from slower-changing competitors.

> Learn from companies that planned to disrupt their models and Create Value.

Top executives are active champions in such changes.

There are so many Value creating examples of people taking advantage of sales, such as when Ballmer started the disruption to Microsoft's successful license and desktop-based business model. And he drove the shifting from software-sales to a cloud-based business model to build Azure, Microsoft's cloud platform. Similarly, he set in motion the process of transforming Microsoft Office from a software product to a cloud-based service.[9]

Seventy percent of the $8.7 billion R&D budget went into this change. Nadella predicted in 2015 this cloud-platform business would grow from $6 billion to $18 billion in 2018, which seems possible now. Microsoft's stock price has almost doubled. Other legacy companies had their stock prices reduced almost by half!

Clark Golestani,[10] CIO at Merck, suggests that there are three time frames for investment: Short-term investments are primarily operational, and are focused on driving service levels up and lowering costs over the next 18 months. A second portfolio of investments aims to drive revenue from customer activities between 18 months and three years out. Finally, longer-term investments – those that enable disruptive capabilities – are intended to drive revenue within three to four years. Golestani says: Looking at investments in this way is how we went from nothing to having an engineered-from-the-ground-up data lake with advanced machine learning for intake of medically based information, very advanced search capabilities, and machine learning for looking at unstructured data.

For example, increased data, analytics and insights are changing the ways that health care companies can Create Value. Health care companies have to invest in digital technology for payments and incentives, and customer experience. Digital technology can improve communications and improve clinical delivery to the patient. Also, pharmacies can use their access to customers to help them with better lifestyles.

The Seeds of Disruption

Horse carriages to cars to driverless cars to drones to hyperloops to supersonics, all are prone to disruption. See the table below to understand disruptors:

---

[9] https://www.bcg.com/publications/2017/Value-creation-strategy-transformation-creating-Value-disruption-others-disappear.aspx

[10] https://www2.deloitte.com/insights/us/en/focus/cio-insider-business-insights/technology-investments-Value-creation.html

> *Technology by itself is not the disruptor, destroying value or not creating new Customer Value is the disruptor.*[11]

NETFLIX did not kill Blockbuster
RIDICULOUS FEES DID

UBER did not kill the Taxi Business.
LIMITED ACCESS AND FARE CONTROL DID

APPLE did not kill the Music Business.
FORCING PEOPLE TO BUY FULL LENGTH ALBUMS DID

AMAZON did not kill other Retailers
POOR CUSTOMER SERVICE AND EXPERIENCE DID

AIRBNB did not kill The Hotel Business.
LIMITED AVAILABILITY AND PRICING OPTIONS DID

Disruption has always existed, but it took a long time. It was not called disruption then, because it happened over a period of time...horse carriages to cars, film cameras to digital. Today disruption is much faster, because supply chains and the communication and the speed of change make disruption more apparent, and it can spread geographically much faster. The pace is even faster when no physical products have to be invented; instead net-based and internet-of-things-based changes can be extremely fast.

Technology alone does not create disruption. Value creation from a new source for the user, or the lack of Value improvement (creation) from the existing supplier is the source of disruption.

Measuring the Value of Disruption: It's Not Always About the Money

Jim Spohrer of IBM and I discussed disruption due to technology or social changes. Typically, the expected impact is measured in dollars and cents and not in the Value (benefits vs. expended effort in a competitive context).

Jim and I discussed driverless cars and their impact. Most people are looking at the impact from a monetary viewpoint. We would like to also look at this from a Value viewpoint.

This will force us to define Value for society, and how to measure these (see, for example Porter et al.[12]). Sadly, few companies follow shared Value as it is meant to be, though many more talk about it.

---

[11] Alberto Brea, LinkedIn with his permission.
[12] http://www.hbs.edu/faculty/Publication%20Files/Measuring_Shared_Value_57032487-9e5c-46a1-9bd8-90bd7f1f9cef.pdf

We will then be able to tell where Value is created and where it is destroyed. Thus, for developing countries, increasing wages may improve the Value to labour over the short term, but long term would force them to be replaced by automation/AI/robots. What

> VDL agrees keeping people well is a major disruptor in the health industry. VDL makes you think beyond the obvious.

happens to the Value to these unemployed people, and the societal impact, and what should governments and companies gear towards?

We could expand this to other areas. Irene Ng's business thought[13] of health care companies focusing on well people and keeping them well, versus concentrating on unwell people is an example. What will this mean to the medical ecosystem, and where will Value be created and destroyed? What role do the players have in viewing the consequences and reversing the destruction of Value by proposing alternatives to those who might lose jobs, or those whose businesses might be impacted? Or should they look at the greater good for those for whom Value is being created in hitherto unthought of, but huge way? How do you view these gains from Value to society?

Figure 2.1 Shows my thoughts a few years after the introduction of driverless cars (say 5 years from now). At maturity there will be more Value created. Value creation will be higher.

Disruption and Way of Life and VDL

It will be there, it will be a way of life, but some disruptors will have a long stay, especially when they create more Value than they receive. Facebook is an example of giving more than it receives, or Google search.

> When the rate of change outside exceeds the rate of change inside, the end is in sight...
> Jack Welch

People like you and me have to live in and participate in this disruption as it will impact us and our way of life. As we get used to one disruptor another one will come up, that dictates our living and living spaces, our transportation, our work, our ability to change careers, our health and health care, our leisure, and our resilience, and sense of humour and persistence, and above all our desire to conquer all, or at least survive.

---

[13] Creating New Markets in the Digital Economy: Value and Worth, February 20, 2014 by Irene C. L. Ng.

With Value-creating thinking we start to think beyond what is obvious. Driverless cars will put drivers out of jobs. Maybe we can retrain professional drivers who are losing jobs to make them monitor driverless cars on the road.

VDL through its first principle suggests improvement of well-being, and the seventh principle that suggests disruption must create more Value than it destroys. The fifth principle says that our potential to live with, and even overcome disruption, is important. And making decisions vis-a-vis disruption and dilemmas can be helped by the sixth principle.

Value Creation and Dilemmas

All actors are faced with dilemmas. What major should a student seek, where to work or whether to start one's own company, to discard polyester film photography for digital, to use bias belt tires or radials etc.? Buyers have similar dilemmas. Use Value and Value-added techniques.[14]

Ethical and Social Dilemmas

Value Dominant Logic helps you look at dilemmas by observing opposing views or different possibilities from their Value creation and Value destruction viewpoint. There are so many examples of business, ethical and social dilemmas.

I can relate one from my own personal experience:

My team and I designed the plastic PET bottle petaloid base used on Pepsi, Coke and other carbonated plastic bottles, and have a few patents on such bases. I also commercialised the half-litre bottles in 1978 in Newark, Ohio. Today, I see PET bottles around the world.

While immersed in this project we could only see the joy of success and the determination to win. We never thought about sustainability. In fact, we talked about the energy required to produce bottles in one plant in a year as being the same as the energy required by a Boeing 747 to fly across the US and back. And we talked about recycling, or getting the energy back by incinerating, or re-using the PET for lower uses such as fibre etc.

> Can we look at Value destruction and creation and not be one sided, looking only at the company's good and not at the harm to people and society?

Were we one-sided Value creators? Because we did not know what Value creation meant, we looked at success and winning. We created Value for the customers (Coke and Pepsi) and perhaps not for the environment. We were not

---

[14] Shown in Kordupleski, Mastering Customer Value Management, Pinnaflex 2003.

concerned about the potential destruction of Value or not truly exposed to the debate.

Should we have been part of the dilemma of the good versus the bad? Of creating Value for the company and customers or for creating Value for society and sustainability? Perhaps, we could have come to the conclusion Coke and Pepsi are bad, or they are good. That this packaging alternative is better…

I think Value creation should look at both sides and not be one sided. Decisions should then be made for the best good or Value (for whom? The company, for society? For consumers?).

Another example from the PET bottle experience was that we had the one-piece bottle, the petaloid bottle. The competition (which had about 70% market share) had a base cup two-piece bottle, which initially was easier to produce, and cheaper. But in due course of time, the petaloid bottle became competitive, the two-piece bottle had ecological issues, and the extra step of making a base cup, adhesively adhering it to the PET bottle, matching colours etc. made it less ecologically friendly and less preferable. The separation of the PET bottle from the polythene base for recycling became a major issue.

The petaloid bottle was protected by patents (expiring in 1986). Our bottle looked different. We were under pressure to look at making base cup bottles. But instead we chose to license a Coke bottler in Texas and also into the UK. Very soon Coke decided to move to the one-piece bottle and with the expiration of the patents the entire world moved to the one-piece bottle. The reason was that the one-piece bottle was more ecological.

> VDL suggests you look at business from different viewpoints, and go away from only thinking proprietary technology and look at sharing.

Value was created by opening the door to customers and competitors to use by licensing the petaloid bottle.

One could draw a Value tree from the company's point of view Figure, 2.2.

The people looking at sustainability would have a different Value tree, Fig. 2.3.

You can see an entirely different argument. Unfortunately, neither side looks at the other's Value tree. You, the reader can take a stab at looking at both sides.

The same thing happens during a war, should we kill or let live? Or be killed? Again, the question is whether Value is being created for one party or the other, or whether the avoidance of war is creating Value.

Politicians have the same dilemma. Should they do good (Create Value) for the citizens or for the vote banks to get re-elected?

In the social scene, job creation for the poor creates Value but has to be balanced by efficiency needs from low-cost robotic manufacture. These are true dilemmas, and the solution is to look at alternatives to traditional jobs with the

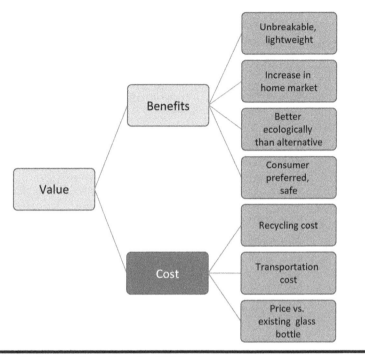

Figure 2.2   Value Attribute Tree for PET Bottles

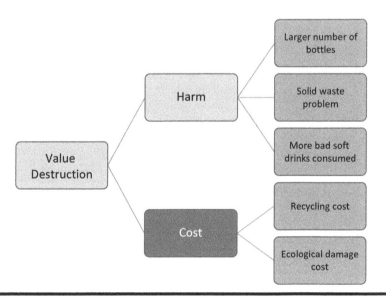

Figure 2.3   Value Attribute Tree for PET and Its Value Destruction

changing social and technological scenes. Emerging nations have a dilemma, whether to automate or continue on with mechanical jobs.

Nadella feels that automation with a human touch will improve country dynamics and also new jobs will emerge. Also, we need to balance return on capital with higher level job skills, and re-arrange the countries work force. It really stops being a dilemma if the standard of living increases and percolates throughout.

> VDL suggests you look at the entire ecosystem and not just at profits or the good of the company. The overall good is good for the company.

In conclusion, should we worry about joblessness versus efficiency/cost and the future for people?

What does progress mean? More cars? More consumption? More needs? New technology and obsolescence of the past? Or does it mean better lives?

A time may come when robots may wish to make humans obsolete, or make humans more efficient with fewer parts (energy and nutrition and oxygen being passed through the skin via nano-bots into the blood of human beings, reducing the need for the heart, the lungs and the intestines)?

These are dilemmas we have to face and solve. Often, dilemmas get solved by a lack of action, and progress takes over.

Value Dominant Logic helps in such thinking, especially through the 7th principle that Value creation should be greater than Value destruction. The principle of creating Value for others, and to go beyond our functional thinking, and its impact on all stakeholders. In doing all this we must keep in mind our values.

By using Value trees, and other tools of Value, one can very carefully examine the best path to take in business dilemmas. Examples have been given using VDL. Disruption, its prevention and also its execution through VDL has been discussed.

Chapter 3

Value, Society and Technology

Value Dominant Logic is concerned with creating Value for and in society, including but not limited to sustainability, social media, technology and innovation. You will notice that in many cases Value is just waiting to happen. There is a great Value potential from social networking which was not that easily seen in the past. More and more organizations like Delivering Happiness, Creating Value Alliance, Conscious Capitalism, Customer Value Foundation, BSR (Business for Social Responsibility) and Forum for the Future are all helping create sustainable businesses. Also, some companies like Whole Foods and Unilever are embracing sustainability and conscious capitalism.

We have added technology to this chapter because of the profound impact technology will have on the future, on people, on society and sustainability. Till you understand where technology creates or destroys Value and for whom, and why technology must have a sustainable face, you will never get the best Value, and so VDL thinking is important in understanding this chapter.

> Next to our moral obligations to address global challenges, it is also a business opportunity. . .
> Paul Polman, Chairman, Unilever.

> VDL suggests you Create Value over social media and networking. Look at what Customer Value can do for you.

It is extremely important that society, technology and value come together. We are working with leading Japanese technology institutes to have technology thinkers immerse in social thinking to come up with technology that is society focused.

Tremendous improvements have taken place in the last two hundred years, see chart on page 43 by Max Roser (Figure 3.1).[1] The question is will this be self-sustaining or will there be a reversal, with the uncertainty of technology, society and employment. You will notice all the currently used terminology for good and well-being (Value) have improved considerably.

But along with this there are people like Dr Jose Foglia[2] from Uruguay who believe that the abuse of digital technology will damage the brain, its short-term memory as well as long-term memory. What the long-term impact will be on human beings and their becoming addicted to tools of technology remains to be seen.

AI is becoming a curator of content, and through deep learning is orchestrating future action for the customer's benefit.

Value and Society

I could expound on the role of Value and society. It is better I do this through the living example of Soka Gakkai. It shows the importance of Value creation in life and in our day-to-day living:

The idea of Value creation is central to the philosophy of Soka Gakkai;[3] the name of the organization in fact means "society for the creation of Value," which focuses on human happiness, responsibility and empowerment.

"Values" refer to moral standards, as we have learnt earlier. Value indicates that which is important to people, those things and conditions that enhance the experience of living. As the term is used in the SGI, Value points to the positive aspects of reality that are brought forth or generated

> Soka Gakkai is among the societies embracing VDL and driving their thinking from Value creation.

when we creatively engage with the challenges of daily life.

So Soka Gakkai focuses on all of us on a day-to-day basis. Further, they say we can Create Value at each moment through our responses to our environment.

---

[1] https://ourworldindata.org/wp-content/uploads/2017/01/Two-centuries-World-as-100-people.png with permission from Max Roser

[2] The Hindu Newspaper Edge, March 5, 2018

[3] http://www.sgi.org/about-us/buddhism-in-daily-life/creating-Value.html

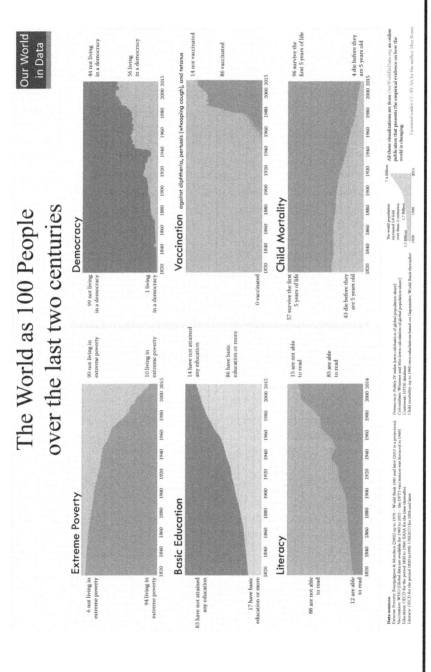

Figure 3.1   The World Has Improved in Many Ways

Depending on our determination and direction, the Value created from any given situation can be positive or negative, minimal or infinitely great.

Even what may seem, at first sight, to be an intensely negative situation can serve as an opportunity for the creation of positive Value.

SGI goes on to state that Buddhists, because they live their lives within networks of interrelatedness and interdependence, so that the positive Value we create for ourselves is communicated and shared with others. Thus, what started out as the inner determination of one individual to transform their circumstances can encourage, inspire and create lasting Value within society.

It is also important to note that, unlike some of his contemporaries, Makiguchi rejected the idea that "the sacred" could be a form of Value unto itself, and he asserted that human happiness was the authentic measure of religion.

The philosophy of Value creation is thus a call to action – "as we are and where we are – in the cause of human happiness, and to dedicate ourselves to a cause, a goal that is larger than us."

So, we learn Value Creation is critical in our daily life, and that forms one of the bases of Value Dominant Logic. Thus, Value and Value Creation are necessary for human beings and for living.

Hence VDL suggests a bigger focus on human beings and how to Create Value for them, and how they can Create Value for each other.

Society and Technology and Value

It may sound obvious that technology must have social thinking. However, combining a Value creation thinking into social thinking and technology makes technologists think beyond technology to

> Use VDL to marry technology and societal thinking.

Value creation in society. As an example, one of the Value destroyers in driverless cars is the loss of jobs and Value for professional drivers who will lose their jobs. Value creating thinking and societal focus will suggest such drivers can be re-trained to monitor cars via computers, and suggest improvements, parking ideas, movement of cars and so on.

Teachers should think of how to teach students to use what they learnt to Create Value for society.

As an example, teaching engineering structures and beam theory, should require teachers to suggest the global applicability of beams: a beam could be a baseball bat, a table, a shaft, a pen, a machine sitting on the ground and just not a beam holding up your roof.

Another example is using artificial intelligence and technology for smart cities. VDL would suggest that first the society leaders must have a Value creation mindset to want to solve problems. Let me give you an example. Dharamsala in India (the Dalai Lama city). The traffic to get to the Dalai Lama temple is horrendous. The mindset is not one of solving the problem but of having smart sensors. The problem cannot be solved quickly only with technology. It needs the coming together of technology, society and a creating Value mindset. People working in smart cities must have a VDL mindset.

Sustainability

VDL promotes and incorporates the concept of sustainability.

One important part of creating Value for society is through sustainability: being aware of and positively contributing to sustainability. Thus, for

> People need the earth to survive. The earth can survive without people.

example, Value creation for sustainability starts with creating awareness. The next step is proactiveness. Unilever took proactive steps to stop using (cheaper) palm oil which was ecologically damaging and using more expensive options that were less damaging. Unilever's customers were willing to pay more for this option and supported the company. Sustainability helps others and society. Focusing on sustainability can also create a new business model. Being ambidextrous helps, by focusing on the business the way it is and how it might be impacted through sustainability.

One example of sustainability is the democracy of energy. Using your own energy (solar or wind) that is on your property and then selling the excess, as opposed to buying from the grid. The energy ladder is replacing kerosene light with a light bulb, and with your own

> The democratization of technology is empowering more people with information and creating Value like never before.

electricity available to you, upgrading to other appliances such as televisions and refrigerators. Energy for everyone using solar is also a low-carbon economy... a dignified energy system. We are already re-charging drones, robots and electric scooters, or using irrigation pumps run off solar. This usage will increase in the future.

Better storage of energy and more efficient appliances... and working capital for more energy will accelerate solar energy from homes into the grid.

Value Creation thinking would suggest to white goods manufacturers to provide solar solutions along with white goods sales to penetrate villages in emerging nations.

Sustainable businesses, or green businesses, have a low negative impact on the environment, community, society or economy – often, sustainable businesses have progressive environmental and human rights policies.

Harvard Business Review (HBR) states that sustainable companies tend to have a better ROI, as using clean alternatives in energy are cheaper.

Sustainable businesses employ a three-pronged strategy:

1. Preserve the environment and conserve natural resources.
2. Build social equity, support employee well-being and promote fair trade.
3. Maximise long-term profitability and promote growth.

This holistic view of doing business places equal emphasis on the planet, people and profit. You'll often see the concept referred to as the *triple bottom line* (People, Planet, Profit).

Examples of fair trade (include work done by Fairtrasa run by Patrick Struebi) are also a case of sustainability and creating Value for farmers in Latin America, by improving their productivity and selling at remunerative prices in Europe.

Unfortunately, there is no persistent (or sustained) focus on sustainability. It is relatively slow in happening but for notable exceptions. Most of America's largest companies aren't taking the action needed to tackle climate change, according to a new report by Ceres.[4]

Only a third of the Boards oversee sustainability objectives and progress in biodiversity, in human rights, in water management, in procurement etc.

Walmart for example has incentives for buyers using sustainability-based supplies. This includes eschewing unfair practices, child labour, under payment of labour or poor labour practices.

> VDL helps you look at means to get societal focus and doing good things will get you good returns. See the examples.

Sergey Brin, President of Alphabet, declares that technology companies must take greater responsibility for the social impact of their work.

This raises the question of monitoring and regulations. Should we have a sustainability standards boards? How do we challenge the essence of capitalism?

- A major brewer identified some 150 possible improvements that could reduce GHG (Greenhouse Gas) emissions – while saving $200 million over five years.
- When a water utility benchmarked its performance against that of other utilities, it figured out where the biggest opportunities were – in this case energy and chemicals. After four years, the results were in: less leakage, fewer customer complaints – and $178 million in savings – a 25% reduction in operating costs.

---

[4] https://www.theguardian.com/sustainable-business/blog/ceres-us-corporations-climate-change-sustainability

▪ A state-owned industrial company in China increased the energy yield of its coal significantly simply by tracking it better, making sure the first mined was the first used. That improved energy efficiency as well as carbon intensity, while reducing costs 13%.

Kellogg's, a US-based multinational food manufacturer, is one example. "We see good opportunities to grow Kellogg's brands as we invest in climate adaptation solutions such as climate-smart agriculture," says Diane Holdorf, chief sustainability officer at Kellogg Company.[5]

The company has committed to reducing energy use and greenhouse gas emissions in its plants by 15% per tonne of food produced by 2020, from a 2015 baseline.

GE's Ecomagination initiative has helped the company to sell more goods and services. In 2015, its Ecomagination revenue had reached $36bn, up to six-fold from when it launched the initiative in 2005.

Consumers are scrutinizing the environmental footprint of the products they buy. "Consumers increasingly want to know how their food is grown,"

This is the start of eco-imagination and eco-innovation.

Fortune[6] says the nitty-gritty of sustainability programs can get complicated. But the principles are actually pretty simple – and should be familiar to executives. First, and most important, is to acknowledge that sustainability is serious. The case is not that difficult to make. In a McKinsey survey of 340 executives, more than 90% said risk management – whether from consumers, regulators or the market (for example, high resource prices) – was an important factor in pushing them toward sustainability initiatives.

Real sustainability efforts are (or should be) core business efforts.

Fortune stated that a Harvard Business School study drew similar conclusions (higher return on equity and assets for higher-sustainability companies), the authors concluded that developing a corporate culture of sustainability could be a source of competitive advantage in the long run.

> Higher-sustainability companies get a higher return on equity and assets companies.

Fortune goes on to say that to think of sustainability as a niche gets it wrong. To do it right, companies need to be rigorous, goal-oriented and accountable. The evidence is building not only

---

[5] http://perspectives.eiu.com/strategy-leadership/moving-needle-corporate-climate-action-low-carbon-world/case-study/case-study/powering-future-driving-business-growth-low-carbon-strategies

[6] http://fortune.com/2015/09/24/sustainability-practices-in-business-intel-unilever-wal-mart-dupont/

that sustainability initiatives work, but that they are an important factor in creating long-term Value.

Walt Disney Company,[7] recognizing its investment in the next generation, has taken a number of steps to strengthen its sustainable practices. It:

- Discloses performance.
- Integrates environmental practices (such as running Disneyland trains on biodiesel made with hotel waste cooking oil). Company figures in the Global Reporting Initiative (GRI), an independent body that covers the economic, environmental and ethical impacts in each of its resorts.
- Employs an International Labour Standards (ILS) program that evaluates and helps address working conditions in facilities producing Disney-branded products around the world.

Olam International, winner of the Guardian's 2013 Sustainable Business Award for "Society – impact," is a global agribusiness company that sources its produce from 3.5 million smallholder farmers. In 2011, the company launched the Olam Livelihood Charter (OLC) to formalise the company's commitment to invest in the rural communities of emerging countries. This charter is built on eight key principles, including improved yield, market access, social investment and environmental impact.

Ajit Pattnaik is the General Manager and Head of Tailoring at Raymond Ltd. At Raymond, he drives sustainable Value creation for communities and consumers through skill development and entrepreneurship development. The 4 C program (Capability, Capacity, Community connection and Consumers) under his leadership at Raymond has gained considerable national attention as a unique Shared Value Creation/Sustainability Initiative.

Value creation through sustainability is then a source of competitive advantage and increased profits. Hence companies should pursue VDL.

We have to self-regulate efforts on sustainability not only for profits and for society and to avoid regulation from society and the government. Value Dominant Logic demands such sustainability efforts.

CECP (CEO Force for Good) who are creating a better world through business suggest questions every CEO of a public company should answer.[8]

"What are the key risk factors and mega trends (such as climate change) your business faces over the next three to seven years and how have these influenced corporate strategy?"

---

[7] https://www.sustainabilitydegrees.com/what-is-sustainability/sustainable-business/
[8] Vanguard's Chairman, Bill McNabb

"How do you identify your financially material business issues and which frameworks do you use for reporting on these issues? How do these figure into your future strategy and capital allocation plans?"

"How do you describe your corporate purpose and how do you help your employees share your vision for the company's role in society? How does this shape your long-term strategy? How does your future strategy act upon this purpose?"

"How do you manage your future human capital requirements over the long term and how do you communicate your future human capital management to your investors?"

"What are the corporation's framework/strategies for interacting with its shareholders and key stakeholders?"

"How will the composition of your board (today and in the future) help guide the company to its long-term strategic goals?"

"What is the role of the board in setting corporate strategy, setting incentives for and overseeing management? How does the corporation ensure a well-functioning and diverse board accountable to its key stakeholders?"

All this behoves well for the future. Note the CEO Force wants to create good, which is Value. VDL thus applies more broadly.

Why Do We Need a Framework for Sustainability?

Porritt[9] suggests that because there are so many issues such as climate change, poverty, resource depletion, peak oil, overfishing etc., that a sustainability framework is necessary. It becomes an aide to the CEO to understand the problems and solutions. He advocates a capital model,[10] wherein sustainability is considered based on wealth creation or capital. Such capital has to be increased and not depleted, as well as how these social issues impact profitability. Going along with Wayne Visser, we should (and Porritt agrees) look at these in an integrated[11] way so that trade-offs and maximization of sustainability can happen. A vision can then emerge. I prefer to call them assets.

The capitals include nature or ecological or environmental capital (which consists of natural resources consumed, and sinks that absorb waste, renewable resources and processes to regulate damage), human capital (and here from all we have talked about concerning people Value we add the ability to manage and

---

[9] The Five Capitals Model – a framework for sustainability
Capitalism As If The World Matters by Jonathon Porritt, available from Earthscan
[10] http://www.metsagroup.com/en/Sustainability/Value-creation/Value-creation-in-society/Pages/default.aspx
[11] Metsa group in forest products, focuses on sustainability of forests. This is an example of integrated Value because renewal of forests and natural resources builds other capital Kari. Jordan@metsagroup.com

create sustainability), social capital which consists of the extended ecosystem into families, government and trade unions.

Manufactured capital consisting of infrastructure, material goods technologies, ecological manufacturing, zero waste and emission.

Financial capital is next and I would add here customer capital to the list of important capitals.

Another term called inclusive capitalism is now being used to determine the real Value a company is delivering, to make capitalism more equitable, sustainable and inclusive. Lady Lynn Forester de Rothschild has founded a group to discuss and develop a measurement that will better reflect the full Value companies develop through human, financial and intellectual capitalism and the impact on the world.[12]

Creating Entrepreneurs at the Bottom of the Pyramid

As part of our effort on Value creation, our Value Creation Forum on entrepreneurship suggested two ideas: Creating entrepreneurs at the BOP and the second idea is creating extrapreneurs.

Our creating entrepreneurs at the BOP started in Himachal Pradesh, District Kangra in India, and includes tourism (creating home stays, tour guides, opening up tourism trails from Amritsar to Dharamsala [before this Amritsar tourists came and went back from Amritsar, as did Dharamsala tourists, start and end in Dharamsala]).

By creating the trail, tourists see and spend time and even nights in homestays in between the two cities.

Other projects being considered are home decoration, adventure tourism specifically for women, bird photography guides, mediation centres, telemedicine centres etc., working with women's cooperatives for better products.

We also realised that we should create and teach people to think like employers, not employees and not think of being just employable.

The concept of extrapreneurs marries corporate intrapreneur thinking with external entrepreneurs who are invited to partner with the corporates to start entrepreneurial projects.

Social Networks Including Social Media

To promote Value for society, we have to use our social networks. An example is using social media. Social media can create and destroy Value.

---

[12] https://www.entrepreneur.com/article/309648fink

Value has to be created equitably across all social networks,[13] through the principles of Reciprocity, Exchange and Similarity. Value creation increases as these three principles are adhered to and maximise Value for all stakeholders.

The first is the principle of reciprocity, which is giving and taking equitably with others or trading favours equitably. Reciprocity works better when actors are different and then they go into exchange of favours. The Value of the exchange increases, it is co-created.

Lastly, the third principle of similarity which works best with people with common backgrounds, values and interests.

Penelope Trunk, author of "The Brazen Careerist" column and blog[14] says building a network is adding Value many peoples' lives so that they, in turn, will want to add Value to yours. Another useful strategy is to network proactively rather than reacting.

IBM found in Creating Value from Knowledge,[15] that the SNA (Social Network Analysis) is uniquely effective in:

■ Promoting effective collaboration within a strategically important group.
■ Supporting critical junctures in networks that cross functional, hierarchical or geographic boundaries.
■ Ensuring integration within groups following strategic restructuring initiatives.

Connect and Develop

Procter & Gamble (P&G) took to social media through the concept of *connect and develop*, which refers to developing new products and services through a vast social network spanning parts of P&G and many other external organizations and people, going away from their traditional model of using their internal capabilities and those of a network of trusted suppliers to invent, develop and deliver new products and services to the market. It did not actively seek to connect with potential external partners.

> VDL suggests looking in your ecosystem to get Value waiting to happen ideas.

However, around 2003 P&G[16] realised there were millions of scientists, engineers, and other companies globally they were connected with.[17] This open innovation is

---

[13] Reciprocity, Exchange, and Similarity Principles of Management, v. 1.1.1 by Mason Carpenter, Talya Bauer, and Berrin Erdogan adapted by: Melissa Fender (v1.1.1 – Published)

[14] blog.penelopetrunk.com

[15] Creating Value with knowledge, Insights from IBM Institute of Business Value in important networks by Eric Lesser and Laurence Prusak, Editors

[16] http://www.pgconnectdevelop.com

[17] Adapted from http://www.pg.com

"Connect + Develop." This open innovation network at P&G works both ways – inbound and outbound – and encompasses everything from trademarks to packaging, marketing models to engineering, and business services to design.

On the inbound side, P&G is aggressively looking for solutions for its needs, but also will consider any innovation – packaging, design, marketing models, research methods, engineering and technology – that would improve its products and services. On the outbound side, P&G has a number of assets available for license: trademarks, technologies, engineering solutions, business services, market research methods and models, and more.

As of 2005, P&G's Connect + Develop strategy had already resulted in more than 1,000 active agreements. P&G interacts with business partners, from individual inventors or entrepreneurs to smaller companies and those listed in the FORTUNE 500 – even competitors. Some of the success stories are shown below:

Olay Regenerist, for example, came from acquiring a small French company that had an anti-wrinkle technology for their skin care products, but came to P&G through a conference contact.

P&G also started to license technology such as Calsura, a more absorbable calcium that builds stronger bones faster that keeps them stronger for life. Calsura is proven to be 30% more absorbable than regular calcium.

Moreover, they have started their University Collaboration with the University of Cincinnati using design labs, university students and P&G researchers collaborate to study the unique needs of the over-50 consumer. The goal is to develop and commercialise products that are designed for this consumer bracket.

New technologies allow P&G to engage consumers, stakeholders and employees through the use of a wide variety of social media. Their Global Social Media policy outlines principles for its responsible use by employees and partners, ensuring they protect consumers, stakeholders and P&G.

Nike started their Considered Index, to check environmental impact, on items such as waste, solvent use, material usage and reuse, using a circularity principle.

The plastics fraternity has started a big program for the circularity of plastics. They are taking action on new products that are amenable to being reused and recycling, are better for collection and recovery, and encouraging consumers to participate in ecology.

An example is the new polymer diaper from IIT Madras, that uses the first biodegradable super absorbent polymer made from chitosan (a kind of sugar polymer extracted from seafood, urea and citric acid).

Elkington's the Zeronauts discusses how to drive carbon, waste, toxics and poverty to zero. He suggested a Race to Zero.

Steven Kotler[18] suggests the 6Ds of exponential technology, using Digitization, Deception, Disruption, Dematerialization, Demonetization, Democratization which

---

[18] https://thoughtcatalog.com/steven-kotler/2015/02/the-6-ds-of-exponentials/

allows entrepreneurs to take on established companies. Such companies can benefit from trust and collaboration on technology, frienemies (making friends of enemies) and extrapreneurs. Another example of using your social network to your benefit. This is what VDL is about. The boundaries between providers and users are blurring, and so, also, are the roles of the participants.

Thus, social media itself should take on the role of a social network platform promoting B2B and B2C interaction and an innovation/technology collaboration and idea generator between businesses and customers and other collaborators. Value creation through social media platforms will therefore remain limited until the moment firms and customers start sharing information on a larger scale[19]

All of us must understand and use social media-based Value co-creation within the different organizational processes (e.g., in product and service development and customer services). Attention to new technologies will allow us to adopt new, innovative, social media-based Value (co)-creation tools and operation models.[20]

Technology and Value

Automation and AI will lift productivity and economic growth, but millions of people worldwide may need to switch occupations or upgrade skills. It is estimated 5 million jobs will be lost due to automation by 2020.[21] Software, caregiving, social media and interaction, lifelong learning related jobs are likely to grow.

Matthew Taylor asks what we mean by good work. We know that wages matter to people, particularly to those who earn less. In a way, people are less concerned with the relationship between their wage and the superrich than they are between their wage and the person who might be one step above them in the hierarchy, for example. People want to see a decent wage, and they want to see fairness. But once you move beyond that – and indeed, overall surveys show that people are saying that pay is a less important part of what determines whether work is better

> VDL suggests looking at employee Value through belonging, autonomous and meaningful work.

---

[19] https://norbertbol.wordpress.com/2016/04/24/social-media-Value-creation-through-interaction/comment-page-1/

[20] Ketonen-Oksi, S., Jussila, J. J., & Kärkkäinen, H. (2016). Social media -based Value creation and business models. Industrial Management and Data Systems, 116(8), 1820–1838. DOI: 10.1108/IMDS-05-2015-0199.

[21] The World Economic Forum, the Future of Jobs, 2016

than it used to be in the past – you come up against the same kinds of things, meaning people want a sense that their work is meaningful and that they are doing something useful, something that they can feel proud of, take ownership of. These Create Value for the employee.

Autonomy – people want to feel that they are able to make judgments and make choices at work; they will not simply be a cog in a machine. What might be called mastery: the sense that, "I am getting better at something, and in getting better at something, I am enabling myself to have more choices in life as a consequence of the job that I'm doing." And then teamwork, camaraderie and the sense that, "I am part of an organization that is inclusive and fair." All these are Value creating.

We need to show more imagination about how we can bring those things to lower-paid, lower-skill jobs. Many of us who are middle class and work in great organizations are used to these things. But there's no reason why jobs in caring, jobs in retail, jobs in security, transportation – can't have those qualities, if we're clever about the way in which we manage our organizations.

We learn that technology capability and human capital investment contribute directly to the overall Value-creation firms. A company's technology capability should be seen as an integral tool for creating economic Value instead of just business infrastructure that makes business operations efficient.

On the other hand, Mitch Barns,[22] CEO of Nielsen says when a company creates a successful new product or process, it is because it has somehow trimmed waste, and thus created Value. Henry Ford's car made it possible for average American families to travel as only the rich had been able to do just a few years earlier. Ford passed much of the cost savings from his technological innovations on to the consumer. Such innovations include the creation of the first tools to the building of the international space station.

Some think that the internet of things, artificial intelligence, advanced robotics, wearables and 3D printing are exciting technologies with the most future promise. Readers may want to read more from Frost & Sullivan[23] and others. As an example, they cite tomatoes and spinach crops, for example can be tested for pathogens within 15 minutes in the field, a great use for IoT.

Elsewhere Health Sense[24] talks about augmented reality to help treat phobias, provide physiotherapy and promote wellness.

---

[22] http://www.nielsen.com/cn/en/press-room/2014/how-technological-innovation-creates-Value-en.html

[23] https://www.tatacommunications.com/wp-content/uploads/2018/02/Gaining-Customer-Value-from-IoT.pdf

[24] http://www.healthcareitnews.com/news/mixed-reality-extrasensory-and-other-trends-health care-vr

Dov Seidman author of *HOW: Why* How *We Do Anything Means Everything* says that technology creates possibility for new behaviour and experiences and connection…but it takes humans to make the behaviour principled, the experiences meaningful and the connections deeper. In short, how to Create Value or not destroy Value.

The Value of technology depends on us and how we use it to impact our own lives and those around us and society. It allows us to connect, to share, to aspire, to grow and to control (if we can avoid being controlled).

Technology has the potential to create immense Value and destroy immense Value. Of course, what it creates and destroys depends on our point of view and our relationship to the result. So, for driverless cars, Value is destroyed for professionally employed drivers, whereas it is created for casual drivers. Soon with Uber's driverless cars, we will have a different taxi system all controlled from a hub. Cars would become 24/7 with no rest needed except for maintenance.

How can we finish the Race to Zero (to get homes to be energy efficient and only dependent on self-generation? Or get electric cars to be self-generating and self-sustainable?).

Technology has little in emotions. Can you download the smile on your grandmother's face when you walk in, or the aroma of mother's cooking, or the hug from your brother, or the sharing a snack with a stranger on a train, or the giggle of delight of a baby being tickled? Or a bystander sending you down the wrong street or going up the wrong way on a one-way street or the exhilarating air on a ski slope with powder snow on your beard?

The surgeon general of the US said the number one disease in the US was isolation, not being adequately connected to others. Some feel technology can help by replacing humans. I am not so sure.

In another example, Cisco Systems developed everything-as-a-service (XaaS)[25] initiative that allows it to break down silos, deploy and leverage technology more effectively, and align IT services with both customers and the business. Cisco views XaaS as an opportunity to control costs, create efficiencies and rethink the way it engages customers and partners. "We realized that we needed to rethink the way we were working, how we thought about Value streams, and the way we organized ourselves," says Will Tan, Cisco's senior director of operations. "Likewise, we began reviewing the relevance of our architecture to determine how our money is being spent. When we look at allocations of technology budget, 57% is spent on business operations, 26% on incremental business change, and only 16% on business innovation. Is this right for your business. Should you spend more on business innovation?"[26]

---

[25] https://www2.deloitte.com/insights/us/en/focus/cio-insider-business-insights/technology-investments-Value-creation.html

[26] Taken from 2016–17 Global CIO survey, Deloitte insignts

Where is it going in our budget? Reviewing the relevance of our architecture to determine what kind of money? Only 16% goes into new innovation, and 57% in improving existing systems.

What can make digital transformation/technology[27] work?

- Understand how technology will impact your business model
- They should be customer centric and not technology centric
- Be clear on what you want, and do not get stuck in all of the technology clutter
- Make sure you understand the scalability required before you start

Long Run: Think of the Future

This was written to look at education and unemployment in India, but the thought is universal. Prof. Luiz Moutinho contributed ideas on this through a PowerPoint presentation he sent me.

There was a time there were humans, and then humans and machines; and humans who are data informed; and humans and machine assisted; and then maybe only machines in the future. One robot, called Sophie, has been given Saudi Arabian citizenship! This could be a frightening scenario, but also an opportunistic one. Another robot built in China can dance in competitions better than humans.

I come away from my travels overseas wondering why most emerging countries are thinking today of what they should have done 10 years ago, whereas the Americans are thinking of the world and what to do 30 years from now.

> Future thinking must be factored in with the here and now in VDL thinking.

If we can factor some of the long-term Value creating trends into our short-term thinking we will become a smarter and will truly become a superpower.

By just focusing on now, we will not improve our competitive power, and may even increase poverty and unemployment.

Kaizen thinking of doing many small steps to improve productivity is now being modified with ideas from the Ambidextrous Organisation by Charles A. O'Reilly III, Michael L. Tuchman where they talk about companies exploiting

---

[27] https://bluecanyonpartners.com/4-roadblocks-digital-transformation/?utm_campaign=New sletters&utm_source=hs_email&utm_medium=email&utm_content=60,325,737&_hsenc= p2ANqtz-_3o2ia4D6kYGVGk7sGf9V8bQLv4wPRRFeTg7KV_wKK-zpHY7HJtY- lpPXgKQINOQCHkS-x4nOttOx8-4euYg3egVCRgA&_hsmi=60,325,737

the present and exploring the future. This is creating Value from now and from the future.

India needs to do just this. Our pre-occupation with catching up in education, skilling, energy, employment, education and food has to be modified with positioning ourselves for the (not today but distant) future.

Energy: It is likely that renewable energy and better energy efficiency will result in substantially free energy.

Skilling and employment: Thirty years from now, unemployment will increase as most routine jobs will be lost to robots and AI. By 2040, computers the size of a cricket ball will be smarter than human beings. And because they're computers, they never get tired, they're never ill-tempered, they never make mistakes and they have instant access to all of human knowledge. In fact, Osborne in the Future of Employment feels that 47% of US jobs will be at high risk in 20 years. Fukoku Mutual Life Insurance in Japan is laying off employees[30] replacing them with an artificial intelligence system that can calculate payouts to policyholders. Productivity will improve by 30% and the investment will be paid off in two years, after which costs will reduce further. Most automobile plants have robot systems and Tesla is almost all robotics.

But what is more worrisome, that we are not working on alternatives for humans as fast. Large-scale thinking and modification of our education system to tackle the future is necessary. I will discuss this later.

Food: Chances are that better nutrients and food supply systems will change, and food requirements may also change.

Re-design of the nutrition system may not require the human digestive tract, as auto-nutrition through special clothing, and nano-bots going in and out of the skin providing nutrition and removing waste. Nano-bots could supply oxygen to cells, making the blood system obsolete, and no heart or lung will be required. What will be left will be the skeletal system and parts of the nervous system! Sound far-fetched?

So, this brings us into education and re-employment 30 years from now. But first, let us understand the background.

Stephen Hawking said the rise of powerful AI will be either the best, or the worst thing, ever to happen to humanity. We do not yet know which. He went on to say that the biological brain could be emulated and even exceeded by computer intelligence. And I add that once this happens AI growth might be exponential.

Robot nannies, robot pets, robot spiritual gurus are now available.

Already, AI is playing a bigger role in visual perception, speech recognition, decision-making and language translation.

It also might be this new intelligence will find unheard of solutions. After all the Wright Brothers' aircraft did not emulate a flapping-wing bird, and Google's driverless car does not use brain sensing and thinking. Nor do gyroscopes use the human body's action in keeping a cup of tea from tipping when climbing stairs.

Narrative science will replace journalists producing news stories, headlines and information reports without humans. It is up to us to Create Value from these and prevent Value destruction.

Artificial Intelligence and Emotional Intelligence

Many people tell me machines will never take over as they do not have emotional intelligence. That is needed as much as AI. But AI will force us to re-skill. Humans will have to discover new opportunities to stay ahead of AI and robots. And because of a sudden disruption instead of a gradual change, we do not have much time to adapt. Everything dumb and disconnected is getting more intelligent, wired and connected, cities, our bodies and our homes. Things that cannot be automated or digitised may still be available to us humans, such as EI (emotional intelligence), creativity, imagination and intuition. Human thinking to look at the future of re-skilling and re-deployment is necessary to build the new landscape of human endeavour. Create Value, master technology.[28]

After all, people are the source of Value. People, with their talent, knowledge, skills and experience constitute the ultimate source of Value. Will this pervade with the onslaught of AI?

An example is restaurants. Tom Krouse, President and CEO of Donatos Pizza, said that restaurants aren't about $13.89 for a pizza from our customers, and he said "but consider all that we give in return: quality and Value, to be sure. But we also give hospitality, smiles, training, development, careers, first jobs, second chances, family connections, and a strong and valuable community connection, too." And this human touch is what can keep AI in check.

Technology and Sustainability

Technology has the ability to impact sustainability, but the technological changes have been minimal and not radical. Much of this has to do with the strength of the corporate system (big business), and the inability or the resolve of the government.

According to the University of Wisconsin, the tools of sustainable development are economic instruments, legislative measures and consumer pressures, are aimed at achieving technological changes such as recycling, waste minimisation, substitution of materials, changed production processes, pollution control and more efficient usage of resources, all to Create Value.

Undesirable side effects of technology include climate change. An example is aircrafts that transport us but impact climate change. Thus, sustainable

---

[28] Change, a film by Gerd Leonhard, VID-20,171,002-WA0017

technology should be highly efficient, benefit health, be renewable, reusable, socially affordable etc. – to mention but a few criteria and not destroy Value.[29]

Research by McKinsey shows that improvements in resource productivity in energy, land, water and materials – based on better deployment of current innovative technologies – could meet up to 30% of total 2030 demand, with 70% to 85% of these opportunities occurring in developing countries. Capturing the total resource productivity opportunity could save $2.9tn in 2030.[30]

The Productivity Conundrum, Why Is Productivity Declining?

Productivity declined 0.5% in the last five years globally till the end of 2017, whereas it gained 2.5% in some previous decades. Puzzling: McKinsey[31] states the three factors include waning productivity growth rates in the last 15 years, the global slowdown due to the financial crisis 2008, and that digitisation has not caught on.

Job growth has happened in the last few years, but not with productivity gains.

While productivity declined 1% in the 1990s, growth due to computers and digitisation was ending in 2005.

Mckinsey feels that digitisation and computerization has led to cannibalisation and reduction in footfalls (up to 10% in retail). Transition barriers and lag effects are culprits. Operating and business models are changing and transforming generating a lag.

The cooperation in the world to bring various countries and trickle down benefits to SMEs is taking place, further accelerating technology gains and productivity. Those interested can read the World Economic Forum White Paper: Technology and Innovation for the Future of Production: Accelerating Value Creation.[32]

There is a feeling that productivity growth will be about 2% per year in the coming decade, 60% coming from digitisation gains.

I would imagine that low growth in the economy, low investments and changing workloads are reducing the effectiveness of people. This is combined with user unfriendly systems (Value starvation).

---

[29] https://www.oeaw.ac.at/ita/en/topics/technology-and-sustainability/
[30] https://www.theguardian.com/sustainable-business/technological-innovation-sustainability-energy-green-investment
[31] https://www.mckinsey.com/global-themes/meeting-societys-expectations/solving-the-productivity-puzzle
[32] http://www3.weforum.org/docs/WEF_White_Paper_Technology_Innovation_Future_of_Production_2017.pdf

Let me give you an example:

I am asked to do more and more on the net like paying bills and e-transactions. But when something goes wrong I cannot access the provider and get answers easily. That reduces my productivity as I have to spend unnecessary time. Companies need to rethink this and think about the customer and the convenience of the customer.

Big companies like LinkedIn, Amazon, State Bank of India, HDFC Bank, Bank of America and Uber are all guilty of this.

We cannot have a lopsided productivity view: the convenience of the company at the expense of the convenience of the customer. Let me give an example: If on Uber your location is not precise due to their location system, then there is a productivity loss for them and for me. Their map showed the cab was four minutes away and the driver thought he had arrived.

In the State Bank of India e-statements, full details of payments and receipts are not given and it is not possible to get this easily from the net or by a personal visit.

I can go on and on. Productivity gains must take into account the customer also, not just the company for it to be pervasive. If you decide not to Create Value, you will get nowhere. Except to use robots for productivity gains without corresponding gains for the customer, and consequently for you. Value should be created for customers first, and not just for the companies.

Value Creation and Innovation

Innovation is like children. It has to be nurtured all of the time, and a mindset of innovation must permeate the company, according to VDL.

This nurturing is more necessary in companies. Therefore, just increasing the number of people in innovation will not increase innovation unless simultaneous internal changes to engender innovation and innovation culture are instituted. This includes understanding the Value drivers of improving innovatability. Value drivers include understanding what creates Value for customers, where you could create greater Value than competition, and new ideas such as Value waiting to happen. Your innovations should increase the Value drivers. Lastly your innovation program has to be Value driven and must Create Value for your stakeholders, including customers, suppliers and delivery chain partners, employees and the firm. Just viewing innovation as increasing Value for the owners does not work.

In the old days, standardisation and scale were very important. Examples include Ford, and standardisation (you can have any colour as long as it is black) and no options, better materials, cost cutting, increasing wages, sharing cost savings with customers after he started the moving assembly line.

Thus, you can have something new (the car) or the process and cost innovation or better benefits including service.

The mobile phone/internet has made e-commerce possible. Farmers in India can find places where prices are higher to sell produce. Plumbers and electricians in India are on call because of cell phones. Before that they were dependent on an electrical or plumbing store to take requests for electricians and plumbers and would often not get the requests till very late. So, customers did not have on-call help.

Since many Indian mobile phone users cannot read or write, voice activated apps have become imperative, adding value to these people to use their mobile devices effectively. These voice-activated apps also made different language capabilities in apps a reality.

Instead of using print media for ads to sell cars, homes and other products, very focused sites allow buyers and sellers to interact.

Production lines are changing because of robotics, 3D printing, artificial intelligence and IoT wearables.

The World Economic Forum[33] asks the following eleven "What if. . ." questions:

For government and business leaders to reflect on the impact of technology and innovation in global production systems:

What if. . .

1. The factories of the future are small, mobile, invisible and located in urban undergrounds?
2. The best robot on the factory floor is the technology-augmented operator?
3. You can track in real time the performance of every machine, employee and supplier in your network, as well as your products in the hands of the consumer?
4. You can produce at the same cost and quality anywhere in the world?
5. Your customers are willing to pay only for performance and all the Value of your flagship products comes from their digital and cognitive features?
6. With hyper-personalization, brands become irrelevant?
7. You can turn your recycled products into raw materials for a new production batch?
8. Technologies do not diffuse beyond select large producers and technology giants
9. Over 80% of global production output is produced and delivered through contract manufacturing?
10. Technologies enable labour relations to become self-organised?
11. Technologies fail to deliver on their promised Value?

These are all VDL-related questions, and with this mind set we could add:
Energy is almost free;

---

[33] www3.weforum.org/. . ./WEF_White_Paper_Technology_Innovation_Future_of_Prod. . .

Governments have to deal with large unemployment;

Leisure time becomes huge;

Governments to deal with changing tax sources;

What happens to insurance companies and banks?

Will society be safer (think privacy)?

Will technology be customer led?

And the Guardian suggests cheap water filters converting toxic water to drinkable, energy producing homes, bladeless windmills, smog scrubbing towers and designing carbon catchers.

Strategy consultant McKinsey & Company, citing recent academic research that finds differences in individual creativity and intelligence matter far less for organizational innovation than connections and networks. That is, networked employees can be more innovative and can catch on more quickly than non-networked employees can.

So, *connect* key people in the organization with an innovation mindset. Have diverse people for generating ideas, researching and validating them. You have started a network. Next, *set boundaries and engage*, defining the network's goals and objectives. In the third step, *support and govern*, set the leadership, processes and reporting. Finally, the fourth step involves *managing and tracking*.

For humans, empathy (especially to get humans to lead technology), education (more equitable, upgrading to implement and run new technologies), creativity (to keep searching), judgement and accountability are musts.

On the basis of what was found by Cross and colleagues across many large firms, within P&G in particular, and in their own research, McKinsey has observed four important steps in the innovation network process.[34] These four critical steps in designing, implementing and managing an innovation network are summarised in the following Figure 3.2 in the Innovative Network.

McKinsey suggests people fit several archetypes. Which one are you?

> Companies must re-position to grow and profit from the world's pressing challenges.

■ *Idea generators* prefer to come up with ideas, believe that asking the right questions is more important than having the right answers, and are willing to take risks on high-profile experiments.

---

[34] https://catalog.flatworldknowledge.com/bookhub/reader/9361?e=fwk-127,512-ch09_s02#ftn. fn-8

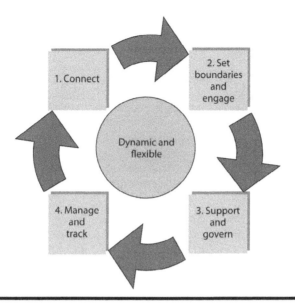

Figure 3.2   Managing the Innovation Network. (Adapted from http://www. mckinseyquarterly.com (retrieved June 4, 2008).)

- *Researchers* mine data to find patterns, which they use as a source of new ideas. They are the most likely members of the network to seek consumer insights and to regard such insights as a primary input.
- *Experts* Value proficiency in a single domain and relish opportunities to get things done.
- *Producers* orchestrate the activities of the network. Others come to them for new ideas or to get things done. They are also the most likely members of the network to be making connections across teams and groups.

Gib Hedstrom[35] suggests the four stages of sustainable transformation. He asks if we are positioning ourselves as sustainability transformation unfolds, or are we missing the boat by doing business as usual, as Borders Book-stores did?

Extreme weather events, failure of climate change mitigation and adaptation, water crises and large-scale involuntary migration are four major risks per World Economic Forum. These risks – interwoven with other societal challenges (inequality, technology impact of digital transformation on job creation and

---

[35] https://www.greenbiz.com/article/four-stages-sustainable-transformation

more) – will impact different industry sectors in different ways, says Gib. He states there are four stages of sustainability transformation in a company. Engaging, Accelerating, Leading, Transforming. Most companies are in stage 1 (engaging), some are in stage 2 (accelerating), but almost none have gone into stage 3 or 4.

Gib also shows how many different types of managers are also in stage 1 and 2 in their thinking. Much needs to be changed, using VDL thinking, echoed by Gib.

Value and Government

VDL suggests that government – apart from spending time on economic activity, regulation, civic and judicial and political activities and the like – should provide the institutional framework for all human activity.

John J Kirlin[36] develops the Value creation roles of governments, namely constitutional, jurisdictional and civic infrastructure, policy strategy and policy infrastructure. The measure is the social Value created.

Governments also have to see where they can create the most Value, where to step in and where to step aside. Value Dominant Logic can get them to decide on the best possible option, and to plan for disruption, job losses and retraining/re-skilling, and the use of technology, VR and AI and the like, such as in smart cities, smart systems etc.

The Capital System for Sustainability

Visser suggests sustainable development is development that meets the needs of the present without compromising the ability of future generations to meet their own needs. It contains within it two key concepts:

- The concept of "needs," in particular, the essential needs of the world's poor, to which overriding priority should be given; and
- The idea of limitations imposed by the state of technology and social organization on the environment's ability to meet present and future needs.
  - World Commission on Environment and Development, Our Common Future (1987)

This leads us to the triple Bottom line:
The Triple Bottom Line is one way for businesses, and includes the profits that your business makes socially, environmentally and economically. This allows you to judge how sustainable your business is, and how profitable it really is.

---

[36] Journal of Public Administration Research and Theory, 6(1), January 1, 1996, 161–185, https://doi.org/10.1093/oxfordjournals.jpart.a024298

In short, environmental and social concerns can't be separated from the economics of business – an uncertain, disruptive future means profits will depend on reducing environmental risk, identifying more sustainable ways of running operations and supply chains while developing stronger relationships and trust with society as a whole. VDL preaches this also.[37]

There has to be a shift from short-term to long-term thinking.

EU[38] suggests 5 R's starting with capital **R**eallocation. **R**isk management, setting core **R**esponsibilities of financial institutions, improving **R**eporting and a system **R**eset in thinking on strategic challenges and opportunities.

Forum for the Future[39] suggests five capitals that one must follow for a sustainable future, similar to VDL teachings:

Natural Capital is any stock or flow of energy and material that produces goods and services. It includes:

Resources – renewable and non-renewable materials;

Sinks – that absorb, neutralise or recycle wastes;

Processes – such as climate regulation;

Natural capital is the basis not only of production but of life itself!

Human Capital consists of people's health, knowledge, skills and motivation. All these things are needed for productive work.

Enhancing human capital through education and training is central to a flourishing economy.

Social Capital concerns the institutions that help us maintain and develop human capital in partnership with others; e.g. families, communities, businesses, trade unions, schools and voluntary organizations.

Manufactured Capital comprises material goods or fixed assets which contribute to the production process rather than being the output itself – e.g. tools, machines and buildings.

Financial Capital plays an important role in our economy, enabling the other types of Capital to be owned and traded. But unlike the other types, it has no real Value itself but is representative of natural, human, social or manufactured capital; e.g. shares, bonds or banknotes.

Customer Capital is another capital we should add.

We are facing a sustainability crisis because we're consuming our stocks of natural, human and social capital faster than they are being produced. Unless we control the rate of this consumption, we can't sustain these vital stocks in the long-term.

---

[37] https://fsinsights.ey.com/big-issues/Society-and-sustainability/transforming-capitalism-for-a-sustainable-future

[38] http://unepinquiry.org/wp-content/uploads/2016/04/Building_a_Sustainable_Financial_System_in_the_European_Union.pdf

[39] https://www.forumforthefuture.org/project/five-capitals/overview

To do this we have to impact culture, politics, architecture, income, businesses, transport, technology, manufacturing, energy, environmental economics and agriculture. VDL helps you do this by following its principles.

Ellen Weinreb, in "Calling all Value Creators, Futurists and Change Agents"[40] talks about the BSR (Business for Social Responsibility) report: Redefining Sustainable Business, which showcases how sustainability is implemented inside companies.

BSR's report calls on sustainable business leaders to redefine the purpose of sustainable business, from a separate function that is integrated into business to the very thing that forms the foundation of business itself. Sustainability, BSR argues, should be used as a frame for growth and Value creation.

To reorient business around sustainability, BSR proposes its "Act, Enable, Influence" blueprint: Companies can act by creating resilient business strategies, governance and leadership approaches; they can enable sustainability by partnering with others and reporting in a meaningful and transparent way, and they can influence by advocating for policies that "strengthen the relationship between commercial success and the achievement of a just and sustainable world."

What Leaders Need to Know

Ellen says that sustainability practitioners and leaders are more than risk assessors and mitigators; they're the Value creators, futurist, change agents and coalition builders. VDL states each one can be a Value creator.

Here's how BSR defines these roles:

1. **Value creators:** These people identify and pursue opportunities to build Value for the business.
2. **Change agents:** They draw on influence and change-management skills to, as one interviewee put it, "move lines."
3. **Coalition-builders:** These quiet leaders look for areas where the company's thinking and movement is already aligned with sustainability progress, and they build coalitions to scale up that work.
4. **Futurists:** These people are the long-term thinkers who understand risk, but also see opportunities to Create Value, even in the face of complexity.

Each of these roles requires new job descriptions that place a premium on different skills and competencies, such as an orientation toward change and progress, and the ability to engage with people and organizations beyond the usual suspects – particularly underserved populations. Importantly, BSR noted,

---

[40] https://www.greenbiz.com/article/calling-all-Value-creators-futurists-and-change-agents

sustainability leaders must focus on innovation and "explore the creation of market opportunities, not only the adverse social impact of market failures."

You should also see Ellen's article[41] The expanding role of sustainability leadership: Sustainability has become a defining part of the business purpose, and this requires sustainability practitioners to embrace new skills. Brand new competencies are needed. These competencies include VDL mindsets.

Alison Taylor of BSR says "We need to move beyond a 'whatever works' mindset and think carefully about governance, management structures and equipping sustainability professionals of the future with change-management expertise."

There is no core sustainability skill set; rather a group of relevant competencies, she noted.

Ellen asks: What would it take for you to reimagine your role as a change agent? How can you build a coalition to redefine the role of sustainability in your company? Become Value creators.

Wayne Visser[42] takes this further by suggesting CSR has to be rethought as Creating Integrated Value. Further, he outlines the 5Ds leading to global Systemic problems and the global innovative solutions with the 5Ss in Figure 3.3:

VDL, Sustainability and Technology

The first principle of VDL suggests that sustainability and technology can be good for people and society, as long as you follow the seventh principle and ensure Value creation exceeds Value destruction. The third principle suggests that you have to Create Value for your ecosystem. Value should impact all stakeholders per the fourth principle. The fifth principle helps you to leverage the organizations potential, and the sixth principle allow you to make decisions on sustainability and technology effectively, following the eight principles Value creation. Creating Integrated Value is part of VDL thinking.

VDL helps you look at technology, look at your business outside its normal purview, and look at Value waiting to happen. VDL suggests a long-term approach that takes into account Value for society and sustainability and goes beyond just the profit motive. This will create more profit. The examples we have given should inspire you to do more with VDL, and also you should ask the questions we have posed.

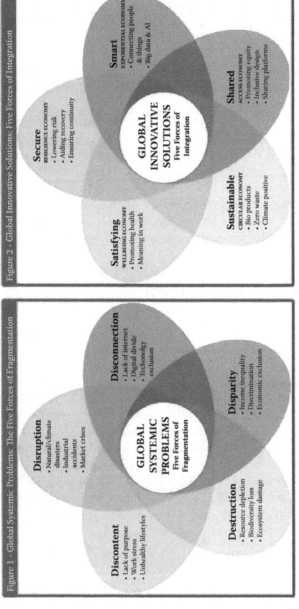

Figure 3.3   The Global Systemic Problems and Global Innovative Solutions from Wayne Visser

Chapter 4

Value and Education

Satya Nadella says: The sum of education and innovation, multiplied by the intensity of technology use = economic growth.[1] Value-added education then can also enhance the growth of people by using innovative Value-creating techniques and technology.

Value Dominant Logic requires educationists to think differently. They have to teach how to Create Value versus functional teaching, and ready students to adapt to the changing world, and to become Value creators.

Teaching Value Creation

CEOs might have noticed our main Value creation discussion in education has focused on business schools. In fact, we are developing course content for a Value Creation major in MBA schools. I just taught a course on Value Creation in Engineering to students, faculty and staff at IIT, Mandi, and IIT, Gandhinagar, to faculty and staff at IIT Jammu and to staff at IIT Delhi.

We all know there is a disconnect between academics and practitioners. Practitioners are looking for short-term, here-and-now solutions. Academics work on long-term research which rigor and relevance (and it is often said that academics publish for themselves). Academics debate SDL, SL and other logics, but practitioners are not even aware of these. The practitioners are concerned about creating Value and need guidance for this.

---

[1] Nadella, S. (2017). *Hit refresh*. HarperCollins, New Delhi.

These academics produce students who industry lament are not usable. Why is there such a disconnect? Does it come from what academics must do to get ahead in their profession? Why not teach Value Creation?

First, who is education's customer? The accrediting body, the students, the parents, or the employers or society at large? And for how long should the education last? Or in today's changing technology world, should education make people ready to face and manage the future as it changes, and not get swept up by the technology and disruption wave. If we were to assess how valuable students are, should we do this on the basis of the grade or on the basis of the feedback from the employers? Or on the basis of the future?

Whom should we be creating Value for? Of course, for all of these, but also for the teachers. And for readying the students for the future.

We also have to see if we want to teach employability or make students think like employers: be capable of adapting, changing and facing challenges.

> As Value creators in education, teach how to Create Value, versus teaching just functional matter. You must graduate Value creators.

> The illiterate of the 21st Century will not be those who cannot read and write, but those who cannot learn, unlearn and relearn.
>
> - Alvin Toffler

> VDL suggests ready students to face the changing future and keep ahead and not get disrupted.

Thus, we first have to make Value creation an important part of our education agenda. After each lecture, teachers should spend five minutes talking about how what they taught created Value, for whom and how, and how students could use the learnings to create more Value.

Lackeus suggests: The Value creation approach in education is fundamentally about letting students learn by applying their knowledge to create something of Value to external stakeholders. Empirical studies have shown that such an approach is capable of escaping the teacher dilemma by allowing for strong development of entrepreneurial competencies, deep integration into the core curriculum and good alignment with many teachers' humanistic values.[2]

First we have to bring in Value creation thinking/initiatives into education. That the role of education is to produce Value creators, and Value creation thinking. Such people will be more employable and capable of creating greater Value at work.

---

[2] Lackéus, M. (2017). ECSB Entrepreneurship Education Conference. Cork, Ireland, May 10–12.

Current teaching produces functional executives, focused on efficiency and improving profits, and being good administrators. We do not produce too many Value creators. Those who succeed, do so because they Create Value intuitively and not consciously. Imagine how much more Value they would create if they were doing so consciously, and destroying less Value.

To make the students receptive to the idea of creating Value, we must teach them what Value is and how to Create Value for themselves. Short courses on Creating Value for Yourself can make the students think about Value creation and become Value creators. They start to understand that they can Create Value for themselves and for others.

Then these courses can be designed from the point of view of creating Value. Next, we can consider adding a lecture per course on Value creation and in-depth thinking of how to use the course content in the real world and how Value creation research can be done.

> VDL suggests people must learn how to Create Value for themselves first and then they become comfortable with creating Value.

Along with this we must work on courses like HRD and IT. In today's world humanising and humanities will become increasingly important to balance technology gains. We have to ask why HR and IT/Technology people do not become CEOs. We soon realise most are functional managers and not

> A teachable moment is about understanding where, when and how you can Create Value

Value creators. Once points A and B are defined, they can tell you the best way from A to B, but do not ask them to define point A and point B. They cannot, because they are not taught to do so. Once we have teachers teaching about Value creation, we can have at least one lecture in each course on creating Value. The first step is for teachers to spend a few minutes every week suggesting how the topic that they taught created Value in the real world and how people used the learnings and the knowledge. They can show how the student can Create Value from this topic and how the learning can Create Value for them. This will make the student more engaged and a better Value creator.

We also must ensure technical courses including technology, IT, engineering, accounting have a societal bent and thinking, apart from Value creation thinking.

The next step is to create a Value Creation Elective.[3]

---

[3] Much of this is taken from my book, *Value Creation, Sage* and *Value Imperative*, BEP per author's agreement.

Lastly we need courses on Value creation, and a Value Creation Elective. This will lead to Masters of Value Creation and Masters of Value Management instead of a normal MBA degree.

For Business Schools and Other Institutions

Changing the education and B-school paradigm, and teaching Value creation as the prime role of a leader and general managers. Teachers should Create Value for the students while teaching and interacting with them. Teachers should show students how value is created from what they teach and how students can Create Value with the learnings in future. The B-school program has to be modified to make Value Creation a General Management elective. Current courses can be modified to show how to Create Value. For example, engineering students can be taught how to Create Value in the real world.

The Business School of the Future

So if you accept the concept of a CEO being the Chief Value Creator, then are we really looking to employ business administrators, or Value creators? The MBA in the future will be replaced by MVM or Masters of Value Management, or MVC, Masters of Value Creation. The business schools will become Value crea-tion schools teaching executives about Value creation for the shareholder and for the Customer, and to teach them that this is natural and the two are complementary. Using VDL analogy, Customer Value = Business Value or CV=BV!

> VDL suggests the CEO is the Chief Value Creator, and so B schools should teach Value Creation and give a Masters in Value Creation.

Students will be taught to manage short-term Value and long-term Value. They will also look at optimisation between Customer Value and the Value of the company, the Customer life time Value, and learn how to measure CVA (Customer Value Added), ROC (Return on Customer), and Customer assets, how to increase these and the relationship between Total Shareholder Value and the Customer Value and ROC.

All the supporting current MBA courses will be modified from a Value, shareholder and Customer perspective.

Some Examples

A few days ago, I had a discussion with an Economics Professor. She was telling me about the various courses she teaches. I asked her if she talked about Value creation to her students. How would they use their knowledge? How would they Create Value for themselves, their employers and the society at large?

She felt it was a great idea, and something she must include in her teaching.

She asked about simple examples of Value creation she could give her class. I told her about my assistant who sent an income tax notice I had received to my tax lawyer. A few days later, I asked him if he had confirmed if the tax lawyer was going to attend the hearing. He had not. If he had confirmed the attendance of the tax lawyer, he would have created Value for me. Just going the extra step creates Value. You can find so many examples of Value creation. A Customer service person solves a problem for me. He realises this problem is prevalent, but he does not try to get the company to change the process/procedure so that other customers do not face the same problem I had faced. He missed a chance to Create Value for the customers, his company and himself.

> Teachers should discuss with students how they could create Value and what Value-creating idea they have.

There are just as many examples of Value destruction. The run around you get when you call a company to complain is a typical example. Taxis that come later than ordered and make you almost miss a plane. A service person who does not arrive when promised. The list is endless.

The first step to companies and executives converting to Value creation is awareness. Awareness that they can create or destroy Value, and what they can do to Create Value is necessary and has to be taught. Awareness starts with secure people who have self-esteem. Else we have to build self-esteem. As part of my course at IIT Mandi I had the students go through an awareness exercise. And suddenly they started to notice things they had never "seen" before.

The concept of Value creation has to be taught to college faculty, and to companies' senior executives, so that they can teach Value creation and set up an enabling environment. The concept is simple. The role of a teacher goes beyond imparting knowledge. It goes into how the knowledge can be used; it goes into how the knowledge has been used by others, and how the student can Create Value in the real world with the knowledge.

We are also setting up Value Creation Councils at IIT Mandi consisting of various stakeholders to create more Value.

- Value creation should be taught in universities.
- It should be taught to executives in companies and should start with creating Value for yourself.
- Teachers should strive to Create Value.
- Examples of Value creation and Value destruction are useful in getting people to understand Value, its creation and destruction.

- Awareness is a necessary step in creating Value.
- Value creation should be taught to faculty and to executives, so that they can teach Value creation and set up an enabling environment.
- Value Creation Councils should also be established.

What Does Value Creation Mean to Students?

Here we discuss Value creation for students and how to figure out what students Value. CEOs can use these learnings in creating Value for their Customers and employees.

When we look at how to Create Value for students, we must understand what Value means to them. Value is very personal: it is a feeling of a sense of fulfilment. And some of it comes from a sense of ownership (of one's life or job), a sense of involvement, of realising a vision (if you have one).

For a student, it could be "Am I employable?" and Value creation could help him with "How can I become employable?" (I would prefer they asked, can I become an employer).

And so campus interviewers have to ask what the student considers Value and how will you Create Value? What are you passionate about? What keeps you or will keep you awake at night?

And for employees it is a sense of involvement that creates Value for them. The employee's sense of ownership adds Value to the company. What can I do to make my job better and get better results for the company, how do I take pride in doing things better? How do I take the extra step?

How does one marry the individual aspiration to the organisational aspiration? And to Create Value?

As an example, a business owner's child may wish to make films, but the father can only see the kid in his business. Both have to understand the key to adding Value for each other.

Security and self-esteem in a person help to add greater Value.

So teachers and executives have to go through refresher courses, and understand the question of Value creation. And they have then to suggest how students can use the learnings of the course to Create Value for themselves and their employer and society at large. And students should start to think about Value creation as their role rather than just to be subject learners.

Role of Faculty

There are two major areas for Faculty Members to learn about Value creation:

1. To Create Value for the students and the institution
2. To teach Value creation and its importance in Life and in Business

Value for students is a feeling of a sense of fulfilment. And some of it comes from a sense of ownership (of one's life or job), a sense of involvement, of fulfilling a vision (if you have one). Value comes from not only gaining knowledge from the teacher but also how to use the knowledge to Create Value for others, including society, thereby fulfilling the student and making him feel more useful and capable. Value creation is building the students security and self-esteem and belief in himself and that he can be useful.

How does the student learn to Create Value for himself, his institution and for the company he might work for, and for its Customers?

The faculty has to weave this into the course so that the student buys into Value creation.

The second part of the course is to teach Value creation to the faculty member, what it is, how to Create Value, and how Value is created for companies though its employees, its customers and partners and thereby for society and the investors.

Tsunesaburo Makiguchi[4] (1871–1944) post-war revitalised and grew the movement he established in 1930, the Soka Kyoiku Gakkai (Value Creation Educational Society). This has grown into today's Soka Gakkai (Value Creation Society).[5]

Daisaku Ikeda, the great Buddhist leader, has defined Value creation essentially as "the capacity to find meaning, to enhance one's own existence and contribute to the well-being of others, under any circumstance." This capacity then is what Ikeda and Makiguchi mean by happiness. The concept of Value creation is also at the heart of the Soka Gakkai movement.

Makiguchi's definition and thinking about Value, "beauty, gain, and good" to enhance the personal and collective lives of people... Considering the lifelong happiness of learners to be the authentic goal of education,

His educational philosophy and efforts is developing the Value-creating potentialities of students. For Makiguchi the creation of Value is the "ultimate purpose of human existence, defining a happy life as one in which the capacity to discover and Create Value has been fully deployed."

The System of Value-Creating Pedagogy (Soka Kyoiku Gak Taikei) published in 1930. Makiguchi's understanding of happiness as the goal of both life and education begins with the recognition that although humans cannot create matter:

"What we can create, however, is Value and Value only. When we praise persons for their 'strength of character,' we are really acknowledging their superior ability to Create Value".[6]

---

[4] Makiguchi *The Value Creator* (Bethel 1973).

[5] Much of this section has been taken from Soka Gakkai literature.

[6] (1983–1988, vol. 5, p. 13; in Bethel, 1989, p. 6).

Soka education today is not defined so much by curriculum elements as by its underlying philosophical stance: its emphasis on close student-teacher relationships, and on each student's unique capacity to learn, grow and 'Create Value.'

There is also a strong emphasis on fostering humane and life-affirming values, on peace and on encouraging students to lead contributive lives. "Education must inspire the faith that each of us has both the power and the responsibility to effect positive change on a global scale," Ikeda writes. A list of principles formulated by Ikeda for the Soka schools in Japan demonstrates the general orientation of such values: (1) Uphold the dignity of life; (2) Respect individuality; (3) Build bonds of lasting friendship; (4) Oppose violence; (5) Lead a life based on both knowledge and wisdom. Visiting educators to the Soka schools have noted as characteristic of Soka students a strong sense of commitment to making positive contributions to humanity, a highly developed sense of purpose, concern for others, sincere interest in peaceful values and a strong sense of responsibility.

A key perspective in Ikeda's philosophy is that "the fulfilment of the individual cannot be realised in conflict with or at the expense of others." Ignorance of this principle might be said to be at the root of the global problems that humankind faces today, and students are imbued with an awareness of this as a central tenet of global citizenship.

DePaul University is offering a Master's in Education on Value-Creating Education for Global Citizenship.

Martin Lackeus[7] in his thesis on *Value Creation as Educational Practice – Towards a new Educational Philosophy grounded in Entrepreneurship?* suggests letting students learn through creating Value for others, giving teachers prescriptive advice on the what, how and why issues of education.

Satinder Sharma feels quality education is necessary for Value creation in society.[8] Further, Educational institutes apart from granting degrees, have produced people who strive authority, power and materialistic wealth. However, they must foster and create wiser future leaders who Create Value in their own lives, families, workplaces, society and in countries. Such individuals without fail can also create materialist wealth in a sustainable manner which can be appropriately used for making a Value-creating society.

Value creation is not something distant and separate from our lives. How can we use education as a weapon to Create Value in every aspect of human life?

---

[7] http://publications.lib.chalmers.se/records/fulltext/236812/236812.pdf

[8] https://www.linkedin.com/pulse/quality-education-Value-creation-society-sk-sharma/

Education and Technology

Eric Cooke, University of Southampton, feels universities as we know them now have no future. In 15 years, we will have no students to teach (I think the time might stretch). Students want a good, professional job and degrees are evaluated against employability. But the professional jobs for which we currently prepare students will be done by intelligent machines.

So why would students take on the debts involved in undertaking a degree course as it is conceived of today, he asks.

This is not necessarily about technology but about humanity and learning. There is a school of thought that says that if you can be replaced by a robot then you probably ought to be!

Haptic screens (based on touch and vibrations), deep learning, deep qualia (of deep learning and blockchain) machines, sense-making networks, convolutional neural networks, smart network convergence, cognitive systems and cognitive computing to the future of teaching, uncollege and experience university, brain-computer interfaces, nanodegrees, micro-careers, are all reasons why our education system must change.

Experience universities, experience degrees, more hands-on learning, applied sciences, intuitive ways of knowing, and answering questions, and knowing what is all in the offing. Digitisation and virtualisation of education by following music, news, brain computer interface to learn or teach; Centre for the Unknown; Human-centred design, community as curriculum.

> What will we teach in 15 years and for what jobs? Since we do not know, VDL suggests a mind-set change of current employees to become re-assignable.

Since we do not know what the job market will be like in 30 years, what are we to teach? 60% of the best jobs in 20 years have not been invented yet! Learning and working will give way to lifelong learning or learning and re-learning. A more complex workplace and a portfolio of micro-careers will happen.

Some of the new jobs created will be:

Productivity counsellors, personal digital organiser, organisational disorganiser, personal life loggers, hackschool counsellors (hack rather than go to

> People need to think like employers, and not just about being employable. This will help them face the future as they lose jobs.

school), medical nanotechnologist, digital history analyst, cyber security professionals, work transformers, social media manager, sustainability officers, unemployment service managers, keeping-unemployed-people-occupied managers, retirement service managers, classroom avatar managers, deep learning specialists using computers to figure out what something is, recognise how a brain recognises, machine human interaction specialists, big data and information specialists, cognitive using knowledge specialists, bio-AI interface/nanobot interface specialists, humanising experts.[9]

Corporate CEOs should worry, too. For a while, everything will seem great for them: falling labour costs will produce heftier profits and bigger bonuses. But then it will all come crashing down... After all, robots might be able to produce goods and services, but they can't consume them.

And eventually computers will become pretty good CEOs as well.

The lesson for emerging countries is that while focussing on the here and now, start a parallel program for new universities based on technology and artificial intelligence, focusing on jobs of the future, and re-employment.

Value can be created/destroyed by focusing on now, we may create some short-term Value, but will be big losers in the future.

How can executives use this? These lessons are to be learnt by executives as they think through the future and disruption. That they have to be aware and agile and anticipate the future.

Example of Value Creation in Education

At the Michener Center, University of Texas, Austin

I have been writing about Value creation in education. Much of the discussion has been generic. That the role of a teacher is to go beyond just imparting knowledge but to Create Value by showing the student how the knowledge is used by others, what they do with the knowledge, and how the student can use the knowledge and benefit from it and enhance his environment (employer, society, etc.)

A few days ago I had the privilege of witnessing this Value creation in action. This was at the Michener Center at the University of Texas at Austin. The Michener Center has assembled brilliant talent in fiction, screenwriting, poetry and playwriting. Students in the MFA (Master of Fine Arts) were graduating, and the graduating class spoke about their amazing, life-changing experience.

The one thing all those graduating said was that the teachers and staff just gave and gave and the students just took and took. The giving was selfless. I wondered what Value was being created for the teacher. Was it just satisfaction? Was it more, the pleasure of helping people become creative and successful? And I remembered my essay that creative people did not need incentives for creating

---

[9] Much suggested by Luiz Moutinho.

and helping others Create Value.[10] Incentivisation does not increase creative power, but may create the environment (like the grants to the students). But the teachers were not incentivised by higher salaries for creating the Value they created. They gave because that is the nature of secure and creative people to create more Value, and to get satisfaction from doing a better job than others.

The students went on to talk about how their fellow students created Value for each other – by example, when they wrote or did something well; by witnessing the disappointment and disillusionment and the lows their fellow students experienced, and helping each other to get going and try again; by giving emotional support. Much like what the teachers gave them.

The teachers gave them the enthusiasm, the secure environment, the emotional strength to go through the winning and losing, and helped them manage the emotional highs and lows. The staff gave them emotional support in their private lives, their special needs etc. and a sense of being part of a family and being at home.

But what was common was building the sense of security in the students, when they felt insecure, inadequate and unable to cope, or unable to find that whiff of genius that could help them with a flow of brilliance, and happiness.

What struck me were the enormous emotional bonds that the students had formed with the teachers and their fellow students, the gratefulness to them. Many cried, as they related their story of growing at the Michener Center.

I had written earlier about the need to be secure to Create Value. Insecurity can come from when you are growing up or in your work or personal environment. And so the teachers and staff created the environment for fostering talent and security.

One teacher told me that the students were inherently talented, and the teacher's role was to make the student use the talent and grow. An environment of trust, of belonging, of self-belief, of relying on colleagues and helping each other (Creating Value for each other),[11] by building emotional strength and bonds helped the students rise to their inherent abilities. And that is what the teachers did. They also helped the students to unlearn so that they could learn faster.

And the importance of unlearning and learning and unlearning.

So this is an example of Value creation in education by teachers and students, and how you too can Create Value.

It is not incentives! It is not self-aggrandisement that makes creative teachers Create Value. The students too will realise that their creativity will flow despite incentives or lack of it…and as they grow, they will find that if they can Create Value for their readers, by getting them to learn, or to get an emotional bond with the writer, or making the readers feel good about themselves. Then the writer will become even more successful.

---

[10] Mahajan, https://customerthink.com/does-value-creation-need-financial-incentives/

[11] Mahajan http://customervaluecreation.blogspot.in/2013/10/value-creation-is-good-idea.html

As one teacher said, when you leave, walk backwards so that it appears you are coming in. Or that you are still with us and you belong.

And when you walk away, ask if it is the experience or the memory of the experience that was more important.

And if you as students and teachers consciously start to think of Value creation as your role, you will find that all of you will enhance your offerings because now you have added yet another dimension to your creativity and work.

Will you, the student become a Value creator? Will you use the special ability the teachers helped you find and hone to become Value creative writers?

What We Learn Is

- Security, belonging, encouragement, emotional support all Create Value;
- Value creators do not need incentives, they are self-incentivised;
- The Value-creating environment is important, and fellow students can Create Value for others.

What do you think about "Value Creation" as a part of education system? How can you use this in your company?

How VDL Applies

The first principle is that education is basic for human endeavour and well-being, and good. Education is important. The second principle is that education expects you to exceed beyond what you thought you were capable of and the third principle applies, which says that you have to use your education and abilities to Create Value for others so that they can Create Value for you. The fourth principle is that your learnings impact all of those around you. The fifth principle also applies, and it suggests that education will help you leverage your potential. The seventh principle implies that you must use your education to create more Value than you destroy. Education should teach you values, as per the eighth principle.

You can see the all 8 principles apply: Creating Value is basic, creating Value goes beyond what is expected of you, and you have to Create Value for others. The fifth principle of leveraging people's potential, the sixth on decision-making not to destroy Value, the seventh on not destroying Value and the eighth that values Create Value.

- First understand what Value the student is looking for;
- Next, what Value is he expected to create and where;
- Also, what Value is the employer, his family and the society expecting;
- Faculty must understand their role in Value creation and Create Value for students;
- Colleges and companies must teach Value creation.

Chapter 5

Value Destruction

There is a mistaken belief that all actions or Value-creating activities Create Value for everyone. We have seen how disruption can destroy Value for some while it might Create Value for others. And because Value is a perception, the same action may be seen to be destructive for some, while for others it can Create Value. VDL suggests that you be aware of Value destruction and avoid it. If you do not notice this and are not aware, you will continue to destroy value unconsciously. Value destruction can also occur when you starve a customer of Value, or when you indulge in non-Value-adding tasks.

Loic Ple[1] suggested, probably because of the etymology of Value, the generalised consensus that because it was co-created, Value could only improve through these interactions – a phenomenon that he called "co-creation myopia."

Thus, Value co-destruction may also co-exist with Value imbalances among interacting actors. This situation can be either accidental or intentional.

Is it possible to consider that one kind of Value could compensate for another one? Stated otherwise, can an interaction result, for the same actor, in economic Value co-destruction on the one hand, whereas it would also result in experiential or relational Value co-creation on the other hand? If so, this would mean that for a single actor, an interaction could simultaneously result in Value co-creation and in Value co-destruction – yet, with Value being of two different kinds. Thus, an

---

[1] Loic Ple, with permission.

illegal act can create economic Value and may destroy moral or ethical Value and may cause risk to the actor.

Loic gives an example:

"As a personal shopper, I have bought several times on Amazon, whether directly from Amazon or from vendors that sell on Amazon's marketplace. I have shared my opinion about many of the products that I bought, so that it can potentially benefit other buyers by informing them about the characteristics, advantages and limitations of the products. Sometimes, my opinion is positive, sometimes it is negative. Lately, I gave a 1-star mark to earphones that I had bought a few months before on the marketplace from a Chinese vendor. Overnight, the vendor's 'director of customer service' sent me an email to apologise, explaining how much she cared about my experience. She proposed to compensate for my poor experience by exchanging or refunding the earphones (without my sending back the defective ones, 'so that I do not have to support any extra-cost'). According to her email, all I had to do was to reply if I agreed with this proposal – which I did, asking for another product to replace the previous one. The following day, I received another email, which I was asked to forward to another mailbox with my order number, accompanied with the link towards the replacement product I could choose among a pre-selection made by the vendor. In the same email, the vendor apologised several times once again, and ensured me that my case had been forwarded to the engineers so that the products be improved. I thus followed this procedure. The day after, I received a third email that surprised me much more than the previous ones. This email confirmed that I could place the order to receive a brand-new free product, but that first, I would have to either change or remove my 1-star comment on Amazon. Only after that would I receive the coupon for the free product (the exact sentence, translated from the French version of the message, was:

> Would you be ready to help us by modifying your comment (to 4 or 5 stars) or to remove it given our after-sales service? We ask for your understanding and thank you for your kindness. All our customers can benefit from our after-sales service that would live up to their expectations. Once the comment is changed or removed, we will immediately send you a coupon. After some hesitation, I eventually did that, and received my coupon to get my replacement product.

"How does this anecdote inform us on Value co-creation and co-destruction dynamics? It shows that in the context of an ecosystem that involves several stakeholders (Amazon's marketplace, the vendor, me as a buyer and other potential buyers of the same product) with different or even opposed objectives, Value is not just either co-created or co-destroyed. My initial negative comment about the product informed other potential buyers about the quality of the product in the context of my own experience. Thus, it was a resource that they could integrate with their own resources to co-create Value, as it would enlighten their decision to buy or not to buy this product. On the other hand, the vendor regarded this comment as a negative resource that would participate in Value co-destruction. The proposal intentionally issued by the vendor aimed to change this situation by removing this negative resource (or by transforming it into a positive one, i.e. one that would participate in Value co-creation from his standpoint). Yet, on the other hand, this would negatively affect the purchasing decision of other potential buyers. Indeed, this would increase information asymmetry, as they would not be able to access nor integrate this resource anymore, increasing the odds for their purchasing decision to result in co-destruction. Moreover, I as a buyer could have paid little attention to the difference between the vendor and Amazon (since I bought the product on Amazon consider that Amazon allowed vendors' unethical behaviours – even though Amazon had little or even nothing to do with the vendor's practice. Indeed, one can legitimately wonder whether asking for a change in the comment in exchange for a new product is ethical or not."

"Therefore, this could have negatively influenced my perception of Amazon. In co-creation or co-destruction terminology, this would result in my integrating a new resource (a poor image of the company) that would lead to co-destruction for Amazon because of the vendor's poor ethical behaviour. Thus, in this web of interactions between several actors, co-creation and co-destruction may co-exist, co-creation and co-destruction might be opposite results of a Value process that involves different actors, and co-destruction might be a step on the path towards co-creation (and vice-versa)."

Kaldor-Hicks suggests reallocation (called a Pareto improvement) if at least one person is made better off and nobody is made worse off. Does this example fit into this?

Co-Destruction

The author was judging PhD students' poster session at Leicester Castle Business School and the First Global Conference on Creating Value and was struck by one poster on co-destruction where the student went on to look at corruption as co-destruction.

> The only alternative to coexistence is co-destruction...Nehru

Our difficulty was how two rational people would start a co-destruction process. While co-creation refers to the process whereby providers and customers collaboratively Create Value, co-destruction refers to the collaborative destruction, or diminishment of Value by providers and customers.

Can you think of any?

After reflection we came up with two football teams willing to destroy each other or co-destruct, or openly starting a war.

Ok, that is easy to understand. But does Value co-creation and Value co-destruction mean:

Prahalad and Ramaswamy define the co-creation of Value thus: "The consumer and the firm are intimately involved in jointly creating Value that is unique to the individual consumer. . .The interaction between consumers and firms becomes the new locus of co-creation of Value."

When referring to one particular case, for instance, they infer that "not everyone enjoys such an interactive co-creation process. . .Nor are all co-creation experiences positive."

You can see the definition is going from a collaborative process to an unplanned process. I think we need to be clear about whether co-destruction is

1. Intentional and collaborative co-destruction
2. Collaborative but unintentional co-destruction
3. Unintentional one-sided destruction (non-collaborative) or
4. Intentional one-sided destruction (non-collaborative)

Thus, for any collaborative process, co-creation or co-destruction, companies and customers should align their mutual expectations. This means that firms should communicate precisely about the manner they expect their consumers to integrate and apply the resources needed for co-creating Value. At eYeka, a co-creation platform, the brief always details what the brand expects from a call for entry, and the content is moderated appropriately. It might not unleash immoderate passion. . . but it will also avoid negative side-effects!

EYeka also states some disappointing results of a co-innovation initiative, for instance, which can be seen as co-destruction because time and money have been spent on something that merely leads to an incremental innovation. Thus, this is an unintentional result.

Against this backdrop, we suggest defining Value co-destruction as a relationship process between focal actors and their networks that results in a decline in at least one of the focal actors and/or their networks' well-being.[2]

> VDL teaches us how to avoid unintentional co-destruction.

An associate gave an example of a financial services firm getting together with an ailing firm with pension liabilities and a large amount of debt to co-destruct the company in order to make a profit. According to S-D logic, Value creation is then

---

[2] http://www.naplesforumonservice.it/uploads//files/Lefebvre%2C%20Ple.pdf

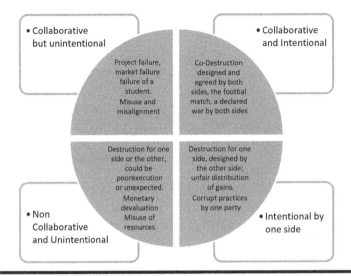

Figure 5.1 Co-Destruction (Author)

an interactive and collaborative process that occurs through the exchange of service between entities. Here we have collaborative and intentional co-destruction.

Non-collaborative and unintentional co-destruction is when I buy a new device such as a cell phone and it does not work. This can be devaluation of your money, or something in a network that does not work.

Intentional co-destruction is when someone goes out to cheat a partner, or does not share the gains as agreed, or engages in corrupt practices.

Collaborative projects that fail include M&As that do not work or yield the desired results, or projects that do not sell or sell at a loss.

Misuse and misalignment, intentional vs. accidental co-destruction can exist. Figure 5.1 shows these.

Non-Value-Added Tasks

Companies have many non-Value-added tasks, processes, events, wastage that are non-Value-adding. These include starting meetings late (wasting the time of many participants waiting for the meeting to start; reading unnecessary

> VDL shows how non-Value-adding tasks are Value destroying.

e-mails; correcting mistakes (especially for Customers as well as in production or in tax reporting); unnecessary travel which could be replaced by calls or video calls;

20 people picking up bosses at airports; not doing legal or moral work; being stuck in a traffic jam.

Non-Value-added tasks are actually Value-destructive tasks. A whole discipline has been brought into play where Value destroyed has become important. This, in and of itself, is an important discipline because it looks at net Value which is Value created minus Value destroyed minus non-Value-added activities.

Value co-destruction occurs mostly when there is a misuse of resources, either incorrectly, inaptly or unpredictably. This happens when the available resources are used, say in an interaction. Companies can misuse their processes to create more Value for themselves, thereby destroying Value for others such as employees and customers. This is planned misuse. Accidental misuse can also be disastrous for customers and destroy Value for them. The reader has examples of what has happened in his or her ecosystem. An unplanned Value destruction happens when a bus or train is cancelled. Accidental misuse could be throwing a cell phone battery into the fireplace.

Corruption destroys Value for some while adding Value for others.

However, very few researchers have looked into the possible downside of Value co-destruction. The risk of losing customers this way is highly likely, as 40% of customers who had a bad experience will discontinue doing business with the offending firm. To prevent nearly half of consumers from churning after a bad experience, it is therefore crucial that both parties communicate their expectations extensively to each other so Value can be co-created instead of destructed.

Value co-creation has implied that both sides are benefited and that it is mutually acceptable. I get what I deserved. Value is destroyed when I feel I got less than I deserved or if something is unfair.

We also find in a generally positive Value-creating merger of two companies, certain entrenched managers destroy Value by their non-cooperation, their attitudes etc.

Chief financial officers[3] often exercise discretion – even sacrifice economic Value – to deliver earnings. Destruction of shareholder Value through legal means is pervasive, perhaps even a routine way of doing business. Indeed, the amount of Value destroyed by companies striving to hit earnings targets exceeds the Value lost in recent high-profile fraud cases.

The same issue arises when looking at executive salaries. Should we look at short-term results that may destroy long-term Value or look at long-term Value that may reduce short-term wealth? Value creation and Value extraction must be viewed in a continuum. We must have better metrics for long-term results, perhaps better strategic long-term management, we should then have a strategic management system that allows managers to provide current results while driving

---

[3] https://www.cfapubs.org/doi/abs/10.2469/faj.v62.n6.4351

towards long-term Value. How do we look at potential growth and innovation? Strategic management performance metrics and incentive design are then also aligned with sustainability and Value creation that benefits the ecosystem: This may destroy short-term Value, and this has to be taken into account.

Value can be created and destroyed in process improvement and service when we ignore other items such as waste created, jobs destroyed.

Total Value created or seen is Value-created work minus non-Value-creating work minus Value-destructive activities.

Waste can include non-Value-added work (this can be seen in the third and fourth quadrant in the chart in Figure 5.2.

When any resource is misused or badly used, Value is destroyed. For example, providing a poor experience to a customer. There is a net Value concept to customers where benefits and negative benefits/sacrifices are considered. This, of course, should be obvious from the definition of Value, what you get for what you give or sacrifice.

So, is destruction included in the Value definition?

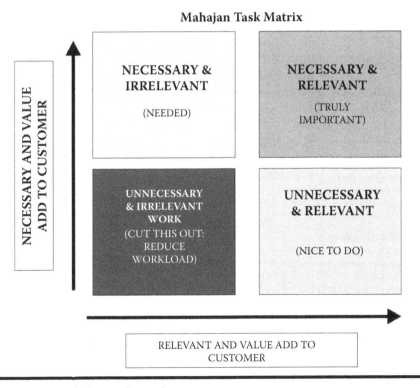

Mahajan Task Matrix

Figure 5.2   Mahajan Task Matrix

Value destruction can also occur when values are abrogated a la Enron...fraud, lack of integrity. Value can be destroyed in deceptive marketing, see Pfizer agreeing to pay $2.3 billion to settle civil and criminal allegations that it violated federal rules governing drug sales. The pharmaceutical manufacturer was charged with illegally promoting its painkiller Bextra and three other medications by offering doctors speaking fees and subsidised trips to resorts, among other benefits.

Value destruction happens when real estate values fall, for example.

Value Destruction: Non-Value-Added Tasks Destroy Value

Companies have many non-Value-added tasks, processes, events, wastage that are non-Value-adding. Some examples have been given earlier of non-Value-added tasks.

Value co-destruction occurs mostly when there is a misuse of resources, either incorrectly, inaptly or unpredictably. This happens when the available resources are used, say in an interaction. Companies can misuse their processes to create more Value for themselves, thereby destroying Value for others such as employees and customers. This is planned misuse. Accidental misuse can also be disastrous for customers and destroy Value for them. The reader has examples of what has happened in his or her ecosystem Corruption destroys Value for some while adding Value for others.

Or the Value co-creation was one sided. Value starvation is an example.

And then there is the question of whether or not Value can be co-destroyed. It can, as I explained earlier.

Value is also seen as benefits minus cost. Others call this, benefits minus sacrifice. Whatever you sacrifice could be construed as Value destruction... Ouch, this takes too much time or effort, or they make me feel like a fool.

However, very few researchers have looked into the possible downsides of Value co-destruction. Some of the risks have been shown earlier.

For Customers

Necessary work is essential for, vital to, indispensable to, important to, crucial to, needed by, compulsorily required by or requisite for the Customer.

Relevant work is pertinent to, applicable or germane to, or appropriate to the Customer. This is work that can be eliminated without deterioration of present service or product.

What work is the Customer willing to pay for? Every business enterprise has at least eight stakeholder groups, whose concerns must be considered when analysing business processes: customers, suppliers and partners, managers, employees, creditors, investors, governments and community groups

Customer Value added of task: (Value to Customer after the task)
MINUS (Value to the Customer prior to the task)

Who is the Customer? Are some classes of work for internal customers[4] necessary? If such work is free now, would someone pay for these services or work?

It is the final bill-paying Customer at the end of the entire Value chain who determines if the work/task adds Value to him/her.

Similarly, for Businesses

Necessary work is essential for, vital to, indispensable to, important to, crucial to, needed by, compulsory required or requisite for the Business.

Relevant work is pertinent to, applicable or germane to, or appropriate to the Business. This is work that can be eliminated without deterioration of present service or product.

Let us list some of these tasks:

Task		Relevant to	Necessary for	Relevant to	Necessary for
		CUSTOMER		*BUSINESS*	
S	Sales and Marketing	Sometimes Yes	Sometimes Yes		Yes
A	Advertising	Sometimes Yes	Sometimes Yes		Yes
A/C	Accounting	Yes			Yes
T	Tax related	Yes			Yes
O	Offsite meetings				Yes
S	Strategy	Yes			Yes
B	Business Meetings			Yes	yes
T	Training			Yes	Yes
C	Customer Meetings	Sometimes Yes	Sometimes Yes	Sometimes Yes	Sometimes Yes
CT	Customer training	Yes			Yes
M	Manufacturing	Yes			Yes
R&D	R&D	Yes			Yes
SM	Social media	Yes			yes

(*Continued*)

---

[4] I think the concept of internal customers' builds silos, and therefore should be avoided

(Cont.)

Task		Relevant to	Necessary for	Relevant to	Necessary for
		CUSTOMER		BUSINESS	
IT	IT	Yes			Yes
PR	Public Relations	Yes			Yes
P	Profit making	Yes			Yes
PRICE	Pricing	Yes	Yes		Yes
CR	Customer Redressal		Yes	Sometimes Yes	Sometimes Yes
CS	Customer Service		Yes	Sometimes Yes	Sometimes Yes
CP	Company People		Yes		Yes
REL	Relationship with Customer		Yes		Yes
VALUES	Values of company		Yes		Yes
PR	Relationship with Partners	Yes			Yes
SCR	Supply chain relationship	Yes			Yes
DC	Delivery chain	Yes			Yes
O	Posh offices			Yes	
D	Data and data analysis				Yes
H	HR Department				Yes
CV	Customer Value		Yes	Yes	
CE	Customer time and effort		Yes	Yes	

Figure 5.3 Relevant and Necessary Tasks

The more companies can align their priorities with the those of the customers and make the tasks that are relevant and necessary for customers, that is make their business priorities the one's important for the customers, the more successful they will be.

Customer anxiety, keeping them waiting, ignoring them, Unnecessary contact, annoying customers and poor quality all are a wasted effort for the company and the Customer and should be cut out. These are relevant to the customer as they are exposed to these all the time.

As an example, if the company was to take customer Value, customer experience and effort, customer redressal seriously and move them into the top right-hand quadrant, then customer needs and company needs would start to coincide.

This is shown in the Figure 5.2.

Morality and Legality

There is a mistaken belief that ends justify the means. There are some who believe creating Value just for themselves is good. If they have done something illegally or immorally, have they destroyed Value for others?

Many times, businessmen cheat the banks, especially public-sector banks. They also cheat on taxes. Both of these actions lead to Value destruction for the banks, the tax system, the country and honest tax payers. Sometimes the government has to bail out such banks, causing a greater Value destruction for honest tax payers.

There are many examples you can give from your experience.

How VDL Applies

The message is: Create Value and avoid destruction of Value.

Obviously, creating Value is natural (First principle). However, if you do nothing or do not exceed what is expected of you, you could destroy Value. Non-Value-adding tasks are an example (Second principle). You could destroy Value by not creating Value for others (Third principle). The Fourth principle suggests all stakeholders must be impacted positively or else you could destroy Value for some. The Seventh principle specifically talks about Value destruction. The Eighth principle talks about morals and values and how a lack of these can destroy Value.

This chapter shows how you and your business can view Value destruction and avoid it.

Chapter 6

The Fundamentals of Value

Nuances of Value

In Chapter 1, we concentrated on the Principles of Value Creation and on VDL. Here we will discuss other aspects of Value. This is a chapter that can be skipped if the reader does not want to get into the philosophy of Value. This philosophy is important to understand VDL.

In this discussion we use Value to mean the Value of a product (or what the worth of a product is), service to someone, or the Value of an institution (like society, or a company, or a person, or a group of people) and the Value (good and well-being) created for the institution or the actor.

We also talk about measurement of Value, which leads us into Customer Value, which is one of the fundamental areas where VDL has been used. Business Value and VDL is shown in the next chapter.

Aaron Fullan asks: Why does every human life have Value? Is our Value based on how much money we make? How many people we influence? What gender we are? What country we come from? What gifts and talents we have? Our physical and intellectual abilities?

He suggests this is a question of morality. Our moral convictions must be based on something outside of ourselves. Otherwise, what one person would consider "morally wrong" might be assumed "morally right" by another, in which case morality becomes an opinion rather than an absolute. So, we all need Values that exist within us. Values are normally absolute, and do not depend on individuals. Individuals may choose to follow or not follow Values for themselves.

Is Value an absolute term? The only place "absolute" Value is used is in determining the Value of a firm through discounted cash flow. So economic Value can be absolute, though generally it is based on perceptions (and therefore assumptions) and may not be absolute. In our definition of Value, Value is always relative (to other alternatives, or to the perceiver depending on his context).

The term surplus Value is really what we call Value added. Its concept started in the economic sense (including its use by Karl Marx to denote new Value added by workers). In the Value creation field, Value added is the increase in Value over what exists or over competitive offerings and goes beyond just economic results.

This chapter then discusses Value as seen by various dominant logics, and then goes into Customer Value, its principles and measurement, and integrated Value.

Innate, Latent, Potential, Inherent, Intrinsic and Extrinsic Value

Unlike what exists in the general Value literature, Value Dominant Logic suggests that Value can be innate, intrinsic, potential, inherent and/or latent Value. This thinking helps people to create greater Value by noticing and developing innate Value and Value waiting to happen.

> To know more about VDL and yourself, you must understand what latent, potential, innate and inherent Value means in your case and the case of others, and how you can relate to them, and become a better Value creator.

What are innate Value, intrinsic Value, potential Value, inherent Value and latent Value?

Innate Value is existing and natural Value – as in a person. The hidden talents of a person may be latent (existing or present, but concealed or inactive). The inherent Value this person has is that s/he has something such as a degree, or a specific knowledge or trait. Innate Value is what someone is born with or has.

Intrinsic is closer to innate. Innate is inborn, native or natural. Thus, it is innate to be able to judge between good and evil.

Intrinsic is like innate but means essential. The intrinsic Value of gold or silver, or the intrinsic Value of the Bhagavad Gita are examples.

The concept of intrinsic Value has been described variously as what is valuable for its own sake, in itself, on its own, in its own right. By contrast, extrinsic Value has been characterised mainly as what is valuable as a means, or for something or someone else's sake. If there is inherent or latent Value in an item, it is called intrinsic Value:

Michael Zimmerman states there should also be something called "extrinsic Value." Here we look at something not for its own sake but for the sake of others, (are things good or bad for themselves or for the sake of others?). Plato in fact said philosophers have tended to focus on just one particular causal relation, the means-end relation. This is the relation at issue in the example given earlier: helping others is a means

> VDL suggests creating Value for the sake of others.

to their needs being satisfied, which is itself a means to their experiencing pleasure or gaining Value.

So, we deal with intrinsic Value and Value which is perceived is extrinsic. This has also been referred to as phenomenological Value as described in Vargo and Lusch's book, *Toward a Better Understanding of the Role of Value in Markets and Marketing*, such Value has to be seen in context.

Take an example of a painting which as of itself has Value that some have called "inherent Value."[1] ("Inherent Value" may not be the most suitable term to use here, since it may well suggest intrinsic Value, whereas the sort of Value at issue is supposed to be a type of extrinsic Value. The Value attributed to the painting is one that it is said to have in virtue of its relation to something else that would supposedly be intrinsically good if it occurred, namely, the appreciation of its beauty.) Many other instances could be given of cases in which we are inclined to call something good in virtue of its relation to something else that is or would be intrinsically good, even though the relation in question is not a means-end relation.

One final point. It is sometimes said that there can be no extrinsic Value (or be extrinsically good) without intrinsic Value (or intrinsically good). Second, it might mean that nothing can occur that is either extrinsically good or extrinsically bad unless something else occurs that is either intrinsically good or intrinsically bad. Both these interpretations may not hold good, as the base argument is questionable. Suppose that no one ever appreciates the beauty of Leonardo's masterpiece, and that nothing else that is intrinsically either good or bad ever occurs; still his painting may be said to be inherently good.[2]

Moreover, Value depends on context and the user. Value creation for one may be Value destruction for another.

For our discussion, we can say that Value exists in some form or other, waiting to be noticed and perceived, before it can be worked on.

In the real world, such Value is worked on and further Value is added so that the Value can be readied to be perceived (awareness) and then exchanged.

The question is that in this process is Value truly enhanced and to what extent?

Why is this of interest to us? Something is valuable for its own sake as opposed to being valuable for the sake of something else. These are issues we often face in life or business.

---

[1] (Lewis 1946, p. 391; cf. Frankena 1973, p. 82)
[2] https://plato.stanford.edu/entries/value-intrinsic-extrinsic/

In what we are discussing Value is based not just on its intrinsic Value but when the Value is perceived by someone else, and in the context it is perceived.

So, let us take the notion of driverless cars. Is it a notion that existed or the Value of a driverless car that existed? This Value was not seen by many, not considered by others or ignored by some others. Those that saw the potential Value, worked on it to create more Value. But they can create only so much Value (which is seen in exchange) but the true Value comes in the use and the further co-creation of such Value.

In this book, we do not differentiate between different Value, and sometimes use Value terms interchangeable to mean Value that is hidden or not seen or noticed. Value creation is an unfolding process, with no end state.

Then we have the philosophical thinking on Value where they distinguish between instrumental and intrinsic Value. Plato was the first to discuss this. He says instrumental Value is worth having as a tool to create something else that is good. A cell phone to receive calls is an example.

Axiology is the science of Value in philosophy, Value theory.

The Value possessed by a property which has potential for redevelopment because it is currently not used optimally is the intrinsic Value of the property.

Does Innate Value Remain? Is It Constant?

Is Value a constant, and do we view components of Value depending on our vantage point? Value, it turns out is not a constant. Value is unlike energy (which can neither be created nor destroyed but can be transformed).

Value exists in some form or other, waiting to be perceived, and when perceived, the Value is enhanced or diminished depending on the viewer of the Value and on the perception of the user or recipient of Value. Value is perception-defined, it can be created, it migrates, is captured and stopped, co-created and can also be lost and found. This is discussed later.

If Value exists in some form or other, it is potential or latent Value. When perceived, worked on, enhanced or improved, Value becomes different, maybe less potential and more useful.

Does innate Value remain, or does it sometimes extinguish itself. So, if you have a diamond, and if artificial diamonds flood the market, the Value of your diamond may reduce or increase. Value can change, intrinsically and in the perception of the receiver/customer.

Moreover, there is a lifecycle, where the need and the perceived Value is high. But this can be reduced a great deal because of supply and demand, changing needs, changing habits.

So, do not take Value for granted. It may not always be there or remain forever. Be awake.

Let's assume you have a car, and you paint it and add Value from your point of view. Two different people view the paint and it creates different Value. Does it mean Value is not constant? And if not viewed completely where is the extra Value?

Or is there potential Value? The answer is that you perceive a Value with the paint. The moment you have painted the car, there is Value for you (you like it, the car looks good, I am happy to drive it). The people who look at it have a perception which may be different from you and may or may not like the colour or the looks of the car. Each perceives different Value, especially if they were thinking of buying the car.

So, the actual Value you perceive as you use the car, which may be different from the market Value of the car or the Value the buyers perceive.

And is actual Value as used or as perceived? Even in use there is a perception.

Is Value only a reality (or a perception) once in someone's mind? Before that there is potential Value not noticed or perceived.

Some define potential Value as the present Value of the best possible outcome in the future and take away the temporal time element of Value.

I may think I have much Value to offer, but you see me as offering only a small amount of Value. So, Value is not absolute but relative.

Absolute Value and standard (expected) Value are relative as perceived.

Is Value Constant?

Value does not exist in the absence of consciousness, ergo Value is relative.[3]

We will see how Value can increase, dissipate and re-emerge in future chapters.

Any discussion of Value is not precise as long as the definition of Value is not precise and is subjective. Value measurement and the border lines of Value have to be in focus.

One question of Value is: Is there a given absolute Value scale – or is it just, and only, a relative relation of a given Value of one part of the economy to the other parts or the total sum.

The overwhelming answer is that Value is relative, because it is perceived, because it is subjective. A number of business-related measurements are based on perceptions but have a correlation with business results, because generally measurement of perceptions is related to the marketplace or the perceiver. Value created by someone is related to, or compared to Value created by someone else. Is this writer creating Value? The answer is based on the Value you think other writers create for you.

Just doing your job is not enough[4] to Create Value. You have to go beyond what is expected of you to Create Value.

---

[3] Olaf Schilgen in a research Gate blog on Value – is it relative or absolute?

[4] https://www.linkedin.com/pulse/Value-waiting-happen-what-you-can-do-creating-yourself-gautam-mahajan/

This brings us to an important point:

You can only create so much Value by yourself, but the true Value comes from creating Value for someone who turns around and says you have created Value. Value is created for you by others using your potential Value. See figure 1.2 in Chapter 1, shown here as Figure 6.1.

Others suggest Value can have an ethical and philosophical property. It is the ethical philosophic Value that an object has 'in itself'; 'for its own sake,' an intrinsic property. An object with intrinsic Value may be regarded as an end or (in Kantian terminology) end-in-itself.[5]

So, Value in an ethical sense is whether it improves or is good for someone. So, pleasure could be good and pain bad, and one has more intrinsic Value than the other. But if pleasure in use causes pain (to someone including the user), its intrinsic Value is lower. So, there could be intrinsic Value in a painting or the natural environment.

Sheth, Newman and Gross[6] suggest five different types of Value: functional, emotional, epistemic, social and conditional Value. Functional Value refers to consumers' perceived utility in terms of product function or performance.

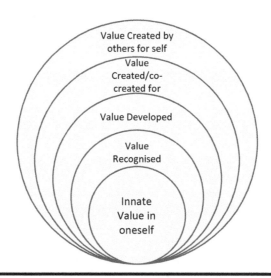

Figure 6.1   Circle of Value Showing How Value Is Interrelated

[5] https://plato.stanford.edu/entries/Value-intrinsic-extrinsic/
[6] Why we buy what we buy: A theory of consumption values: Sheth, J. N., Newman, B. I., & Gross, B. L. (1991). *Journal of Business Research*, 22(2), 159–170.

Emotional Value is what rouses feelings in consumers. Epistemic Value is based on consumers' curiosity, novelty and desire to learn. Social Value is where consumers are in groups.

Other Value Expressions

These include Prudential Value, which includes well-being and is differentiated from Values. Value theory helps understand how people Value things, and why. Value theory separates moral and ethical good, from natural good which has to do with things not people. Ethical good has to do with people.

Value theory, is also called axiology, studies which things are good or bad, how good or bad they are, and, most fundamentally, what it is for a thing to be good or bad. As a philosophical discipline, Value theory branches out in various directions: into ethics, it has implications for philosophy, economics and so on. The conceptualisation of Value cannot be just restricted to what it means. From the 20 odd meanings of Value, it seems that from a business perspective Value means the worth of something versus competitive offers.

Comments Based on SDL and Other Logics Such as Customer Dominant Logic

This section focuses on other logics. It is more theoretical.

Value Dominant Logic is all encompassing. It involves and goes beyond the known and the unnoticed. The goal of all dominant logic is to Create Value. That is to improve the quality of life and Value in a continuous, dynamic, actor-centric manner, in a continual quest for improving well-being of human actors, in an ever-changing context. In a sense companies are also human actors, because they are made up of humans.

We paraphrase some facets of various logics. We only comment when we have a different point of view. Thus, many of the points below are also part of VDL.

Resources are anything actors can draw upon to increase viability and can be tangible and intangible. Resource integration can be used to define the process of innovation. In VDL, resources also have Value, or potential or latent Value. Value can be co-created, consumed, it could be perishable, or it could be re-used.

Value creation/destruction can occur by changing rules and resource relationship, such as re-defining existing markets, or by disruption. Value creation increases with relationships and collaboration. Every interaction then increases resource and learning competence.

One actor creates Value, whereas another actor consumes and maybe destroys Value.

Actors have Value, Create Value (for themselves and others), can consume and destroy Value.

Value also works in dilemmas, as in making decisions in an environment of high uncertainty. Value implies effectiveness versus efficiency.

Service Dominant Logic, SDL states Value is always phenomenological as seen by the beneficiary. Value creation is a service-to-service exchange.

Knowledge has intangible Value that can become a potential resource or used by Value creators, and when applied becomes a service which creates Value. Value Creation takes knowledge beyond the functional and mechanical into useful for Value creation.

SDL explains why Value (even in self-service) is always a co-creation act because every individual is deeply embedded in society and culture. Even a single individual on a desert island is using knowledge derived by society over time to think clearly about self-service Value, like starting a fire or making a shelter. The actor is integrating resources from others and judging those resources as beneficial. The other actors do not have to be physically present for co-creation to be in play.

SDL is based on the idea that service, the application of competences for the benefit of another, is the fundamental basis of Value creation through exchange. That is, service is exchanged for service.[7]

Value is the fundamental *goal* of exchange. Service is the fundamental *basis* of exchange (knowledge and skill are the fundamental basis of exchange) Exchange-Value is what something is worth whereas use-Value is improving well-being. The end result is more important than the process, and so SDL suggests the experience and solutions are more important than the process. Service is the process of one actor doing something for another.

Value transcends processes and is a mindset; and improves the well-being of another actor.

In VDL, Value creation goes beyond the functional (and functional management) and what is expected. Potential customers are also a form of Value creation.

CRM (Customer Relationship Management) assumes customers are operand (tangible and static) resources.

VDL states we can potentially Create Value from anything and add/create/co-create Value with them. Value creation implies a mindset and perspective. Evert Gummesson in 1995 said: Customers buy (I say or use) offerings which render services that Create Value. Operand resources are tangible resources and are static resources according to SDL.

Operant (or intangible) resources are those capable of acting on other resources to Create Value. Providers, customers or actors can include governments, companies,

---

[7] Vargo, S. L., & Akaka, M. A. (2009). Service-dominant logic as a foundation for service science: Clarifications. Service Science, 1(1), 32–41, SSG.

non-governmental organisations, institutions focused on education, knowledge, research and innovation, employees and supply and delivery chain partners.

We will not go into the foundations of SDL, Vargo and Lusch; SL (Service Logic), Gronroos; and CDL (Customer Dominant Logic), Heinonen and Strandvik; and CVDL (Customer Value Dominant Logic), Schlager and Maas, 2012 which are described adequately by the authors.

Because people, businesses including providers and customers, and the business ecosystem of individuals, companies, employees, partners, supply chain and delivery chain and society; government and institutions and other recipients of Value, are all driven by creating and *absorbing* Value, VDL is important to the ecosystem. This is, in spite of the remarkable changes in the ecosystem at large and the business ecosystem in particular, in terms of technological changes, buying and selling changes, marketing and increasingly knowledgeable customers, the primacy of customers and the availability and sharing of information, Value and the creation of Value remain a primary objective of all the actors. CDL and CVDL reiterate the understanding that the customer is of key importance. VDL does not deny this, because the Value design and delivery to and subsequent use and absorption by the customer and actors before creating more Value by the actors to the ecosystem, remains of prime importance.

We do not espouse a Value Creation Logic, as Value creation is the process of creating Value which we all seek, and desire to deliver to gain more Value for ourselves and the ecosystem. SDL and the other logics have Value creation as a goal.

VDL means that ecosystems flourish including business ones, by proactively and consciously becoming aware of, and then developing and creating or co-creating Value and exchanging it with those that perceive that Value is being added to them beyond other alternatives or sources, that leads them to consider, buy, use, improve or co-create and discard products and services. SDL calls for Value co-creation, SL for focusing on Value-in-use, and CDL promotes Value formation and Value-in-life. CVDL suggests the intertwined role of customer's and the firm. VDL embraces all of these and goes beyond to the role of actors is to Create Value for themselves, business and society and ecosystems. The process is important as proposed by SDL, SL, CDL and CVDL but VDL goes beyond processes, and the debates of the primacy of products, services and the customer, because to Create Value for the customer one must Create Value for the providers including employees, supply and delivery chain and society at large, and the imbibing of Values (integrity, moral and ethical etc.) are essential.

Just as the purpose of education is to Create Value in society (though the direct recipient is the student, and the employer); or the purpose of a company goes beyond just the profit motive to creating Value for the customer, to doing something for its stakeholders and society. Value goes beyond the actors, though Value has to be created for them.

Value also exists in inanimate and animate objects. Here Value can mean good, meritorious or worthwhile, or the like. VDL works with any of these definitions. Value has always existed as shown in Figure 6.2.

SL however, states the focus is indeed to provide service and was defined by interactions involving and revolving around customers. Value-in-exchange is created during the exchange process, and then Value-in-use is created. Service should "focus on Value through the lens of the customer" states Edvardsson. CDL places the customer at the centre and is a customer-centric perspective which argues that SDL and GDL (Goods Dominant Logic) are provider focused, and do not emphasise the interaction between the customer and the provider/market.

Gronroos and Voima mooted the Value spheres in 2012 as shown in Figure 6.2.

From an S-D logic perspective, companies cannot provide Value but merely offer propositions of Value; it is the customer that determines Value and co-creates it with the company at a given time and context. Thus, a company's offering, be it intangible, tangible or a combination of the two, is merely Value unrealised, i.e. a "store of potential Value," until the customer realises it

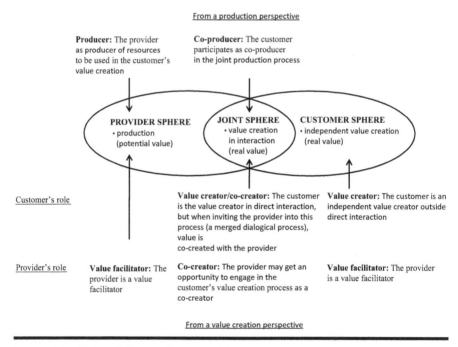

Figure 6.2   Value Spheres, Gronroos 2012

through co-creation in context and gains the benefit.[8] CDL shifted the perspective to a customer one from a provider one, and that providers must be driven by customers. Both service and products must form the basis of Value creation. Customers therefore dominate and control Value creation.

The Service Logic view is shown in Figure 6.2.

Figure 6.3, shows the CDL view of the offerings and actors and their focus (Heinonen and Strandvik 2015). SM is service management.

The CDL view and the consumer cultures view are not outside the purview of VDL, even though customer cultures look at a wider ecosystem, and not so focused on managerial thinking. CDL is a marketing perspective focused on customers.

SDL is further developed by Vargo and Lusch where the axioms and foundational premises of SDL are upgraded. This is best seen as Value creation starting with actors, who integrate resources and exchange service for institutions and institutional arrangements, and in service ecosystems.

They describe a configuration of actors that consists of institutions and an arrangement of institutions and an interdependent assemblage of institutions as the facilitators of Value co-creation in markets and elsewhere.

Co-creation (not just co-production) of Value is the purpose of the exchange of service for service processes, and thus fundamental to markets and marketing. The scope is widened by using beneficiaries instead of customers. Value is co-created by multiple actors including the beneficiary. Value creation takes place in networks.

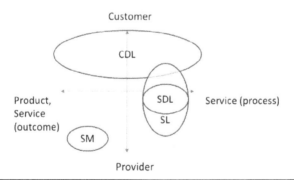

Figure 6.3   Customer Dominant Logic vs. Service Logic and Service Dominant Logic

---

[8] OUTCOME-BASED CONTRACTS FOR BUSINESS-TO-BUSINESS SERVICE. 1. Irene C. L. Ng. Sai S. Nudurupati. Paul Tasker. 077-May-2010. ISSN: 1744-0009

Ng and Smith state:

> The relationship between use and exchange therefore traverses an important macro and aggregated level, that of markets. Individuals source for what is "good" or of Value from the output demand market and make their choices in a similar way that firms source for what is "good" or of Value from the input demand market. This means that the exchange Value for an offering may not be merely driven by its use-Value, but through the transaction by which the individual chooses the offering, of which use-Value may only form part of the reason, with the choice context (availability of substitutes, etc.) taking a dominant position.

Vargo and Lusch discuss resource integrating, reciprocal-service providing actors co-creating Value. They also define Value as idiosyncratic, experiential, contextual and meaning laden.

Gronroos defines the role of marketing as engaging the firm with the customers' processes with an aim to support Value creation in those processes in a mutually beneficial way.

Fisk (private communication to the author, 2017) states Value can be habitual or transformative. He focuses also on choice, which becomes a potential Value creator.

Schlager and Maas, 2012 discuss Customer Value creation and its relationship to SDL and CDL thinking. Value is being determined uniquely and phenomenologically by the customer, Vargo and Lusch 2008, (p. 7).

> Value, which is a perception, needs to be measured. An example of the Customer Value Added measurement is shown and can be replicated for other Value measurements. Thus VDL helps measuring Value.

Value cannot be re-inventoried. Shlager and Maas, 2012 reiterate that CV is contextual and experiential. Mahajan 2011 defines Total Customer Value Management, as the effort of the entire company in creating Value for the customer.

Measurement of Value

We have learnt that Value is not an absolute measure.

It is a relative measure, and so the best measurement of Value is versus alternatives.

While Value is doing good and improving well-being, it is also whether something was worthwhile.

We have been measuring the worth or Value of a product or service using the measure Customer Value Added. Here we measure the market perceptions of Value we add, and the market perceptions of Value added by competitors. We then define a relationship between the two called:

Customer Value Added

$$CVA = \frac{Perceived\ worth\ of\ your\ offer}{Perceived\ worth\ of\ competitive\ offer}$$

One such measurement is Customer Value Added, of which the Vodafone MD Graham Maher said:

Customer Value Added tracks market share to within 1% accuracy. It is a leading predictor of market share. Vodafone's market share went up from 19% in 1997 when Customer Value work started to 70% in 2002 in New Zealand. And his financial director said "the CVA score is more rigid and correct than our financial scores".

Similarly, we can measure the Value added by a company to its employees as perceived by its employees. This is called:

Employee Value Added

$$EVA = \frac{Perceived\ worth\ or\ Value\ added\ by\ your\ company\ to\ your\ employees}{Perceived\ worth\ or\ Value\ added\ by\ your\ competitors\ to\ their\ employees}$$

This is a measurement done by a company to elicit the perception of Value added to its employees versus the Value competitors add.

However, if you are an employee looking to change jobs, you want to figure out whether the new offer is better or not than your current job:

$$Value\ added\ by\ new\ job = \frac{Perceived\ worth\ of\ or\ Value\ created\ by\ new\ job}{Perceived\ Value\ created\ by\ present\ job}$$

So, if the answer is 1 there is no apparent difference between the present and the new job. If the answer is higher than one the proposed job offers more Value to you. EVA is shown in Figure 6.4

You notice from the results we can also get the relative importance of each of the attributes in the attribute tree.

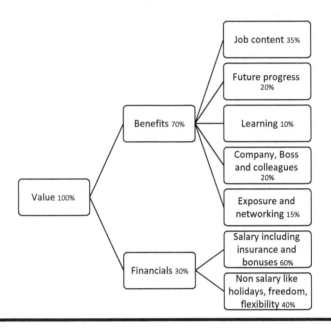

Figure 6.4   Attribute Tree to Value Your Job

You could make a similar attribute tree for your business. You can get details from my book: *Creating Customer Value Makes You a Great Executive.*

Measuring something for doing good, can be done in a similar fashion. India introduced a new GST (Goods and Services Tax). Is it good or not good? Every individual will have a different perception. If we measure a statistically significant number of respondents, we will get a general idea of the good or bad it did (Value created or destroyed) see Figure 6.5. We could also do this for other social causes. We could do this for ourselves, for example when considering entering a college for engineering or for anthropology. Which could be potentially more valuable?

We have shown similar types of attribute trees for disruptive occurrences such as driverless cars, Value destruction for professional drivers, repair services, insurance and Value improvement for drivers, for society etc. These Values will change over time and in various countries.

Customer Value

Customer Value Creation

This section will help you to use Customer Value Creation effectively and effortlessly, and to gain professionally and personally by applying the principles

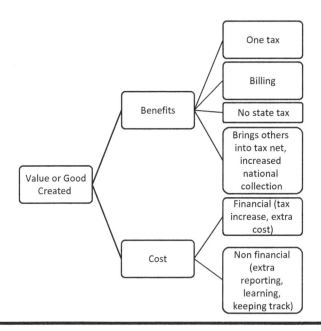

Figure 6.5   Attribute Tree for Value Created by Goods and Service Tax in India

of Customer Value Creation. You and your company will achieve long-term success through the enablement and delivery of Customer Value.

> Value is what something is worth to the Customer. Value creation is therefore a necessary step for management transformation to Customer orientation. Value creation is executing proactive, conscious, inspired and imaginative and actions that create better gains or Value for Customers and all stakeholders.

The first step in your mastering Customer Value Creation is to understand what Customer means, how Value and Creation are used in the context of Customer Value Creation. All of us should use this common terminology.

Once we all agree and understand the definitions, we can move on to the next step. The definitions are shown in the box below.

Customer: a person who buys goods or services from a shop or business, or receives services from anyone be they government, society or NGOs. We differentiate between a Customer and a consumer (who consumes a product but may not buy it).

We have to understand that a consumer could be an influencer for buying and therefore Value has to be created for him (a consumer then is a special case, a non-buying Customer). Another non-buying Customer is a non-Customer. He buys from someone else and not from us and therefore could become our Customer if we provided greater Value to him.

We are also Customers of government and society, and of non-governmental organisations. This is because we get services from them and contribute to them in some sense.

You notice we used the word Value and creation in conjunction with the Customer.

Value: We use Value to mean what something is worth to us. It is used in combination with the benefits we get weighed against the cost of getting these benefits

It is not just the regard, the importance or usefulness of something. These words are used such as "your support is of great Value" or to estimate the monetary amount of something like. His estate was valued at £45,000." Consider (someone or something) to be important or beneficial; have a high opinion of. "She had come to Value her privacy."

Value is a comparative term that compares benefits and costs (which includes price). It will not be used in this book to mean the importance, or usefulness, or monetary amount, or benefits. Value is used as a combination term.

The benefits can include importance, image, brand, emotions, experience, products, people, service and so on. Costs can include the time or effort or energy to buy or deal with someone; it includes the monetary price and payment terms.

If you can catch the significant difference in our usage and the everyday usage (which is a partial usage of one aspect of Value such as price or benefit,) you are ready to become a Customer Value Creator.

Thus, terms like Value for money have no meaning in our concept, because Value includes money. In the vernacular Value for Money means being price conscious. Another phrase is Money for Value meaning that you are willing to pay more for perceived benefits.

Value is a perception in the eyes of a Customer or receiver of Value. The Customer has a perception of costs and benefits and their components.

Creation: In the dictionary, creation refers to something new. In our definition of Customer Value Creation, it is creating something new or beneficial to the Customer or reducing the cost (which includes the effort) of getting that benefit.

Customer Value Creation is the performance of actions that increase the worth of goods, services or even a business in the eyes of the Customer

Customer Value is a compound word meaning what something is worth to a Customer. Customer Value is created when benefits improve over costs and destroyed when costs go beyond benefits.

Second and very important, the Customer has a choice of the product or service he should buy or use, and therefore Customer Value that one organisation creates is compared to the Value the competing organisation creates.

Customers tend to buy or use those products that they perceive creates greater Value for them.

You cannot buy Experience

Remember, the end result of Customer Value Creation is an improvement in business performance such as loyalty market share, profits, efficiency, team work; and the executive gain professionally.

Customer Value Creation is fundamental to a business. Once you understand this, you will find yourself ahead of other executives. You will hear them talk about Loyalty, Customer Experience, Customer Response, Customer Journey, Customer Effort, Customer Satisfaction, Customer Success and so on. Each one of these is a component of Customer Value. Thus, a poor Customer Journey can increase the cost (greater effort, energy or time) to a Customer. Or a poor Customer response (ignoring the Customer, not answering on time, not answering at all) can decrease the benefits and therefor the Customer Value.

You will notice that Customer Value encompasses all of the types of Customer programs being used today. They are all essential components of Customer Value and impact Customer Value Creation (or destruction).

In a generic sense, Customer Value Creation is executing proactive, conscious, inspired and imaginative actions that Create better gains or benefits for Customers and all stakeholders, including enhanced returns on investment.

The role of an executive is to Create Value, and not just be a good administrator or efficiency expert. The executive has to go beyond being a functional manager to being a Value Creator and avoid destroying Value.

Principles of Customer Value Creation

To appreciate Customer Value Creation, you must understand the principles of Customer Value Creation. The principles of Customer Value Creation, enunciated by Gautam Mahajan are:

The 1st Principle: Customers tend to buy or use those products or services that they perceive create greater Value for them than competitive offers. It is therefore essential for executives and leaders to create higher Value for their Customers than competition can.

The 2nd Principle: Customer Value Creation is applicable in all fields, such as business, service, education and academics, society and government, social work, innovation and entrepreneurship. It impacts humanity.

The 3rd Principle: Customer Value Creation touches all stakeholders, you, your colleagues, your employees, your partners (supply chain, delivery chain and unions), and society to create resounding Value for the Customer and thereby for the shareholder. It is the source for creating Customers and retaining existing ones, increasing loyalty, market share and profits.

The 4th Principle: Customer Value Creation is proactively exceeding what is basically expected of you or your job and is going beyond your functional and routine roles to creating Value in your ecosystem. Value creation can be planned or spontaneous, and in both functional and emotional thinking.

The 5th Principle: Customer Value Creation leverages a person's or an organisation's potential, learning and creativity while making it meaningful and worthwhile for people to belong and perform, both physically and emotionally.

The 6th Principle: Customer Value Creation presents a very powerful decision-making tool for companies to decide on actions, programs and strategies for the Customer that can increase the company's longevity and profitability.

The 7th Principle: Value creation must exceed Value destruction or reduce negative Value and be done consciously (not just unconsciously).

The 8th Principle: Values (what you stand for, integrity, honesty, fairness etc.) creates Customer Value (that is Customers Value your Values).

These principles form the foundation of the Customer Value Creation strategy and implementation, resulting in great Value for you and your company.

Why Is Customer Value Creation Important Now?

Customer Value Creation has always been important. It becomes more important today because:

Customers are coming of age. They are more aware, more demanding, more knowledgeable.

Customers can be more malleable by being seduced by technology and exciting new products, and influence where companies make Customers feel that certain things (products and services or ways to get service) are better for them.

Product obsolescence, new products, disruption causes companies to think about the Customer first and creating Value for them.

When a company is in a dilemma on choosing a new product to launch, or which channels of distribution to use, whether digital or physical presence is important, or a business decision, they can solve these by looking at the Customer Value each of the options creates, or can create in the future, and selecting the best one(s).

Can you be a Customer Value Creator today and Create Value for Customers?

Philip Kotler echoes the importance of Customer Value in his book on Principles of Marketing Figure 6.6. Marketing to him means creating Customer Value.

Customer Value, of course is a reflection of the many types of Value the Customer is impacted by: It could be the Product Value, the Brand Value (of the company and the product), the Value and Brand of the Employees who interact with the customer, the Service Value and the Cost Value (both price and non-price).

Preface

The Fourteenth Edition of *Principles of Marketing*! Still Creating More Value for You!

The goal of every marketer is to create more value for customers. So it makes sense that our goal for the fourteenth edition is to continue creating more value for you—*our* customer. Our goal is to introduce new marketing students to the fascinating world of modern marketing in an innovative and comprehensive yet practical and enjoyable way. We've poured over every page, table, figure, fact, and example in an effort to make this the best text from which to learn about and teach marketing. Enhanced by mymarketinglab, our online homework and personalized study tool, the fourteenth edition creates exceptional value for both students and professors.

Marketing: Creating Customer Value and Relationships

Top marketers at outstanding companies share a common goal: putting the consumer at the heart of marketing. Today's marketing is all about creating customer value and building profitable customer relationships. It starts with understanding consumer needs and wants, determining which target markets the organization can serve best, and developing a compelling value proposition by which the organization can attract and grow valued consumers. If the organization does these things well, it will reap the rewards in terms of market share, profits, and customer equity.

Five Major Value Themes

From beginning to end, the fourteenth edition of *Principles of Marketing* develops an innovative customer-value and customer-relationships framework that captures the essence of today's marketing. It builds on five major value themes:

1. *Creating value for customers in order to capture value from customers in return.* Today's marketers must be good at *creating customer value* and *managing customer relationships*. Outstanding marketing companies understand the marketplace and customer needs, design value-creating marketing strategies, develop integrated marketing programs that deliver customer value and delight, and build strong customer relationships. In return, they capture value from customers in the form of sales, profits, and customer loyalty.

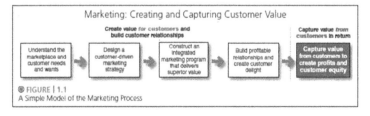

FIGURE | 1.1
A Simple Model of the Marketing Process

xvi

Figure 6.6   Kotler says Marketing is Creating Customer Value

Some Examples of Value Data, and How Companies Have Used This Data

Changing the Rules of the Game in a Service Business

One can change the rules of the game, by using Value data, and understanding Customers and their changing needs. The following example shows how.[9]

Godrej HiCare was a late entrant in the pest control business. This business was the domain of what in India is called the unorganised sector. That means a sector literally run by mom-and-pop operations and where no real large, organised players existed. A few years earlier, one organised player had entered, called Pest Control of India (PCI).

When Customer Value Foundation started work at Godrej, we were convinced that they would have to change the rules of the game. The majority of Godrej's people, though, thought that the Godrej name would play a role, and were unable to get the importance of price from their minds. A Customer Value Foundation study showed how it was possible to change the rules of the game, and how unconsciously, Godrej was actually doing this. We showed Godrej this through our study.

Value

In the marketplace, we see ourselves as we want to. And when we come up against a seemingly price conscious market, we tend to think the market is based only on price. We are not willing to change this perception. But through a value study, we can start to understand how benefits can become more important than price. The table below vividly portrays this.

	Entire Industry	PCI & Godrej	Godrej Only
Attribute		Impact weight	
Overall Benefits	33%	45%	64%
Overall Image	5%	0%	0%
Overall Cost	63%	55%	36%
Overall Value	**100%**	**100%**	**100%**

Even with limited Customers, the actual cost in the case of Godrej is less important.

What does this tell us?

---

[9] Taken partly from Total Customer Value Management

It tells us that the majority of the Customers in the unorganised segment view cost as important as they do not see the differentiated benefit of pest control service as high. Godrej has to find a way of letting them know the importance of the pest control service and the advantages of using Godrej over the competition.

In addition, this tells us by adding value, you can make the price less important in the eyes of the Customer. Over a period of time, brand and image will be built up. Why is it not important now? The reason is that currently, service execution (that is the pest control service works to my satisfaction or elimination of pests) is more important than the HiCare brand, which has to be established.

Similar results were seen in Overall Benefits.

Overall Benefits

It is likely, as Godrej becomes a more important service provider, the package and people will become more significant. If we look at only the organised sector, we can see the weights (importance) change from the perception of the overall market.

Attribute	Entire Industry	PCI & Godrej
	Impact weight	
Pest Control Package	34%	37%
People	19%	34%
Service Execution	47%	28%
Overall Benefits	**100%**	**100%**

The people become more important (34% versus 19% for the entire industry). Thus, teaching our frontline people Customer Value will help as the industry seeks more organised players. Service Execution is more of a given with organised players.

Pest Control Package

In an effort to understand what drives the pest control package, we went beyond what HiCare executives had suggested. The pest control package has to have a warranty and a service execution declaration or history that Customers can see and derive satisfaction from.

The pest control package should include people, service execution warranty and of course, show an understanding of the needs of the Customer. Is HiCare too rigid?

Pest Control Package Importance from Customers	
Attribute	Impact weight
Understands my Needs	23%
People	23%
Service Execution	33%
Warranty	21%
Overall Pest Control Package	**100%**

People

Actually, while working with PCI and Godrej Customers want more skilled people. This is different than the unorganised sector where people are not that important.

	Entire Industry	PCI & Godrej
Attribute	Impact weight	
Skilled	24%	45%
Responsive	22%	0%
Knowledgeable	22%	18%
Accesible	10%	18%
Prompt	21%	19%
Overall People	**100%**	**100%**

In trying to understand the people equation, one also sees the actual **service execution** impacts the Customer. Skilled people will execute the job better and be more responsive! And what does the Customer equate Service execution with? It is the lack of any pests during the contract. If this is not done properly, the service package and people are perceived to be poor.

People Importance from Customers	
Attribute	Impact weight
Skilled	21%
Responsive	12%

(Continued)

(Cont).

People Importance from Customers	
Attribute	*Impact weight*
Knowledgeable	18%
Accessible	6%
Prompt	9%
Service Execution	34%
Overall People	100%

People are reviewed on their service execution, something missed out in looking at how Customers perceive people.

Service Execution

Going further, Crisis Management is a very important part of the Service Execution, even more so in the organised sector (PCI and Godrej). We can see the market need shift from reliable and effective to Crisis control, as the previously important factors become more common and expected in the organised sector.

	Entire Industry	*PCI & Godrej*
Attribute	*Impact weight*	
Reliable	22%	14%
Effective	13%	7%
Quality Assurance	10%	15%
Timely	10%	3%
Technical Support	23%	19%
Crisis Management	21%	43%
Overall Service Execution	**100%**	**100%**

Overall Image

Image is currently not important but is bound to become so.

If we look at the organised sector trust in the company becomes more important, showing Customers latent need is coming out.

	Entire Industry	PCI & Godrej
Attribute	Impact weight	
Brand	0%	0%
Trust	5%	25%
Ethics	44%	45%
Concern for safety	51%	30%
Overall Image	**100%**	**100%**

Overall Cost

Non-price terms are make up 60% of the price and actual price is 40% of the importance in the perception of overall cost.

	Entire Industry	PCI & Godrej
Attribute	Impact weight	
Price itself	44%	60%
Payment Terms	56%	40%
Overall Price Terms	**100%**	**100%**

Payment terms become less important in the organised sector. Actual price is more important, because people suspect the organised sector will be more expensive.

Non-price terms are more important than the price terms.

	Entire Industry	PCI & Godrej
Attribute	Impact weight	
Crisis Support	12%	16%
Partnership – Training, Updates, Safety, Health	56%	40%
Warranty	47%	44%
Price Justification	4%	28%
Overall Image	**100%**	**100%**

Price justification does not show up as being important. Yet when we look at the organised sector, price justification becomes a significant factor! Not as significant, as warranties, but important enough.

The end result is that Godrej was able to increase referral and reduce pressure on price while improving on branding and increase market share.

Frank Perdue and the Chicken Business

The classic example of changing the rules of the game is the one of Frank Perdue and the chicken business.

Frank Perdue inherited the chicken business from his father. He found that it was a real commodity business, with there being no importance to the brand. A chicken, was a chicken, was a chicken! Chicken was being sold frozen. Availability in the store was the most important buying decision. Given below is the purchase criteria.

Chicken Business:
Customer's Purchase Decision

Key Purchase Criteria	Before Frank Customer Rating		
	Relative Weight	Perdue Chicken	Others	Rating Differential
• Product				
— Yellow Bird				
— Meat-To-Bone	5	7	7	0
— No Pinfeathers	10	6	6	0
— Fresh	15	5	5	0
	15	7	7	0
• Service				
— Availability				
— Brand Image	55	8	8	0
	0	6	6	0
	100			

Weight On Quality vs. Price Before Frank	
Quality	10
Price	90
	100

Source: PIMS Principles

CVF   CUSTOMER VALUE FOUNDATION

He decided he needed to change the rules of the game. He met consumers and found that the major need was for chicken to be yellow, fresh, with no pinfeathers and good meat to bone ratio. He therefore decided to sell his birds refrigerated and not frozen. You could then press the bird and it felt fresh compared to a hard-frozen chicken (which definitely did not feel fresh). He also fed the bird well with yellow corn and put them in yellow styrofoam trays to enhance the yellowness and took good care to get rid of the pinfeathers in the production stage. Frank then went on TV and extolled the virtues of his birds, particularly freshness. The resulting purchase decision is shown to have contrasted with the original purchase criteria curve.

After some time, brand had become important (25% importance) and availability had dropped to 10%. More importantly, his product got a positive differential rating versus the competition, showing consumers preferred his product. When he became president of Perdue Farms Inc. in 1952, the company was averaging revenues of $6 million, and exceeded $35 million by 1967, when they decided to enter New York. In

1971, he started his ad campaign built around changing the rules of the game and the rest is the history of Perdue's success. From a negligible market share (3%), they went on to become a leading national chicken player.

Chicken Business: Customer's Purchase Decision

Key Purchase Criteria	After Frank Customer Rating		
	Relative Weight	Perdue Chicken	Others	Rating Differential
• Product				
– Yellow Bird	10	8.1	7.2	+0.9
– Meat-To-Bone	20	9.0	7.3	+1.7
– No Pinfeathers	20	9.2	6.5	+2.7
– Fresh	15	8.0	8.0	0.0
• Service				
– Availability	10	8.0	8.0	0.0
– Brand Image	25	9.3	6.5	+2.8
	100			

Weight On Quality vs. Price After Frank	
Quality	70
Price	30
	100

Source: PIMS Principles

CVF   CUSTOMER VALUE FOUNDATION

You too, can change the rules of the game if you know what Customers truly want, and don't fall into the trap of thinking that you have to compete in what is perceived as their views in the marketplace.

Decommoditizing a Commodity Business

Jeff Immelt, Chairman of GE said that the danger in business was that it would become a commodity business. He suggested the way to prevent this from happening was to add Value. The following example show how.

Another example is where Tata Chemicals' Crop Nutrition business decided to decommoditise their business, by starting a loyalty program and franchised stores which would provide a range of agri-solutions under one roof. The loyalty program called for farmers to be enrolled in a program called *Tata Kisan Parivar*, (TKP) literally, Tata's Farmer Family and the franchisee store is called *Tata Kisan Sansar* TKS (or Tata Farmer World). The normal sales pattern involved traditional channel partners – dealers and retailers, both of whom were multi-brand.

In 2006, the question came up whether these were cost programs or provided real benefits to the Customer, and thereby to the company.

In a Customer Value Study spearheaded by Customer Value Foundation, it was proven that these two programs were seen as providing immense benefits to the farmer and to the company. Even a non-TKP member found the TKS stores adding value to them. TKP members going to normal stores seemed to derive more benefits and had higher brand loyalty to Tata, than normal farmers. The biggest payoff came when TKP members dealt with TKS stores.

Based on this study, Tata Chemicals' decided not only to continue growing the two programs but also decided to increase the focus on TKP through the TKS stores.

The loyalty curves are not true loyalty curves, but are curves based on the percent that would recommend the brand or the retailer. True loyalty curves are based on re-use likelihood, not on recommendations. Recommendation based loyalty curves tend to be more stringent than when you ask people if they would re-purchase. You can see the remarkable improvement in loyalty on TKS and TKP. Loyalty went up from about 15% to 50%.

In the table below, light grey means you are better than, very light means equal to and very dark grey worse than whom you are being compared to. medium grey means you are below par in that attribute.

ANALYSIS OF TATA FARMERS: NON TKP and NON TKS VS. All other combinations

Only for TATA

Non TKP and Non TKS	Normal Tata Farmer buying from normal retailer
TKP	All TKP (buying from normal retailer and from TKS)
TKS	Tata Farmers Buying from TKS (includes TKP buying from TKS)
Non TKP,TKS	Normal Tata Farmer (non TKP) buying from TKS
TKP TKS	TKP Farmer buying from TKS
Impact weight TKP*	Impact weight of TKP shown where there is a significant difference

Value

	Impact weight for all (non TKP, non TKS)	TKP Vs Non TKP / Non TKS				TKS vs. Non TKP / TKS		Non TKP, TKS vs. Non TKP / TKS		TKP . TKS vs. Non TKP / TKS	
		Non TKP and Non TKS	TKP	Ratio TKP Vs Non TKP and Non TKS	Impact wt TKP*	TKS	Ratio TKS vs. Non TKP and TKS	Non TKP, TKP, TKS vs. Non TKP and TKS	Ratio Non TKP TKS vs. Non TKP and TKS	TKP, TKS	Ratio TKP TKS vs. Non TKP and TKS
Overall Quality	22%	8.32	7.16	1.13	20%	7.01	1.11	6.68	1.06	7.2	1.14
Urea Brand image	45%	8.20	8.74	1.07	62%	8.65	1.05	8.21	1.00	8.89	1.08
Overall Price	33%	5.67	6.34	1.12	18%	6.36	1.12	6.35	1.12	6.35	1.12
Overall Value	**100%**	**7.40**	**7.98**	**1.08**		**7.09**	**1.07**	**7.63**	**1.03**	**8.04**	**1.09**
Valid responses		91	121			157		57		100	

Price

	Impact weight	TKP Vs Non TKP / Non TKS				TKS vs. Non TKP / TKS		Non TKP, TKS vs. Non TKP / TKS		TKP . TKS vs. Non TKP / TKS	
		Non TKP and Non TKS	TKP	Ratio TKP Vs Non TKP and Non TKS	Impact wt TKP*	TKS	Ratio TKS vs. Non TKP and TKS	Non TKP, TKP, TKS vs. Non TKP and TKS	Ratio Non TKP TKS vs. Non TKP and TKS	TKP, TKS	Ratio TKP TKS vs. Non TKP and TKS
Competitive Price	30%	7.07	7.69	1.09	33%	7.65	1.08	7.51	1.06	7.73	1.09
Discounts and Other B	18%	3.80	3.85	1.07	23%	3.72	1.03	3.86	1.07	3.64	1.01
Credit Terms	52%	5.02	6.00	1.19	44%	5.93	1.18	5.80	1.15	6	1.19
Overall Price	**100%**	**5.67**	**6.34**	**1.12**		**6.35**	**1.12**	**6.35**	**1.12**	**6.35**	**1.12**
Valid responses		89	121			157		57		100	

Quality

	Impact weight	TKP Vs Non TKP / Non TKS				TKS vs. Non TKP / TKS		Non TKP, TKS vs. Non TKP / TKS		TKP . TKS vs. Non TKP / TKS	
		Non TKP and Non TKS	TKP	Ratio TKP Vs Non TKP and Non TKS	Impact wt TKP*	TKS	Ratio TKS vs. Non TKP and TKS	Non TKP, TKP, TKS vs. Non TKP and TKS	Ratio Non TKP TKS vs. Non TKP and TKS	TKP, TKS	Ratio TKP TKS vs. Non TKP and TKS
Overall Urea	27%	9.10	8.98	0.99	4%	9.03	0.99	8.91	0.98	9.10101	1.00
Overall Retailer	73%	6.97	7.46	1.07	96%	7.43	1.07	7.18	1.03	7.58	1.09
Company's Services											
Overall Quality	**100%**	**6.32**	**7.16**	**1.13**		**7.01**	**1.11**	**6.69**	**1.06**	**7.20**	**1.14**
Valid responses		91	121			157		57		100	

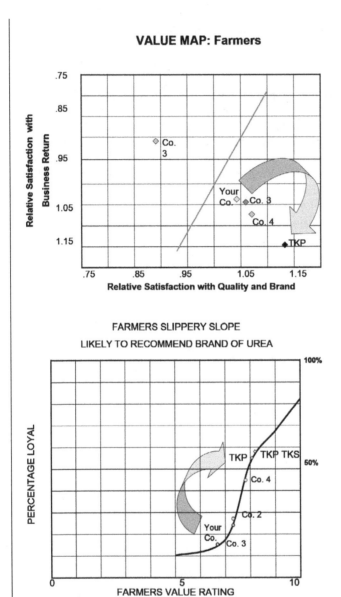

VALUE MAP: Farmers

The end result was that brand became important, price became immaterial, and a methodology for improving loyalty and validating the loyalty programs was installed. Also, it told Tata where to improve to increase value.

So, you can see the power of Value creation and VDL methodologies for your business.

Integrated Value

What Is Integrated Value?

Integrated Value is becoming more important as businesses are now starting to develop a wider role in society.

This goes beyond philanthropy and CSR, and also takes into account incorporating Values, environment, conscious capitalism, happiness, sustainable business and the wider concept of shared Value.

Wayne Visser's definition: integrated Value is the simultaneous building of multiple "non-financial" capitals (notably infrastructural, technological, social, ecological and human capital) through synergistic innovation across the nexus economy (including the resilience, exponential, access, circular and well-being economies) that result in net-positive effects, thus, making our world more secure, smart, shared, sustainable and satisfying.

In short, doing good and improving well-being of the ecosystem.

Natural Capital is any stock or flow of energy and material that produces goods and services. It includes:

- Resources – renewable and non-renewable materials
- Sinks – that absorb, neutralise or recycle wastes
- Processes – such as climate regulation

Natural capital is the basis not only of production but of life itself!

Human Capital consists of people's health, knowledge, skills and motivation. All these things are needed for productive work.

Enhancing human capital through education and training is central to a flourishing economy.

Social Capital concerns the institutions that help us maintain and develop human capital in partnership with others; e.g. families, communities, businesses, trade unions, schools and voluntary organisations.

Manufactured Capital comprises material goods or fixed assets which contribute to the production process rather than being the output itself – e.g. tools, machines and buildings.

Financial Capital plays an important role in our economy, enabling the other types of Capital to be owned and traded. But unlike the other types, it has no real Value itself but is representative of natural, human, social or manufactured capital; e.g. shares, bonds or banknotes.

We also have to add Customer Capital, which is impacted by factors discussed in the previous page.

We are facing a sustainability crisis because we're consuming our stocks of natural, human and social capital faster than they are being produced. Unless we control the rate of this consumption, we can't sustain these vital stocks in the long term.[10] We have to do more Value making and less Value taking.

Integrated Reporting

In a most simplistic sense, we need to report customer scores along with financial scores. Internally we might wish to report employee scores, scores given to us from our suppliers and partners, and sustainability scores. All these add up to integrated reporting of Value.

On balance sheets, put items of real importance to shareholders, your Customer Value Added score, is it going up or down. How many Customers do you have? Spend per customer and so forth. Put the social and employee value.

Research/to do:

1. Become aware of things around you.
2. Notice interactions around you.
3. Notice behaviour (pushing in line, littering).
4. What is needed, why do people litter?
   a. Musical littering bins
   b. Video/Audio littering bins
5. Why don't people use stairs instead of escalators?
6. Why do people like to hang out?
7. Why do people like to interact?

How can we convert these into ideas?
   Who is interested and why?
   What will interest him and Create Value for people?

VDL and This Chapter

We look at Value from different viewpoints, whether latent, potential, innate, inherent, intrinsic or extrinsic. VDL applies to, and is impacted by, all of these. We see examples of Value measurement and Customer Value Added, and how VDL can help you measure Value outside of the Customer world.

All eight principles apply and should be used. We also looked at Customer Value Creation and its principles. We talk about VDL and you, and the nuances of Value and its impact on happiness, Value waiting to happen, disruption and integrated Value. You can use this understanding of Value to your advantage. This chapter shows how business can employ Value data to increase Value, and to change the rules of the game as well as simple ways of adding Value.

---

[10] https://www.forumforthefuture.org/project/five-capitals/overview

Chapter 7

Value Is in The Mind of the Perceiver

Value Dominant Logic recognises that everyone seeks Value or the optimal Value. But what they actually see, or feel, or experience is a perception and perceptions which are relative, and vary. The pursuit of Value is based on perceptions.

Very often the perceiver may not be the intentional recipient of the Value creator. An example is an architect who builds your house and is creating Value for you. As a passer-by, I see and admire the house. I am an unintentional perceiver for whom Value is created.

Because we are perceivers, we confuse what is good and what is good for me. Value that improves the good or well-being of a person may not necessarily be for the good of the person. What is good for the child is to let a child sleep without disturbing him or her. But if the child has fever it may be good for her to wake her up and give her some medicine.

Value is based on perception. Perception starts from the basics. We perceive something is good. Is it good for me or is it actually good? Ice cream may be good, but it may not be good for me if I am lactose intolerant.

Value is in mind of the perceiver and what he wants to perceive. So, a Trump aide says "The point, is that we got a lot of attention, and that alone creates Value." This is the law by which Trump lives his life. Attention creates Value, at least for him. We[1] add Value to others when we...

---

[1] https://www.business2community.com/leadership/add-Value-team-follow-brilliant-leadership-strategies-01434964

1. Truly Value others. Good leaders go out of their way to never subtract Value from their people. They are intentional about adding merit and make it part of their core Values.
2. Make ourselves more valuable to others. The premise of adding Value to the lives of your team members is based on the fact that you have usefulness to add. Are you able to teach a skill? Are you able to make a career changing introduction? Are you able to open the door to a better opportunity?
3. Know and relate to what others Value. As a leader how do you know what your team Values? You listen. Many leaders are too quick to take charge. A good leader takes the opportunity to listen to what every person believes is important, and then leads.

Customers perceive a product based on their needs (and also contextual need, now or later), their awareness (could be based on brand, advertising, personal approach, relationship, their emotions, reviews, their own experience, social media etc.), and their consciousness of the company, the sustainability, the environment etc.

Many people may try to influence you with facts and figures. At the end it is your perception of the Value the product/service adds and whether this Value is higher than your perception of competitive offerings.

Take an investment in the stock market. We seek guidance, we seek knowledge, metrics, investment sites, trends etc. At the end we buy based on our perception. And the moment we buy stock, or a house or anything, we find that its price is not what we paid, but what the next person who will buy it thinks it is worth in his perception!

Sometimes perceived Value is seen as different from common sense, like people waiting overnight to buy a new iPhone, or standing in line for something that is free of charge, like a free shuttle, versus taking a taxi. This also depends on the user's perception of the Value of their time.

Marketers are always trying to find ways of increasing perceived Value.

Value can also be based on knowledge or lack thereof. Let me give you some examples. I once sat one seat away from Robert Redford on a Concorde and once next to Ralph Lauren. Both times I was not aware of them, till my boss pointed them out to me. With this new knowledge my perception changed, and I walked up the aisle just to get a glimpse of Redford. Was Value created for me? Perhaps in my being able to say I saw Redford or sat close to him. Perhaps people would be impressed? Beyond that no Value was created for me, and yet I was anxious to see him. Was Value created or destroyed for Redford?

Ralph Lauren ruined my flight. I was anxious: Should I say hello, talk to him, not talk to him? What would he think if I tried to strike up a conversation?

Once I sat in an aisle seat adjacent to George Harrison of the Beatles who was traveling with Ravi Shankar. The people in the plane had not recognised him.

I said hello, and he said please ignore me, or I will be mobbed! He was happy to be perceived as yet another traveller.

I think it is sad for a celebrity not to be recognised or be over-recognised. It is all in their perception of themselves. Recognition can create and destroy Value.

Value Has to Be Perceived, Seen, Felt, Viewed, Noticed

This is important as we learnt from the previous section. If your company has a great service or a product, and I, as a customer, do not know about it (your company or its product/service) how can I perceive its Value. Thus, awareness becomes important, especially in today's age of social media. Word of mouth brand ambassadors who are your customers then become very important in creating positive awareness or perceptions.

Value Is Therefore Transient

Value is transient for various reasons. The Value the provider creates may change over time (often because of the action, or inaction, of the provider).

Value perception may change in the eyes of the beholder. Thus, if I am hungry, and an ice cream comes in front of me my perception of Value is higher, and I may be tempted to buy it versus when I am full and have no desire to eat.

Needs change, perceptions change. Audesh Paswan and Francisco Guzman wrote about the time aspect of Value in the Journal of Creating Value, JCV 3-2.

Value and Happiness

Happiness requires your attention. It often is difficult to be happy under trying circumstances, but if you can make the best of everything you are on your way to happiness.

Is Value related to happiness? The answer is yes and no, and it depends on the Value you receive and perceive, and whether you feel good about it.

Some actions Create Value for you such as playing with your grandkids, sipping a drink when relaxed, meeting close friends.

Happiness, just like Value, is a perception and depends on circumstances and context. Happiness is not easy to define (the result is). To many, happiness means feeling good, and if Value as defined creates good and increases your well-being then happiness is the result.

Happiness depends on social values, and also on expectations and whether these are met or surpassed. So what matters to you is important and in what context and circumstances.

More people equate happiness to well-being and therefore to Value and its creation to improve your well-being. Some equate happiness to pleasure (happiness being longer duration). Harry Walker[2] states that the power (Value?) of happiness is in the difficulty of defining it. And he asks if morals and values are in conflict with happiness.

Thus, Bhutan's Gross National Happiness is difficult to define and therefore, measure.

Like Value, more happiness is created when you create happiness for others. You cannot easily create Happiness for yourself. It is a result of other Value-creating actions you take for yourself and others.

VDL and Value Perception

Value creation has to do with creating good and well-being (which is another definition of happiness). Creating Value for others could Create Value for you and increase your Value. Just Capital and their list of best companies for customers/employees talks about Value creation by the winner companies. VDL will help in creating Value for you and happiness for others.

---

[2] Values of Happiness, Walker, H., & Kavedžija, I. Hau: Journal of Ethnographic Theory, 5(3), 1–23.

Chapter 8

Value, a Business Perspective

The best way to begin a business section is to show how Philip Kotler began his latest edition of *Principles of Marketing* (see Figure 8.1). He talks about how the book can Create Value for you and that the role of marketing is to Create Value for Customers. How many of you have considered that marketing, means creating Value (see Figure 8.1)? In addition, Normann and Ramirez[1] wrote that strategy is the art of creating Value. American Marketing Association defines Marketing as the activity, set of institutions, and processes for creating, communicating, delivering and exchanging offerings that have Value for customers, clients, partners and society at large.

What does creation of Value do for businesses? It increases the bottom line, by not focusing on it but by creating Value for all stakeholders. To do this, we have to establish a Value creation mindset and thought process. Marketing is about creating Customer Value, for example, as stated by Kotler.

Value co-creation in business is the professed goals of all dominant logics. So how do businesses create and co-create more Value?

Value creation for shareholders has been a mainstay of business. Value Dominant Logic helps business people understand the importance of Value creation and **how and where to Create Value.** Thus, apart from creating Value for customers, VDL also focuses on employees, including front line ones, partners, supply and delivery chain, society and government. VDL suggests Value creation for the entire ecosystem. Value creation and Customer Value connect companies to the customer.

---

[1] HBR JULY–AUGUST 1993 ISSUE.

Preface

The Fourteenth Edition of *Principles of Marketing*! Still Creating More Value for You!

The goal of every marketer is to create more value for customers. So it makes sense that our goal for the fourteenth edition is to continue creating more value for you—*our* customer. Our goal is to introduce new marketing students to the fascinating world of modern marketing in an innovative and comprehensive yet practical and enjoyable way. We've poured over every page, table, figure, fact, and example in an effort to make this the best text from which to learn about and teach marketing. Enhanced by mymarketinglab, our online homework and personalized study tool, the fourteenth edition creates exceptional value for both students and professors.

Marketing: Creating Customer Value and Relationships

Top marketers at outstanding companies share a common goal: putting the consumer at the heart of marketing. Today's marketing is all about creating customer value and building profitable customer relationships. It starts with understanding consumer needs and wants, determining which target markets the organization can serve best, and developing a compelling value proposition by which the organization can attract and grow valued consumers. If the organization does these things well, it will reap the rewards in terms of market share, profits, and customer equity.

Five Major Value Themes

From beginning to end, the fourteenth edition of *Principles of Marketing* develops an innovative customer-value and customer-relationships framework that captures the essence of today's marketing. It builds on five major value themes:

1. *Creating value for customers in order to capture value from customers in return.* Today's marketers must be good at *creating customer value* and *managing customer relationships.* Outstanding marketing companies understand the marketplace and customer needs, design value-creating marketing strategies, develop integrated marketing programs that deliver customer value and delight, and build strong customer relationships. In return, they capture value from customers in the form of sales, profits, and customer loyalty.

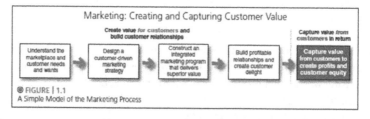

⊚ FIGURE | 1.1
A Simple Model of the Marketing Process

Figure 8.1   Preface from the 14th Edition of Kotler's Principles of Marketing

Businesses know much about creating Value, and how to Create Value. This book helps businesses develop a Value creation mindset for themselves, their employees, partners, executives and leaders. This helps Create more Value and Value thinking, and reduces destruction of Value by the business or its people,

Before I go any further, I must suggest that Value creation for most businesses (and sadly, wrongly) means Value created for the business, not for the customer. Value creation means numbers (even though the Figure 8.2 below is defined by the company as Value creation). They state: The following overview provides examples of how we Create Value for our company, the environment and society. It is modelled on the framework of the International Integrated Reporting Council (IIRC). Both financial and non-financial Value drivers form the foundation of our actions. Our business model transforms these principles and actions into results.[2]

In this chapter we mean to change the thinking.

Value as a Business perspective is still seen as ROI and financials, see "Recognizing when the effort to Create Value outweighs the Value created."[3]

Value is also seen as the cash flows a business generates divided by its risk factors. Put another way, companies can influence the Value of the business by improving cash flows through increasing revenue, reducing expenses and improving efficiencies; or by reducing risk, which is affected by a variety of factors, including the number and types of customers, recurring vs. project-based revenue, the state of the balance sheet, the depth and strength of the management team and the employees (whether functional or Value creators), and how dependent the business is on its owner for its continued success.

This is the classical way of looking at the business, and not at the creators of Value, the customers and employees, partners and society all of whom we will discuss in detail later on. Value is customer defined, Value is created, it migrates, is captured, sometimes disrupted, co-created, re-captured and can also be lost.

Another factor, is where the word Value is not understood in business. An example is shown below.

Dr Robert Pendleton, MD, of the University of Utah states: First, (their) leaders – Jeff Bezos of Amazon, Warren Buffett of Berkshire Hathaway and Jamie Dimon of JPMorgan Chase – must think deeply about what "Value" actually means. It turns out one reason there's been such little progress in creating a Value-based system is that the stakeholders in the US health care system – patients, providers, hospitals, insurers, employee benefit pro-

> VDL states it is important your employees, Customers and shareholders have a common terminology for Value.

viders and policymakers – have no common definition of Value and don't agree on the mix of elements composing it (quality? service? cost? outcomes? access?).[4]

Fundamental Value misalignments include the relative importance of health outcomes for patients.

---

[2] https://bericht.basf.com/2017/en/how-we-Create-Value.html

[3] http://www.sbnonline.com/article/recognizing-effort-Create-Value-outweighs-Value-created/

[4] https://hbr.org/2018/02/we-wont-get-Value-based-health-care-until-we-agree-on-what-Value-means, with permission from Dr Robert Pendleton

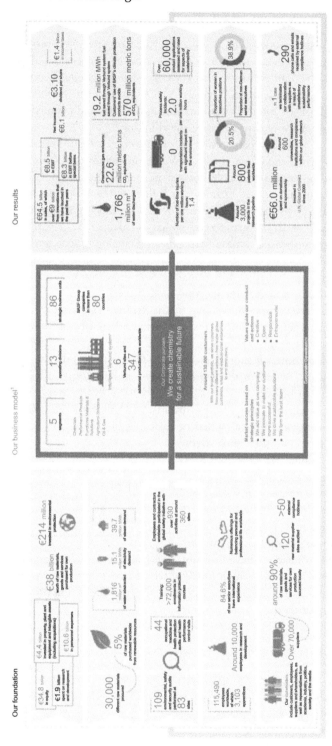

Figure 8.2   What Companies Think of as Value Creation

For physicians like me, clinical outcomes are paramount; health improvement and high-quality care are essential components of health care Value. And we assume that patients share that perspective. But, it seems, they don't. When the Utah survey asked patients to identify key characteristics of high-Value health care, a plurality (45%) chose 'My Out-of-Pocket Costs Are Affordable,' and only 32% chose 'My Health Improves.' (In fact, on patients' list of key Value characteristics, 'My Health Improves' was slightly below 'Staff Are Friendly and Helpful.') Given the chance to select the five most important Value character-istics, 90% of patients chose combinations different from any combi-nation chosen by physicians. In general, cost and service were far more important in determining Value for patients than for physicians.

Are we listening to the customer (the customer assumes he will get good health care) who expects more than just good health care? Do we understand what Value is and what it means?

This is telling because it shows the disconnect between the provider and the receiver!

> It is important that service provi-ders and service receivers are in sync. On what Value is to be cre-ated. For patients it could be cost, and for doctors health outcomes. VDL suggests bridging these.

Boundaries of the Business Ecosystem

We start with a definition of the boundaries of the business, and we argue that business people have to look for Value outside the business boundaries (out of the box thinking or a no-box (invent-your-own-box) thinking) and seek Value waiting to happen and avoid being disrupted by others; and increase an innovative mindset, looking at how leaders can add Value and inculcating the 6As[5] to make executives smarter.

Also discussed are issues of values, beliefs and attitudes, ethics and morals and traits.

Value Added and Value Created

First, we must understand in Value Dominant Logic there is a difference between Value Added and Value Created.

In fact, Value creation is a basic requirement for sustained human flourishing according to the author. Thus, reducing the price adds Value to the customer, but is not truly creating Value. On the other hand, going from a film camera to a

---

[5] See page 141 of this book.

digital camera is a form of Value creation. Value added, Value creation and Value co-creation are words used interchangeably (we too will use the words interchangeably, unless there is a need to do otherwise). Future researchers will need to distinguish this aspect, as everything then is not really co-created but is sometimes only co-added Value. Value is created, for example, through new products, services or business thinking.

Value Dominant Logic is important in business. Much of the Value learning and work is based on business thinking, and extends to leadership, employees and executives, partners and society. Businesses using Value creation and Value Dominant Logic have to examine what Creates Value for each one of their constituents and stakeholders and how to avoid destroying Value. They have to create a VDL culture and mindset, a way of thinking and execution.

Many people define a boundary for Value creation, and very often Value as well. According to many, Value is not created outside the boundaries they define. Some say Value can only be created through co-creation with the customer, and no Value exists otherwise. Defining Value boundaries narrowly makes you an ideal prey to disruption, as we will show later.

Our thinking is different. Value could be present or be latent before business happens. It is present in a design, in a piece of machinery, in a remote location where the business does not sell. This Value is seen differently by different people. Some of these people can add or Create Value to these items, be it design, a piece of machinery or a remote location, by working on them and adding/creating Value, which may be seen by someone else, let's say another employee or a customer as being valuable or not. This is dependent on his perception at a given point in time and based on the alternatives available. Value can change in the mind of that beholder over a period of time, and before and after use. A new beholder may have a higher sense of the Value created and may be willing to create additional Value by buying something, using it or consuming it.

Thus, VDL has a wider business Value canvas than just something that exists only when seen by a customer or a company.

The Boundaries of Business Value

The business and social definition tries to build a boundary for the Value ecosystem. That is Value exists within the boundary defined by a classic company-customer-society ecosystem. We will term this the classic business boundary.

However, in the way I have been defining Value, it exists beyond these boundaries, and exists in a wider ecosystem that goes beyond the classic business/social ecosystem. It can exist even when not perceived (Value waiting to happen). In businesses employees, too work within boundaries and form silos which are so deleterious to business. Thinking outside your silo's boundaries is necessary for greater Value creation.

Value used in any other context is noticed when it comes into a useful state. This is when we *perceive it* and say this actor or product has Value or is creating Value for himself and others.

In Figure 8.3.[6] we can see that Value exists outside the classic business system, while impacting goods, processes, customers and providers. The Value can be in the form of an idea, or an (animate or inanimate) object or a potential service.

> VDL will make your business boundaries wider so that you do not miss opportunities.

Thus, the idea could be one of driverless cars. This idea may be obvious now, but it had little Value a few years ago, as most people did not notice the concept of a driverless car[7]. Those that saw it, discarded it as impractical, or valueless. It remained Value waiting to happen. It was outside most business's boundaries. It is only those who realised the Value of the driverless car and picked up the idea, developed it, created more Value and developed the ecosystem for customers and also for society, including infrastructure for the concept, creating further Value. Awareness (and curiosity) is one lesson to be learnt in creativity and in the creation of Value.

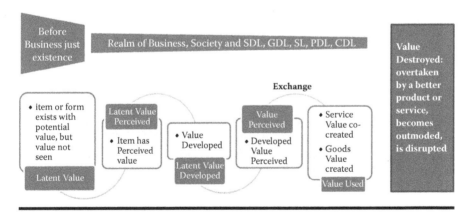

Figure 8.3   The Expanded Value Ecosystem (from Author). (Latent Value is potential Value or Value waiting to happen. Service includes services and goods)

---

[6] Part of this section is taken from the author's article on Value Dominant Logic, partly published by the author and some parts published in Journal of Creating Value, JCV3-2.

[7] I keep using the example of a driverless car because it impacts many of the chapters in this book.

There can be Value destruction in such ideas along with Value creation:

Self-driving cars stand to destroy millions of jobs – and generate trillions in new business. Autonomous vehicles could displace the 3.8 million people who drive for a living. But the changes will also create new jobs and business opportunities – an estimated $7 trillion worth by 2050, according to estimates from Intel. Start-ups like California-based Phantom Auto are developing remote centres where operators can keep tabs on five different autonomous vehicles at a time, intervening only when necessary, reports the San Francisco Chronicle. And when everyone becomes a passenger that could open the door to a brand new in-vehicle services industry, where passengers can receive manicures, health care or even a massage. Vehicles could be used as a source of power and compete with the grid; or as wireless routers!

Much wealth will be concentrated in the hands of battery companies and software companies. Batteries will become a service, where swapping instead of in-situ charging will be the mode, or better charging while driving, through solar or better means such as charging from power supplies embedded in the road.

Traffic policemen might become a way of the past – fewer in number and internet based.

Not looking outside your business ecosystem can have adverse effects. Another example is that of the telephone. The Telegraph Company saw no latent or potential Value for the device offered by Bell. In the case of Kodak, digital cameras were outside their business system, and they were slow to commercialise them even though they were early technology leaders.

At Continental Can, where I worked, fears of cannibalisation of beverage cans with PET bottles (which Continental was developing) were not heeded, as this would happen with or without Continental. Continental was able to take advantage of the growth of this segment of the soft drink packaging business with PET and somewhat with cans. PET bottles were Value waiting to happen when compared to the conventional 2l glass bottles, which were heavy, breakable and under certain circumstances, could explode. Subsequently, new uses such as single serve and recyclable PET bottles, hot fill and aseptic bottles became common.

Potential service examples include shared services such as Uber, and AirBnB, but did not work or exist till these companies came on the scene, took this latent Value and created further Value.

We therefore suggest that for creativity and innovation, one has to be able to see and be aware of latent or potential Value (Value waiting to happen) in things in front of and around us. Thus, looking at trees, may suggest better ideas to detect minerals and other items in soil, and to pump separated or compound items (as trees do: pump up to tall trees, and for the leaves to receive these). Or the ability of seeds to absorb water in volumes larger than the seed itself. Or how zebrafish can repair eye retina damage. Value is waiting to happen.

Examples using trees are mine detection: Danish scientists made a scientific discovery in 2004 with significant humanitarian and environmental potential. They showed that it is possible to produce plants that change colour in the presence of specific compounds within the soil, opening the way for the first bomb and land-mine detection plant.

Recently a team of researchers from MIT (2017) has designed a microfluidic device that mimics plant mechanism and pumps water and sugars through a chip at a steady rate, without requiring external pumps and motors.

Bioinspiration is an example where we study existing bio-entities, and use the ideas to design, develop and create new materials, devices and systems, all of which are inspired by biological items.

Jeffrey Karp, a bioengineer at Brigham and Women's Hospital (BWH) in Cambridge, Massachusetts is an example of a bioinspired person who invented surgical glue from ideas inspired by everyday biological products, trees, plants, animals, etc., and a surgical staple based on the principle of porcupine quills (Value waiting to happen).

> As your awareness and curiosity increases, and with a VDL mindset, you will start to notice Value waiting to happen, and perhaps make it happen.

The nose of the Shinkansen train was bioinspired by birds in flight that could go from low resistance (air) to dive into high resistance (water). This helped reduce drag and vibrations caused by the train entering and traversing a tunnel.

The way birds like kites zoom into their prey is evoking interest from researchers in missile guidance systems.

Have you noticed you can balance a cup when going up stairs, or can insert a key into a lock without really looking? Man-made gyro systems cannot currently match the true intelligence (not artificial intelligence) of the human body.

Just learning from the world around us can Create Value which is waiting to happen.

Thus, Value also exists in a larger ecosystem than a classic business/social ecosystem. And it runs the risk of being destroyed by being overtaken by a better product, idea or system.

This thought process is valid for society, for people, for institutions and outside these boundaries.

There are times, when the Value remains potential, such as in a painting. When the artist goes to sell it, then it has potential Value in his mind. If Value is recognised and someone buys it, then the potential Value is converted to Value-in-exchange for the artist. Then we have to think of increasing the Value potential, and how is that done? Just by facilitation and Value creation, to improve the potential (such as showing in a particular exhibition or adding a frame to the picture making it more attractive or through social media). If he does not want to sell it, he has still created Value for himself, and the exchange has no meaning. The Value potential may still exist in the future.

VDL suggests you must look outside your ecosystem to prevent the impact of obsolescence and disruption.

In VDL thinking, the motivation of all people is to Create Value for themselves and for others so that they, in turn, can create more Value for themselves. Sometimes the beneficiary is oneself. Often the beneficiary sees no Value, or even perceives destruction in Value. Thus, in driverless cars, there is a destruction of Value for one beneficiary of the system, the professional driver (though the driverless car can help part-time drivers like you and me, by making us more efficient). One can argue that he is not a beneficiary, but it is a fact that he exists in the ecosystem.

Another potential change will be that cars will not belong to individuals but to groups, and so in-trunk storage of bags or golf clubs will disappear, causing a new storage industry to grow.

In VDL, as in the real world, Value exists outside networks and can be developed by individuals working in isolation such as a sculptor working on a piece of stone (unless you extend networks to include inanimate objects like stone and other products to become co-creators). The sculptor has to use his accumulated Value (knowledge, ideas and his inherent ability) to create or co-create more Value.

VDL looks at Value that exists, whether we notice and do not notice its potential (Value waiting to happen). VDL wants people to become aware of what is around them and discover the Value and also of the destructive potential. Since the pursuit of Value is basic and actors and networks must increase this Value using all means.

We (including institutions) need a focus on Value and creation, not just satisfaction, not just experience, not just service. We want to create good, we want well-being and we want Value. When someone gives me something of Value, I receive the item and my perceived Value of what I am given is developed (maybe high or low).

Value within the Classic Business/Social Ecosystem

Value is created at every step, it is ever changing, and is not a constant. It has to be continuously and consciously built or it will deteriorate. Thus, in a company or society, every actor has to Create Value. He first must Create Value for himself. He has to learn to do that in the context he is in (as an executive, as a husband, as a father, as a member of society). This could be through learning, through improving his awareness and attitude. He has to do this for himself (no beneficiary except himself) and he should also learn to Create Value for others. He could also collaborate with or learn from others (and Value is created/co-created here). Every actor creates Value for himself and for others, but the greatest Value is created when some other actor, or perhaps a beneficiary, perceives the person delivering or creating the Value to be a Value creator. The company has to Create Value for the employee, the partners, supply and delivery chain, society and the shareholder. Value exists in all these interactions. There should be primacy of Value in the thinking.

Moreover, often the beneficiary sees different stages in his contact with an actor or a service (including a product). We call this the Waterfall of Needs.[8] This is now called the Customer Journey, and later the Value Journey. The beneficiary sees Value (some may call it potential Value) of a product during his product/services search or when someone tells him about it. He investigates further, and he decides to buy it. The seller (physical store, net or a person) adds Value to the buyer (and in this case the beneficiary) through the exchange of knowledge and ideas on the use and advantage of the item. (Value could also be destroyed in this interaction). All this time the customer or beneficiary is weighing the relative Value of each one of the alternatives. And he decides to buy the one that gives him the most Value (of course it is a perceived Value). He gets in exchange the product/service for something (usually the cost), part of which goes to the seller as price and other price terms or potential price terms such as discounts, partial payments, future business, services potential etc.) The beneficiary now owns the product/service, the Value increase or decreases in context and in use. Value is again prime in the transactions, while there is a service exchange. This is shown in Figure 8.4. This figure mirrors the Customer Journey with a Value Journey (Value created/ destroyed at every stage). Note that at each stage, Value is perceived by the customer, even though the graph shows relative Value versus competing alternatives. In fact, Value is destroyed when the product does not work.

There is a feeling one cannot perceive Value before purchase, because it cannot be quantified or measured. I would contend one would have the same difficulty after the purchase and during use. The same method of quantifying Value is used during or before use. Take the example of a phone.

So, Value is created (sometimes destroyed) at every step. It is perceived, it is transferred and it is used and then co-created by the beneficiary. The phone might provide a solution to the user, and the user may add apps and get enhanced outcomes and Value from it. Enhancing outcomes is better than providing solutions. If the phone does not work, Value is destroyed. Its superior perceived benefits/cost (over competitive phones) to the buyer causes the buyer to buy. In its use, Value increases or decreases. If it works as expected, maybe no further Value is added.

Let's assume the phone develops a fault. An unnecessary experience and journey is imposed on the beneficiary and this may be destructive of Value.

---

[8] Kordupleski, Mastering Customer Value Management, Pinaflex, 2003.

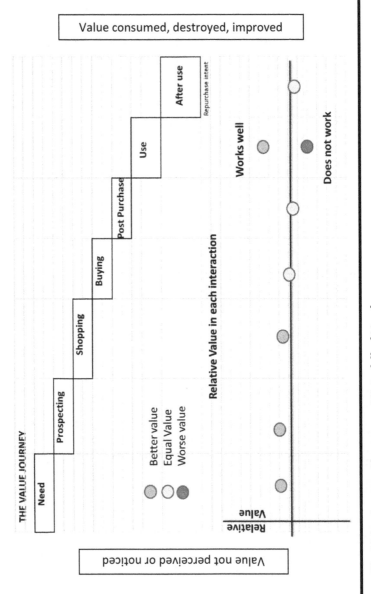

Figure 8.4   The Value Journey Shown as a Waterfall of Needs

Creation and Destruction of Value beyond the Classic Business/Social Boundary

The lay manager/executive has to grasp and to understand this significance and want to be a Value creator. This has to be taught at the individual level, at the school and college level and at work.

Value needs to be taught, because in my interactions with many leaders (there are notable exceptions), they have no real sense of Value or its creation except the profit motive. They do not live, nor do they breathe Value creation. They live in a functional world of short termism. Companies have to Create Value for their entire ecosystem and derive Value for their shareholders and gain longevity both for the CEOs and for the company.

Long-lasting companies are driven by Value and values and focus (on entrepreneurship and innovation). Creating Value drives the oldest business families such as Takenaka in Japan 1610; Merck, Germany 1668; Coors, USA 1786 and Thomson Reuters, Canada 1799.

A sea change and a shift by the large majority to participate in Value creation will change business thinking into long-term success.

Ecosystem

Businesses have to look into the customer ecosystem, into the provider ecosystem and into the product and service ecosystem. Many companies do some of this. Where they have difficulty is in looking outside the ecosystem at what is happening with ideas, with customers, with supply systems and so on, and whether potential Value/Value destruction exists. Or when they define their ecosystem too narrowly. It is difficult for companies to abandon their existing logic, especially if they have been good at it. Examples include Kodak who did not embrace digital photography, or Digital Equipment Corporation, DEC, who failed to see the potential of personal computers. (Or the Telegraph Company and the telephone as described earlier). With VDL, had Kodak looked outside its business/social ecosystem boundary, seen potential destruction, they would have adopted to a better Value creation idea. Value could be overall good or worthwhile.

Does Value Have to Be in the Eyes of the Customer before It Is Seen

This goes back to our discussion that Value is perceived. In business, providers Create Value based on their perception of what the customer wants. A certain amount of Value is created by the company: it increases know how, more employees get involved with the new offering, there is marketing activity. But the company can create only so much Value, and no more, till the customer sees it and perceives Value in the product. This is the real additional Value for the company. Further Value comes when the customer buys it and when he uses it.

The difficulty with Value is that it is an intangible because Value depends on the various actors in the Value ecosystem and their perception of Value.

One can also ask if Value can be received unilaterally or does it have to be bilateral?

The actor could also collaborate with or learn from others (and Value is created/co-created here). Every actor Creates Value for himself and for others, but the greatest Value is created when some other actor, or perhaps a beneficiary, perceives the person delivering or creating the Value to be a Value creator. The company has to Create Value for the employee, the partners, supply and delivery chain, society and the shareholder. Value exists in all these interactions. There should be primacy of Value in the thinking.

> Who will succeed in business? The man who will use his skill and constructive imagination to see how much he can give for a dollar, instead of how little he can give for a dollar is bound to succeed. **Henry Ford**

So, Value is created (sometimes destroyed) at every step. It is perceived, it is transferred, and it is used and then co-created by the beneficiary. Sometimes, the company wants the customer to co-create something they should have done and puts the onus on the customer. Effective co-creation is a two-way street, benefitting the provider and the customer.

Value and Leadership and Executives

In VDL, businesses have to transform themselves to become Value creators. That means the CxOs should lead the charge and aid and abet their executives to become Value creators.

As CxOs work with executives, we find they embrace the idea of Value creation, once they know what Value creation is, but also what will Create Value. They need to know if I am creating Value, how do I measure how much Value I am creating, how do I create meaningful Value (and for whom?), how do I see the impact of Value creation and what it does for me? So, this takes us into the realm of ingenuity, imaginativeness, innovation, pro-activeness and initiative taking, and implementation. And how do organisations transform themselves into helping Value creators[9]?

---

[9] Before the Value role of leaders, one accepted definition is the ability to influence individuals or groups in a manner that encourages cooperation, collaboration, and action towards positive results.

First, I think, companies have to recognise Value creation is an important role of the executive. It enables executives to transcend their functional work and go beyond what is expected of them and consciously Create Value. Companies have to set an environment for Value creation and create a Value mindset. So, they need an enabling organisation, and they have to let go (not ask for conformists). They have to subtly promote Value creation (by building self-esteem, awareness and pro-activeness), while discussing what Value creation will do for the Value creators and the company. How, what and where to Create Value?

> Leaders, Executives and Employees must develop:
> The 6As: Awareness (and Curiosity), Attitude, Ability, Agility, Anticipation, Ambidextrousness.

Value Creation Pointers

■ Before executives can be asked to Create Value, they must know what will Create Value, and for whom and;

■ How do they recognise and understand Value creation;

■ They must realise that just being good functional executives is not good enough. They have to learn to go beyond and Create Value and a Value creation mindset;

■ Companies have to set up a Value creation environment. That means they recognise and promote Value creation.

Value and Leaders

Leaders must have curiosity. They must engender trust, which is a killer app for leaders. Nadella suggests:

Empathy + Shared values + Safety and Responsibility = Trust over time. LinkedIn CEO Jeff Weiner says consistency over time is trust.

Henry Mintzberg wrote in the 1990s that the 10 roles of a leader and managers are to act as figureheads, lead, liaise, monitor, disseminate, be spokespersons, entrepreneurs, disturbance handlers, resource allocators and negotiators. Most of these requires a VDL mindset. Value creation and its mindsets helps you focus on the Value creation part of the job (versus functional) and create more Value. Thus, leaders must not only produce more leaders, but more importantly Value-creating leaders and setting a Value-creating environment.

Leaders according to John Kotter, focus on change, create a vision, communicate and earn commitment, motivate and inspire. Managers deal with and control people and things – more functional work. We want managers to Create Value in whatever way they can.

Hugh Blaine suggests six factors that contribute to a mindset that lowers performance and stifles the well-being of customers and employees. These kill the urge to Create Value: underperformance is tolerated; miscommunication; being tired, worn down and burnt out; not having the skills to manage stress effectively; poor time management and priority setting habits; unaware of the importance of mindset on performance.

We have found that mindset has a great influence on leadership and the ability of leaders to Create Value.

Leaders must be acutely aware of society, of embracing technology to improve their services to citizens, productivity, local entrepreneurship and sustainability.

Leaders should ask: What can we be the best in the world in? (Obviously not in everything.)

Many leaders believe the extraordinary is possible. A health care CEO sees her job as primarily focused on creating cultural transformation. Patient care and safety are paramount, along with engaging employees. A cultural and mindset transformation is necessary. This is Value creation.

Value creation thinking states that someone creates or co-creates (which is what you should do) so that someone else (whoever your customer is) can achieve success and gain Value (what).

Successful leaders are Value creators. Value creating is giving and not taking. Value creating is creating Value for the ecosystem.

Most successful leaders are Value creators, without consciously being so. We want leaders to be aware of creation of Value, and work consciously on reducing destruction of Value and create more Value. They have to be able to see the best Value in dilemmas, wherein Value is created, and some is destroyed. They have also to manage sustainability.

For example, when closing a plant, the company has to let go of people. The leader has to think of options that create the least destruction for the various actors.

Or when promoting someone, the leader has to seek the best Value creator, and ensure Value destruction to the persons not promoted is minimised.

The leader has to change the thinking of his people from functional to a creating Value mindset and encourage Value creation thinking. One way is to put Value creation which goes beyond functional work in the key performance indicators, and trigger bonuses from it. I know one Indian company that has started this program in their KPIs[10].

Leaders can create an innovative culture by daring to dream. Skilled and true leaders create a shared Value or a "higher purpose." Leaders reframe the

---

[10] Key Performance Indicators.

role of employees, by providing a sense of belonging. A societal organisation helps families improve well-being or helps create jobs or moves the country's economy forward. The purpose is not just about the company's future but a mission of the organisation's "big-picture-thinking," grand purpose or why it exists.

The message is to inspire, innovate and look at the Triple Bottom Line (TBL: people, planet, profit).

In "Larry's Letter," Fink said that companies could no longer rely on profits alone. They must create long-term Value and financial performance. Understanding a company's effect on the wider world was also vital, he said. "Society is demanding that companies, both public and private, serve a social purpose," Fink wrote. "To prosper over time, every company must not only deliver financial performance, but also show how it makes a positive contribution to society. Companies must benefit all of their stakeholders, including shareholders, employees, customers and the communities in which they operate," the letter said. These sentiments are supported by Indra Nooyi and Carlos Ghoshn.

PepsiCo CEO Indra Nooyi[11] explained at Davos in 2018 how her long-term strategy for the company eventually paid off, but almost lost her the job. She said that CEOs and shareholders need to have better dialogue around future Value creation, as opposed to solely chasing quarterly results.

In a new book, Dear CEO,[12] we find they say many things Value creation espouses. One is that the CEO is really the Chief Behaviour Officer. Mindsets are extremely important! A Chief entrepreneur is also required to promote innovation and disruption.

We talked about inclusive capital in Chapter 7 on Value, Society and Technology.

Leaders Must Reorganise for VDL to Take Root

Leaders realise that VDL is a mindset. That it must get into the organisation, become part of the culture.

However, there is physical re-organisation one can do to become a Value-creating organisation. The CEO should become the Chief Value Creator, and the Chief Operating Officer (COO) should become the Chief Customer Value

---

[11] https://www.businessinsider.in/pepsico-ceo-indra-nooyis-long-term-strategy-put-her-job-in-jeopardy-but-now-the-numbers-are-in-and-the-analysts-who-doubted-her-will-have-to-eat-their-words/articleshow/62748222.cms

[12] Dear CEO, Bloomsbury 2018 by Thinkers 50.

Creator. This is because everything the COO does is for the customer, such as manufacturing, logistics, service, marketing, sales, design etc.

The head of HR should become the Chief Employee Value Creator, and the head of finance the Chief Shareholder Value Creator. He is responsible for providing the board, customer and employee data at board meetings and alerting the board of potential problems, such as when Customer Value data shows a decline.

The CEO has a person reporting to him on strategy, the future, disruption etc.

Then the organisation has a balance, with individuals tackling different areas where Value has to be created, and not letting the organisation become one sided. An organogram is shown below in Figure 8.5, Organisation of the Future.

Functional Executives vs. Value Creators: Reorganise

Accepting the organogram in Figure 8.5, one then must ask: How do we get functional work done? Everyone cannot be a great Value creator. They may create enough Value to be good performers, but not more than that. Thus, we have

> Create a functional or administrative department (work that can be outsourced.

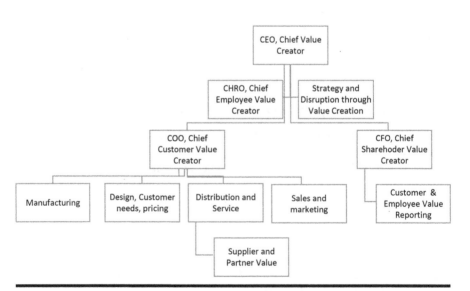

Figure 8.5   Organisation of the Future

to create routine or functional work departments, that is work that can be outsourced, so that the Value-creating executives can be freed up to do better work and Create Value for now and the future.

Items that can be easily outsourced include accounting, market research, human resource administration, some manufacturing or manufactured items, design and software work. This is shown in Figure 8.6.

In India this is even more important because the CXOs have to do an extraordinary amount of routine, administrative and functional work. The have to be relieved of this. Thus, one can have an administrative department reporting to the Chief Value Creator, or just outsource all this work. Or each department could have an administrative department, that should receive minimal attention from the CXO.

> Even functional executives can have a Value Creation performance criterion.

You can add to the list of outsourceable work.

Just as an example, a HR person who is meant to monitor leave, compliance, etc. can be put into the administrative department. Even in such a department one performance criterion should be Value created outside expected work.

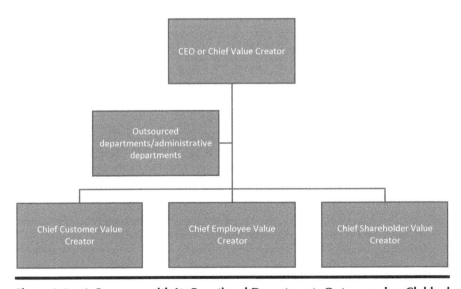

Figure 8.6   A Company with Its Functional Departments Outsourced or Clubbed in a Functional Administrative Department

Leaders Must Have Values

Leaders must have values: morals and ethics, and conviction etc.

We know from experience and data that values Create Value.

This is not to say that leaders without values and morals are unsuccessful. Or those that bend values are unsuccessful.

Morals and ethics are different. Morals are one's own principles and thinking about what is right or wrong. Morals are about our own codes of behaviour. These depend on what we think is right or wrong, based on our faith systems, and the society and environment we live in. There is an overlap in ethics and morals.

Ethics is what is seen or expected by external rules. Ethics are the code of conduct we apply to others and society. Values are about doing good and being good.

Often, morals and ethics can be the same. Killing someone falls into this. Morally and ethically wrong. However, in war, killing an enemy may be ethically sanctioned.

As an example, your morals may include being honest, being religious, being truthful, engendering trust. Ethics could include integrity, honesty, transparency, fairness etc.

Many leadership ideas focus on core values, and they confuse values and traits (core values).

George Mason University cites core values (which are actually traits):

"Respect, as demonstrated by self-respect and respecting others regardless of differences; treating others with dignity, empathy and compassion; and the ability to earn the respect of others, making a difference are all traits. Integrity, authenticity, courage, service, humility, wisdom etc. are values."

A larger list of traits would be:

ambition, competency, individuality, equality, *integrity*, service, responsibility, accuracy, respect, dedication, diversity, improvement, enjoyment/fun, loyalty, credibility, *honesty*, innovativeness, teamwork, excellence, accountability, empowerment, quality, efficiency, dignity, collaboration, stewardship, empathy, accomplishment, courage, wisdom, independence, security, challenge, influence, learning, compassion, friendliness, discipline/order, generosity, persistence, optimism, dependability, flexibility

These are all traits.

Items that fit into values are integrity, honesty. So, leadership training does not focus that highly on values. Traits are often called core values and shape the mission and style and the culture. But the culture and style must reflect basic values.

In business jargon, values are called ethics, and traits are core values. In our definition core values are not traits but actually should be the ethical and moral framework of what is right and what is wrong, fair and not fair.

The combination of these makes a great leader, and if he is a great leader, he Creates Value for the ecosystem. He becomes a Value creator! He creates a culture of creating Value.

Value-based leadership connects to employees' values. This helps in a more inclusive culture and Creates Value. Values, Beliefs and Attitudes (VBA) has an impact on values and ethical climate (see Figure 8.7).

So, you can see that values and high VBA create great values, whereas just a mixture of traits such as respect, commitment and excellence and low VBA can lead to systems failure as in the case of Enron.

As we said in creating Value for yourself, you have to Create Value for others. This is the core message to leaders:

1. We add Value to others when we truly Value others. Good leaders go out of their way to never subtract Value from their people. They are intentional about adding Value and make it part of their core traits.

2. We have the core traits and then have the values (morals and ethics).

3. We have to understand that we cannot create profits without creating Value for the ecosystem.

4. That long-term thinking is important for creating Value.

> By being first-movers and Value makers, not takers, they create better outcomes for everyone, themselves included.
> – Victor Wong, CEO of PaperG

5. With these, the leader has to take the employees and partners, customers and society leaders along with him, and convince the shareholder of long-term thinking. He has to enunciate the purpose of the company that goes beyond the profit motive and routine mission statements.

6. Greater Value for us is created when we Create Value for others. We then make ourselves more valuable to them, and they in turn

> The bottom line in leadership isn't how far we advance ourselves but how far we advance others.
> – John C. Maxwell

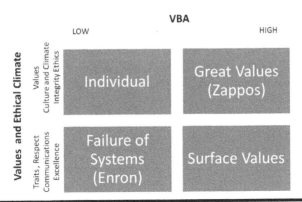

Figure 8.7 VBA, Values Beliefs and Attitudes from Author

will Create Value for the leader, making him a greater leader. Examples of Value creation may be giving emotional support to someone, listening to someone, teaching them to be better executives and Value creators, giving them more opportunities etc.

7. Understanding what other's Value allow us to Create Value for the team. A good leader takes the opportunity to listen to what every person believes is important, and then leads.[13]

Value Dominant Logic treats employees as part of human capital, and Value needs to be created for them.

Companies need to find and convert talent to Value (T2V).[14] This is becoming more important as economies become more dynamic, digital and knowledge based. This is a start to creating human Value.

Andrew Karpie suggests a T2V model and its basic building blocks: digital, platform-based, precision sourcing and the application of external and internal expertise into time-delimited, outcome-specific projects that Create Value for an enterprise. This implies a holistic way to use knowledge, talent, IT and intangible assets and IP to design, co-create with customers and deliver innovative products in dynamic, digitally integrated networks.

Once we have talent and the T2V approach, Value can potentially arise from expertise and capabilities that can be redeployed into future projects. Platform-based talent pools can be employed. We are thus building potential Value for the future.

An important part of employee well-being is creating trust, according to Randy Conley.[15] He cites his ABCD model for creating trust. Leaders must be **A**ble (demonstrate competence), **B**elievable (have values and integrity, and consistency), **C**onnected (show care and concern) and **D**ependable (show reliability).

Creating Value for Employees

Value-creating work definitions vary from one employee to another. Generally, these are challenging opportunities, which also allow people to use their skills and knowledge. Employees love to take part in a common purpose (belonging) where they can Create Value in their work life. Work that creates meaningful Value makes the employee feel good and reduces career stagnation and monotony.

---

[13] http://www.business2community.com/leadership/add-Value-team-follow-brilliant-leader ship-strategies-01434964#LwSEgT5QzmG4lyJW.99

[14] http://spendmatters.com/2018/01/24/talent-Value-t2v-enterprises-need-todays-dynamic-digi tal-knowledge-based-economy-part-1/

[15] https://leadingwithtrust.com/2013/11/17/the-abcds-of-leading-with-trust/

Establishing a common purpose or a shared goal enables employees at every level of the organisation to envisage the company's future and how their roles fit within it. While having people who possess the right skill sets are crucial, building Value adding skills for the future is equally pivotal. (Note we prefer enabling people. True empowerment is rare.)

VDL helps employees to gain an employer mindset with a can-do attitude and become part of the larger purpose of the organisation.

Employees, like most other actors, are deliverers and recipients of Value. They form part of the Value Dominant Logic in Business.

Companies can Create Value for employees, and in turn employees can create more Value for customers and the company and the ecosystem. Employees need to be valued, especially when creating Value. You will notice we have been saying that it is mandatory to have valued employees (employees that feel valued) and customers. How you treat your employees directly reflects your customer satisfaction and Customer Value. Developing, empowering and respecting your employees will result in happy customers! Employee experience is the foundation for customer experience. The HR Chief has to take on the role of the Chief Employee Value Creator.

Much of this is engendered by trust. If we don't treat our employees the way we treat our best customers, they will stop trusting us. And it's very difficult to get that trust back. This is very dangerous for the business! You end up losing the best employees and adding more problems recruiting new employees into the system.

How we treat our colleagues speaks volumes about the way we treat customers. That's why we recommend a Courtesy System so that you are polite and courteous to your colleagues and your employees, and courtesy becomes a habit and a culture, a way of life.

So, start doing some nice things for your employees, pat them on the back, take them out for lunch etc., and make them feel valued.

Most employees do not have a strategy for themselves. They need to ask what they Value, what they want out of life, out of work and what they Value at work. Is it learning, is it getting recognised, is it being given responsibility, is it

> Employees must create or be helped to create a Value-creating strategy for themselves.

a sense of belonging and being part of a group of people, being engaged, is it the values of the company, the growth of the company, the reputation of the company, the challenge, the opportunity to achieve, the management, the colleagues, the prospects for advancement, the money? Which are more important? Monetary gains or other monetary advantages such as free courses, travel and an expense report, etc. or is it the other benefits? How do they balance work and their personal lives? The company must help them understand how to Create Value for themselves.

More and more HR managers and PR managers like Paul MacKenzie-Cummins, managing director of ClearlyPR, are saying, "It's down to individuals to demonstrate the Value they can add to the organisation and 'sell' themselves against that Value. Yet too few people do this well enough and it starts early in their careers."

And if businesses are based on the Value Dominant Logic of creating Value, they too should be thinking about creating Employee Value, or what the employee values. Value means how worthwhile it is for the employee to work for this company versus working somewhere else. Which of the Value terms are most important? The salary and perks or the benefits you think you are getting? So, in terms of importance, is money 60% and benefits 40%, or vice versa?

$$Employee\ Value\ Added\ (EVA) = \frac{Value\ you\ add\ to\ your\ employees}{Value\ your\ competitor\ adds\ to\ its\ employees}$$

This is shown in the Value tree in Figure 8.8:

Facebook[16] says managers can destroy Value. People leave their managers. Even when they quit their jobs, they often are really leaving their managers.

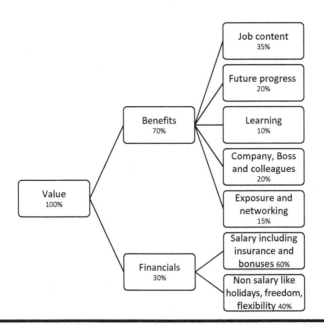

Figure 8.8 Value Attribute Tree for Employee Value Added

---

[16] https://www.peoplematters.in/article/strategic-hr/why-do-employees-quit-lessons-from-facebook-17337

Because a manager is responsible for what the job is like. Tasks depend on people; instead of squeezing them into pre-determined job descriptions. Narrow and functional job descriptions can also hurt.

A Value-added employee cannot stop here. If he wants to get ahead he has to Create Value not just for himself but for his colleagues, his bosses and for his company. Value Dominant Logic suggests Value creation is a two-way street.

In creating Value for himself the employee has to ask, what will make me a more valuable person in this company? What will make the company take notice of me? How do I build my brand equity? How do I use my brand equity to enhance the company's brand equity? Is it just doing what is expected of me or doing a better job than the others? Or going the extra mile? Or creating ideas, methods, thoughts that will make the company or my department more valuable? What are these extra steps I can take? (Remember, creating Value means going beyond the functional aspects of your job and doing your Value-creating job well.)

Doing this builds your brand equity. You are known by the brand you create for yourself. If your name is Jim, what is brand Jim in the eyes of the company? Does brand Jim mean dependability and reliability and getting the job done? Or brand Jim means he not only gets the job done, but he thinks of better ways of doing the job and thinks ahead to the next step. Is Jim a Value Creator?

Having good brand equity means people (your colleagues, bosses, suppliers and customers) want to deal with you. Poor brand equity means they do not want to deal with you or worse still, are saying keep him out of our way.

One of the companies on whose Board I am has set up a bonus system based on employees accomplishing agreed upon results beyond the functional job. And another bonus to go beyond even this in creating Value for themselves, their colleagues, society and the company. This has been proven to be right, as shown below.[17]

Patty McCord, former chief talent officer at Netflix, in her just-published article on corporate pay doesn't mince her words. "The prevailing system is behind the times," she slams. "It's based on what employees have produced, rather than their potential to add Value in the future. Far better to focus on the performance you want and the future you're heading to."

Others have difficulty in measuring Value.

James Reed, chairman of Eponymous reed.co.uk,[18] says: Give staff an indication of their Value. "Incentivise people to control their own development to add more Value and therefore take-home pay."

---

[17] Should employees who add Value or bring in more business get greater reward? RCNT.EU/ R8JOM BY PETER CRUSH, January 30, 2018.

[18] https://www.raconteur.net/hr/reward-top-performers-higher-pay

Value is a term more understood by Stone Junction founder Richard Stone says: "Equality and pay based on Value created are not contradictory concepts; they are complementary."

Paul MacKenzie-Cummins, MD at reputation management agency ClearlyPR thinks: "It's down to individuals to demonstrate the Value they can add to the organisation and 'sell' themselves against that Value," he says. "Yet too few people do this well enough and it starts early in their careers."

Value Dominant Logic will suggest that companies be concerned about the Employee Journey, and what he has to go through to Create Value, and to help the employee answer the question whom does he work for? Himself? The company? And whom is he responsible to and for?

Companies can add Value to the customer by using a connected company concept raised by Dave Gray.[19] CEOs have to think more of the net, the digital and e-world, the internet of things and work through the urgency of getting connected and help their employees become internet savvy. CEOs have to think about creating Value for themselves and their employees and building employee brand equity. And how to make employees feel valued?

Dave suggests employees own a task such as owning the customer's experience, and the employees work holistically, without silos (where specialisation and separation is encouraged). This does not work for creative people or for complex jobs requiring adaptation, or for people driven by purpose.

The message should be:

■ Employee Value is important and should be measured. Valued employees deliver more.

■ Have a Chief Employee Value Creator.

■ Make it easy for the employee to work, including simplified systems (I just go off a call from Tata AIG asking about whether I had been given access to their payment gateway. The poor call agent called four times to check. The system took its own time, making both myself and the call agent anxious.)

■ You should also build your own, and fellow employees', brand-equity.

■ Value-added employees add Value to customers and their companies.

■ Start a Courtesy System so that there is a culture of courtesy which the customer will notice.

Remember employee churn will cost you a bundle of money and problems.

---

[19] Dave Gray, 2014, The Connected Company, O.

Doug McDavid[20] argues that companies need to improve the well-being of employees by designing architecture designed for the well-being of employees. Further he envisages a Human Institution that forces companies to focus on creating architecture for the well-being of all stakeholders.

"Since people spend more time at work than in any other single environment, it behoves leaders to create organisations that foster the well-being of its members."

Value and the Front-line

Often Value creation/destruction is done by front-line people. It is not because they are Value creators/destroyers, but because they are carrying out the diktat of their bosses, some of whom may not be customer centric, or do not understand customers or customer centricity.

The problem is that front-line people become the mouth of the company and often do not have recourse to higher-ups. (Try asking a front-line person to connect you to a decision maker. He cannot and will not as he is also made the gatekeeper). Value Dominant Logic seeks to change all this.

As an example, I got a bill of 12,000 Rupees (Rs) from my cell phone company. I had bought a 10-day call package for Finland, Germany and UK when I left India for a visit. The total cost was 6,000 Rs. The cell phone company activated one 10-day call package for Finland and Germany (which I used for seven days) and a fresh 10-day pack for the UK (where I had a two-day stay). I was made to pay twice. I talked to the call centre and they said that I must have asked for two call packages (which I had not and would not have done). He could not see that the company representative had done anything wrong and advised me to pay it to prevent interest charges.

I called a friend at the company, and he understood the issue and asked billing to look into it. They reversed the 6,000 Rs charge.

First, we need to enable the front-line people, and make them the owners of their action. Second, they have to be able to understand the issues rather than to keep saying the company is right.

I am having this problem with Tata Sky. They asked me to renew my annual subscription for 16,750 Rs. I kept getting messages that the resubscription had been done for six months, and even then, certain features were not available. I was forced to go back to the CEO's office to get this corrected. Why? Why were these errors occurring? Who was going to fix this and prevent this from happening to others?

---

[20] TMTC Journal of Management | April 2012.

Customer-Centric Circles

This is why we need to get customer Advocates, so the front-line people and the mindset of the company become important. See Figure 8.9 from Colin Shaw's[21] Beyond Philosophy with his permission.

The Customer Strategy starts off a customer alignment and culture at all functions and levels as part of our customer-centric objectives. This establishes what we call "Customer Conduits," which are a top-down approach, driven by the CEO, to make the organisation customer-centric.

Customer-Centric Circles (or Customer Circles for short) are a bottom-up approach to customer centricity. The term Customer-Centric Circles is really a misnomer because it is a company-sponsored group of people generally front-line employees and some staff

> With VDL, we must make the front-line people self-directed. To do this and add Value to the employees and the customer, we start Customer-Centric Circles.

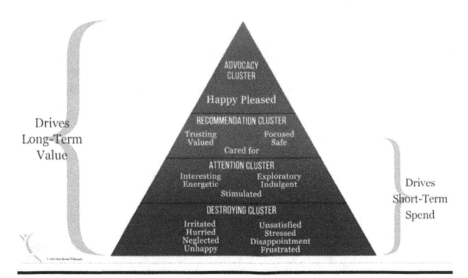

Figure 8.9   How Driving Long-Term Value, Is Different from Driving Short-Term Spending

---

21 https://www.mycustomer.com/experience/engagement/the-20-emotions-that-drive-or-destroy-Value-in-customer-experience?utm_medium=email&utm_campaign=MYCMO N161017&utm_content=MYCMON161017+CID_adfb95270e6b53285b5f91de9d2771 b9&utm_source=internal_cm&utm_term=Research%20reveals%20all

people. Customer Circles may not necessarily have Customers in it per se, but this group of people will focus on the customer.

Some may ask why have Customer-Centric Circles without Customers? Ideally, we would like to have Customers in the Customer Circles. However, it is difficult to get the right type of analytical Customers who could commit the time to be in an on-going initiative. In any event, the Customer Circle is a task force to run a customer-focused project with targets, responsibilities and timetables.

The circles Create Value for the employees. They get them engaged, allow them to feel they are in charge, make them take responsibility for the customer and his well-being, suggest what the company should do to be more customer centric and build the customer's DNA (Do Not Annoy), and uphold the customer's Bill of Rights.

Composition of Customer Circles

First, we have to decide whom to select for the Customer-Centric-Circles. It depends on the size of the company, the number of front-line people, and where they are distributed geographically. If we have to select from a large number, we should start with front-line people who are communicative and proactive and can later widen the circles or manage them. As stated earlier, we should add some staff people and others from support functions mostly having regular contact with Customers, and people from communications, IT, business development, environmental affairs, manufacturing and product development among others. This is because we want these people to participate in and understand the proceedings of the Customer Circles and be able to implement ideas emanating from the Customer Circles.

Typically, you can have 20 people in a Customer Circle. We have worked with 60 people in a Customer Circle.

In larger companies, we have had many different Customer Circles. For example, at Tata Power, we had set up an apex Customer Circle to view the overall customer-centricity of the company and the effectiveness of the various other Customer Circles. We had a Customer Circle in departments such as Finance, Sustainability, customer Service, IT, Field Support and so forth.

You could call the participants Customer Champions.

Running a Customer Circle[22]

First and foremost, we are not to teach or train. We have to make this into a self-learning and self-directed group of people.

---

[22] Much of Customer Circles is taken from Mahajan, 2011 Total Customer Value Management, Sage.

Generally, front-line people are not used to this. They are more used to being told what to do and to following orders and processes. They are not used to being the decision makers on how to treat the customer.

The first step is to raise the self-esteem of employees on Customers. This is necessary so that they can have self-confidence and be honest about customer interactions (and stop saying the customer is always wrong and we are the injured party). We want them to feel good about themselves, to feel confident they can do positive things for the customer, and to put up with the possible poor treatment at the hands of the customer.

The second step is to raise the awareness of the people. We want them to become generally aware of what is happening around them, notice more, "see and hear" more. Are they aware of things around them? Can they perceive the inflexion or the pain in the voice of the customer or the body language of the customer? This will raise consciousness of the importance of the customer.

These two steps to build self-esteem and awareness may require help from an external expert. One will notice that when self-esteem, self-belief and confidence are built up, these Customer Circle members will start to admit that many of the reasons that Customers get angry were caused by them or the company. For example, a person who was

> Value is created for front-line people in Customer Circles, by increasing their self-esteem and awareness, and their taking ownership of the Customer.

promised delivery by a certain time could get aggrieved if after two hours of waiting the delivery has not happened. And you cannot placate her by saying "these things happen". Once participants realise that being late and their casual response caused the customer to be unhappy (often the Customer Circle person would have said the customer is irrational) they will then start to rectify this. Why was the person late? Is it happening often? Are promises being made which cannot be kept? How do we prevent this from happening? How do I change my response to "I am sorry"?

The front-line people develop strategies for dealing with Customers at a local level. They devise ways and means to make it easier for the customer to do business with them. They find methods to touch the customer and to give the customer a great experience. Customer data, information, inputs, complaints or plaudits should be made available to the Customer Circle, as and when it is available, or an effort should be made to collect such feedback.

What you'll find is that the group will come up with better ways to handle a customer. Through this process, awareness of the customer in the company and among the employees will invariably increase. But before all this, we must understand the Voice of the Employee, her pain points, and increase her self-esteem, and awareness on the customer. Along with this, we must capture the Voice of the Customer and the Voice of the Competitor.

We must help the group to build their ability, become agile, to acquire a great attitude and become ambidextrous (along with awareness and anticipation, these are called the 6As, see page 141). These all Create Value.

Basically, this is a bottom-up approach to energising an organisation so that it can become customer centric and Create Value.

The Customer Circles must collect data on the customer, plan on how to track every contact and experience and chart out future touches and experience, keeping the retailer (in a B2C case) in the forefront. They must talk to the customer, get feedback from the marketplace, and learn what they can about the competition in both formal and informal ways. Sometimes because of the large numbers, it is not easy to get data from every contact, and so we settle for a sampling.

Customer-Centric Circles are akin to a level 3 empowerment described by Jan Carlzon of SAS Airlines, where employees are self-managing and can make decisions. They will take ownership of the customer and the customer initiatives because these are their own ideas. This is how we make the employees the owners for customer focus. What the employees propose is common sense. What they suggest is what the company would have wanted the front-line people to do!

Our people will have stopped saying: "these are our rules," "didn't you know our rules?" "you should have known" and other irritating remarks.

Next, they work on the customer's Bill of Rights and what promises are required to uphold such rights. The group examines promises kept, promises capable of being kept and maintainable, and suggests changes in the Bill of Rights.

They also embark on a Continuous Customer Improvement Program.

Customer Circles and Shared Visions

What we notice is that if we show the front-line people the results of their actions through customer feedback, and if this is positive, that the front-line people get a sense of pride and a sense of achievement. The motivation level on serving Customers better goes up.

Customer Circles engender shared vision and teamwork. They are a pillar of a learning organisation, where people work together for shared goals and beliefs. They allow the building of promises and working together to make things happen. They lead to creativity and making people think about mastery; and in this case, mastery of habits, responses, approaches to the customer and of building systems and methods for better customer satisfaction and Customer Value. A shared vision (on how to treat Customers) is not necessarily an idea but a desire or a force in people's minds and hearts that drives them to achieve extraordinary goals; for example, making Customers happy, consistently!

Sharing the vision means people working together. People have to be convinced that they want to do something good for the customer; you cannot force them. You encourage them to have a personal vision and try to build it into a shared vision. During Customer Circle sessions, we have to ask people why Customers become happy with the front-line people and why they become unhappy. Often, they respond that the Customers' unhappiness is caused because Customers are unreasonable or have high, unmet expectations. On introspection, the group often reaches the conclusion that it is their own actions or inactions that cause dissatisfaction in the customer's mind. With this awareness, they search for solutions, including modification of their own behaviour and how to create more Value.

The group builds its own (its members' or participants') self-esteem and awareness and decides on action steps, including building the Customers' satisfaction factors and Do Not Annoy (DNA) factors. Such factors include:

> A customer Culture means the Customer Comes First.

consideration for the customer's time, energy, respect convenience, image and so on.

The problem with a top-down approach is that top management 'dictates' a vision, does not build it with a buy-in of key players at all levels, nor is it built on personal and shared visions. Shared visions spread because of commitment, enrolment, clarity, enthusiasm, reinforcement and communication.

Understanding current reality and accepting it, without clouding it with perceptions and blame avoidance, are important to shared visions and Customer Circles. Cynicism, being ordered or told to do things, of being taught rather than self-learning and organisational structure, all conspire against success of Customer Circles. Value is created for the employees, and through them, for the customer.

Customer Circles and Team-Learning

Customer Circles are interdisciplinary teams. The success of Customer Circles depends on individual excellence and learning and how well the team members work together. It depends on managing individual skills and merit with team spirit. Unaligned teams waste energy. Therefore, teams have to learn to align themselves and develop the capacity of the individuals in a team effort to Create Value for customers.

Examples of Customer Circles

The Tata Power Customer Circles led to the introduction of the courtesy system (smiling and greeting at work). The Customer Circles realised that the Customers were being inconvenienced when they visited the Tata Power office. The Circles designed special signs and put them up for the Customers to get to the customer department. Soon thereafter, an existing office was converted into a comfortable customer meeting room. The customer did not have to search for the right Tata Power representative. The customer just picked up the intercom as they came off the elevator.

The person who responded ensured the right person came to meet them in the meeting room. Individual customer-facing employees started to put customer-related quotes on their desktops. They made laminated cards they carry showing Customers' Do Not Annoy (DNA). On the reverse side of the card are the customer's delight factors.

An example of this card is given in Figures 8.10 and 8.11.

Service people who fix customer problems have started to carry cards showing how to save energy and leave these with Customers, as shown in Figure 8.11.

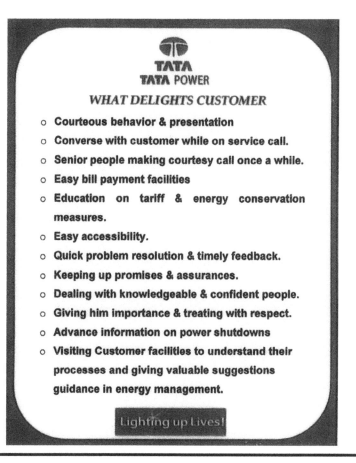

Figure 8.10   Customer's Delight Factors

ENERGY CONSERVATION TIPS

- Minimize/Shift usage during the 10 am–8 pm peak time and avoid adding to the load.
- Switch on AC an hour after starting work and switch off an hour before closing.
- Run all ACs at 24° C.
- Switch off all electrical appliances from the plug point.
- Set computers to sleep and Hibernate mode.
- Replace incandescent bulbs with compact fluorescent lamps (CFLs) in your homes and premises to save upto 75% of electricity.

Figure 8.11   Cards for Saving Energy

Substation managers invite important Customers to the substation to show the Customers they have dedicated control panels for them with the customer's name on them.

Call Centres have better co-ordination on answering billing-related enquiries.

Complaints fell from 9 per 1,000 to 2.7 per 1,000 in the quarter following the formation of Customer Circles.

Results from Godrej Customer Circles

Three months after the inception of Customer Circles, they (the employees) are feeling happier about work. Sales per salesperson has gone up by 30%, service technicians are able to make five calls per day – up from three (on average) per day – because of better addresses being noted, better sequencing of technicians (sending them to contiguous addresses rather than criss-crossing the territory, and better understanding of the work to be done on the client's premises) and Customer Value Added had increased. Teamwork and coordination has improved considerably.

The co-ordination has improved, the mistakes have been reduced and bickering in the team has decreased. Addresses and telephone numbers are properly being given to the service technicians and appointments are confirmed. The service technicians are smiling and greeting the Customers better, and briefing them better, so much so that many Customers prefer their team and ask for them by name for future services. Customer Circles help the team to deliver more than the individual can.

Teams are dependent on the members, who need each other to achieve more and deliver. It requires listening and respect, such that you let your own opinions be overridden. It teaches you to overcome conflict and use dialog to work together, and it builds team-learning discipline. Dialogue causes people to observe and improve their own ideas and thinking.

Teamwork and team learning requires a facilitator or a catalyst and requires people to suspend their beliefs to listen to others and to regard each other and colleagues who are present to help them.

We have to celebrate the successes and learn from the failures.

These Customer Circles can become a self-learning system. With Customer Circles, the organisation is bound to become creative and innovative. People want to be part of such an organisation and participate in the innovation.

The principle has to be that no one should be too proud to learn. And not be too proud to learn from anyone. Continuous learning and participation will lead to customer excellence and Value creation.

The Customer's Bill of Rights

We now know how to measure Customer Value. In the previous chapters, we have also been exposed to the softer side of Customer Value Management. Tools of Total Customer Value Management include building a Customer Strategy and the Customer-Centric Circles, both of which we have seen.

In this section, we discuss the customer's Bill of Rights, and why it is important for Customer Value and for building a customer culture.

We have all seen the customer's Bill of Rights. How often are these really honoured? More importantly, how many executives/employees know about the Bill of Rights and how to uphold them?

I bet you that in most companies the executives do not know the Bill of Rights. So, in one Tata company, at the customer centre, the company put the Bill of Rights on the wall behind the executive, so that the customer could see her rights. Very soon, they put one on the wall behind the customer's seat... So that the executive could also see it. And what a difference it made.

There are a number of steps in making a customer's Bill of Rights. Some are self-evident, like the right to get a product to work and honour the warranty. Less obvious are the rights to expect a product to work trouble free, be easy to understand and use, return a product, get it fixed, access to a knowledgeable, friendly, empathetic service person, no price gouging, no bait and sell, and so on.

Second, how do you find out whether a particular right is upholdable? Let's say the country you sell in insists on a maximum retail price on the package. How do you prevent someone from selling at a higher price during shortages?

> VDL steps like Customer Circles, the Customer's Bill of Rights, and the Circle of Promises all Create Value.

Third, if there is a problem how do you uphold the Bill of Rights? Let's say the Bill of Rights says a product will be repaired in two days. The front-line person may say that to the customer also, but does she know that this will happen? This requires all the people responsible to repair the product in a timely fashion to ensure this happens. This is the Circle of Promises.

This brings together everyone to Create Value and focus on the Customers and engenders teamwork and a customer focus.

Examining the Bill of Rights

The Customer Circle examines the Bill of Rights. Can they indeed be honoured? Are they being kept? When are they not being respected? Why? Can the Bill of Rights be upheld? If not, we should discard that particular right. If it is not being fulfilled due to a company or employee error, how do we prevent future occurrences?

Building a Customer's Bill of Rights

To build a meaningful Bill of Rights, we must understand what will be useful and reverberate with the customer? Has the company understood the customer's expectations?

What are the components that are important? Fairness, being well treated, great service, repair facilities, return policy, respect for the customer her time and her energy?

The Bill of Rights should be vetted by the Customer Circles (and of course, the legal department to prevent legal issues). We have to build support and enthusiasm for the Bill of Rights.

As stated earlier, a good Bill of Rights should also make the customer comfortable and wanting to do business with the company. It should also build trust and closeness to the customer. Of course, the company should be caring and engaging.

The wording should not be ambiguous, and the Bill of Rights should be upholdable.

The Bill of Rights should also lead to some idea of how to handle the Rights and some rules.

Basic rights should include:

- The right to safety.
- The right to be informed, and what to do when you have a problem.
- The right to be treated with dignity.
- The right to choose.
- The right to be heard and to redressal and access to someone who is customer friendly in solving problems, and not have to deal always with gatekeepers.

- The right to know how to access someone who can solve the customer's problem.
- The right to satisfaction of basic needs.

These rights state that businesses should always provide consumers with enough appropriate information to make intelligent and informed product choices. Product information provided by a business should always be complete and truthful. Aiming to achieve protection against misleading information in the areas of financing, advertising, labelling and packaging, the right to be informed is safeguarded by several pieces of legislation passed between 1960 and 1980.

These rights give consumers the ability to voice complaints and concerns about a product in order to have the issue handled efficiently and responsively.

One can take these into account when building one's own Bill of Rights. Some will be generic, and others will be specific to your company and your Customers.

The Circle of Promises

The Circle of Promises is the understanding by people in the company or partners that they are part of a promise to uphold the customer's Bill of Rights. They have to be in the loop and understand the meaning of their promise. More importantly, they should form a customer-Centric Circle to discuss improvements and where promises were not kept and how to solve problems. This will help change mindsets. This is shown in Figure 8.12.

The customer's Bill of Rights must be upholdable.

Value and Partners/Supply and Delivery Chain

Value creation has to extend to partners and suppliers and they in turn have to increase Value in the supply and delivery chain.

Take an example of suppliers. Most companies treat suppliers as vassals. I am paying you, you owe me. Partnership and co-creation exists only in a limited number of companies. Because they were treated badly, Nippon Steel starved Nissan the Japanese car maker of steel during a shortage (see Carlos Cordon of IMD in Customer Value Investment).[23] He suggested that purchasing managers know everything about suppliers, but not what suppliers think of them.

In a seminar-based Customer Value Added study with the Indian Army some years ago we discovered that suppliers, though highly paid, were very dissatisfied because of many changes in orders, procrastination and then demands of quick delivery.

---

[23] Mahajan, Customer Value Investment, Sage 2008.

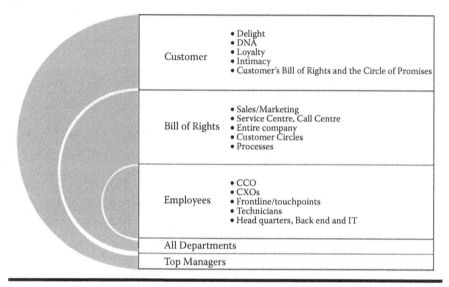

Figure 8.12   The Circle of Promises to Ensure Promises are Kept

In another study of the delivery chain we discovered that the loyalty of the dealer to the company was 50%, and that of the retailer to the company was 50%. The loyalty of the retailer to the dealer was only 20%. And the loyalty of the end customer to the brand was 60% and to the retailer 10%. Obviously, there is a disconnect. Adding more Value to the dealer and retailers by the company and focussing on them changed this because each of them started to add more Value: the dealer to the retailer and the retailer to the customer.

This is what Value creation is all about and its message.

Continuous Customer Improvement Program

A Continuous Customer Improvement Program (CCIP) is necessary to keep ahead of competition. The Customer-Centric Circles and the awareness through the Customer's Bill of Rights and the Circle of Promises condition

> Continuous Customer Improvement Programs add Value to the Customer.

the employees to seek more ways to please Customers. This becomes a Continuous Customer Improvement Program. As the program takes root, we find more and more ideas to improve Customer Value through customer experience or the customer journey. Ideas on customer intimacy, customer satisfaction, CRM, customer delight, customer customisation, customer success and solutions customer experience, customer goodwill and customer channels can all be discussed.

Zero Complaints

Value Dominant Logic suggests that as we work on the CCIP, we could actually incorporate systemic changes that could prevent a problem we have noticed from re-occurring with other Customers. Or we might notice that Customers ask the same question ...

> Value-creating thinking will allow you to acheive zero complaints just like you acheived zero defects.

we cannot find your office in South Delhi. We can then check why that is the case and make it easier for the customer to find the office and not waste their time calling us.

We have to work towards reducing the number of complaints or getting closer to Zero Complaints. Most people believe this is not possible, but we all agree we can strive toward it. Zero complaints create more a positive experience and creates immense Value for Customers.

One tenet of Value creation is to reach zero complaints, following what the Quality movement did towards achieving zero defects. The more we go towards that, the fewer interactions we will require, we will reduce customer journey and so on.

Value and Customers

The Principles of Customer Value Creation have been enunciated in Chapter 6.

We have said before that customers buy from the alternative that provides the most Value to them (Value being defined by the customer). We have shown that you can measure Customer Value Added (page 105). You build the customer's Value Journey (also called the Customer's Waterfall of Needs, or customer journey), the attribute trees and then measure the Customer Value Added.

An example is CVS Pharmacy, where they are trying to become part of the customer's life, and not just a filler of prescriptions. Their smart watch app lets customers take their medication, snap pictures of their prescriptions to expedite refills and scan their insurance cards. In their clinic, customers can receive treatment for minor illnesses, flu shots, cholesterol screening and more than a dozen other medical services – all of which can be booked and paid for online. For people who can't make it to a physical location, CVS Health is also partnering with various telemedicine services like Teladoc. Using IBM Watson technology, they can predict when customers might have emergency needs.

Companies can Create Value for people by using technology, AI and IoT to empower people, and to interact with them and provide better and easier services to them. We call it putting the customer in control (another way of adding Value to the Customer). Others say companies can put power in the hands of the customer.

Beer makers are able to get information from customers to customise their beer to add Value to the customer. Thus, companies must adapt technologies (that are interactive and self-learning) to customers. This is a customer-first approach.

Accenture suggests aligning technology to customer needs and goals. Better still – partner with customers and co-create with them. And as this happens, company and customers merge and become partners. Company goals and customer goals coalesce.

Within the workplace, companies can Create Value by letting employees design how they work and interact, and how work is designed for humans, and look for new (hitherto unknown) methodologies using technology.

AI is helping new interfaces, such as for Echo and Alexa. AI has hit farmers to provide plant-by-plant fertiliser as required when using a Blue Technologies interface.

Accenture predicts that in five years half of your customers will choose company services based on AI. In 10 years, digital assistants will be prevalent.

Customers will look for aggregators to make decision-making simpler, and aggregators will be platform-based systems. Companies will have to choose their platforms carefully. Most of your customers will be buying through digital middlemen. Companies will engage globally through multiple middlemen ecosystems. Maybe the companies will have limited physical infrastructure and fewer people when they rely on external digital platform ecosystems.

Similarly, the management of work is going online (through collaborative platforms). Slack is an example of collaborative work, sharing of ideas, processes and systems. Corporate workforce models like Uptake are becoming the new norm. Public crowd freelance, flexible workers and workplaces will happen. On-demand options are likely.

Companies will start to work for people and not the other way around as has been the case. The digital connected work force will form the core of business employees.

Personalisation and customisation will come into vogue because of technology. An example is Stitch Fix that ships customised clothes. Companies helping customers to choose more easily will be in the fore.

With customer-company Value co-creation and partnership, the company's and customer's goals merge. And therefore, also employee-company Value co-creation and partnerships merge towards a common goal.

Value Dominant Logic asks you to prepare to Create Value jointly for customers, employees and yourself. Value-based AI adaptive analytics helped Virgin to reduce fuel usage.

Partnership through Value co-creation will become the new norm. People and human goals become the new company and AI goals. Customer retention over sales focus becomes more important. All things we have been stated in Value creation.

To Create Value, companies have to work with and even co-create regulations. Government, companies, society will have to work together on a people-first system.[24]

Companies are starting to use neurologists and anthropologists to understand customers and bring in new ideas. So not only technology, but newer thinking and insights. Miele (the premium white goods supplier headquartered in the US) used ethnography to understand culture and values (why people do what they do). They found that some people were very dust averse, and that helped them build a vacuum cleaner that tells the user if the surface is clean.

It is important to note that what people say and what they mean are sometimes different.

So, if you ask them what is important they may say one thing, but if you get an implied importance through statistical or other means you may find the answer to be different.

This is also true when you ask someone a question. When customers are asked to assign a weight or importance for a particular attribute, or to weigh various attributes. (The way this is done is typically to assign an importance to the attributes so that the total of the weights is 100. Thus, if there are 3

> What people say and what they mean are contextual, and may not be the same thing.

attributes, the customer is to ask them to assign a weight to each of these three attributes, such that the total comes to 100.) Sometimes customers can assign a weight to attributes which may not really be important in the buying decisions. Weights assigned by the customer are called Stated Weights.

An example of this is asking customers how important airline safety is. Most customers would respond that safety is definitely extremely important. Ask yourself, when was the last time you bought a ticket based on safety? Safety is important but not important as a purchase criterion.

That is why we prefer not to directly ask customers to assign weights. We derive these through statistical analysis. Most commonly, regression analysis is used. These are called implied weights. Using statistical analysis to derive weights, we may find that airline safety, though truly important, is not a factor in the selection of an airline (assuming there has been no recent crash, and we are looking at major airlines). So, the importance of weight of safety in the buying

---

[24] For more read: https://www.accenture.com/us-en/insight-disruptive-technology-trends-2017?c=ad_giusFY17_10001296&n=bac_0417

decision (or selection of an airline) would be relatively low, unlike what would have come out in the stated response.

Another example is hotel courtesy. It is often uniformly good and ceases to be a distinguishing factor in the purchase decision. However, if a hotel differentiates itself by poor courtesy, or unbelievable courtesy, it becomes important. In both cases, customers will say when asked to assign a direct weight that courtesy is important! These stop being Value creation factors and become expected factors.

The relation between direct and implied weights is shown in Figure 8.13.[25]

This is a goal of many logics like SDL, to co-create Value with the customer.

I have meet with many companies that are market leaders. They may have, let's say, 30% of the market share, and they are proud of it. Their goal is to go to 31 or 32%. I ask them why 70% of the customers in the segment go to their competition. Value Dominant Logic suggests that people buy from you because you create more Value than your competition, and they go to others because they create more Value than you. So, you need to find out if you have segmented wisely, or if segmentation is correct, what is competition doing to attract customers?

While the bulk of Value creation is based on individual customers, Value Dominant Logic suggests going beyond and working with a community of customers, especially where large customer bases or large digital bases exist. Further VDL suggests interacting with society.

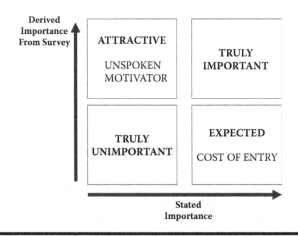

Figure 8.13   What Is Said and What Is Meant (from Survey)

---

[25] From Ray Kordupleski: Mastering customer Value Management.

Two examples are Harley Davidson and Land Rover which have created a community of like-minded customers, who share adventure experiences, get the opportunity to travel together on their bikes or in the Land Rovers, and interact with society and so on.

Thus, we have to find and work with communities that are like minded.

Thus, airlines that I have connections with may not be as good as airlines connecting people going to Croatia for holidays. They can leverage this group and provide more for them.

Value Dominant Logic suggests focusing on heart share and wallet share and not just on market share.

Unfortunately, companies want to be able to contact Customers but not have Customers contact them conveniently. Companies seem to say keep away, you cannot contact me. They set up the one-way contact system. The other unfortunate item is that the convenience of the company takes precedence over the convenience of the customer. Lastly, companies are taking over customer's rights by insisting on knowing their locations, their pictures, their contacts etc.

Customer Obsession/Success Etc.

> *The Mission of Customer Success is to build more <u>proven</u> value faster for both the customers and your company.*
>
> 99

Customer Success Manager, Client Advocates, etc., but regardless of the label, it's about customer relationship, retention and optimisation. And the most effective way to keep your customers is to make them as successful as possible in using your product. And more importantly for them, to create more success. This is a good way of creating Value, though it may not be sufficient. Let's say your product provides 0.5% spoilage in processing at your customer's. Let's say your relationship is great and you work on the customer's success. But your competition provides only 0.25% spoilage. In the end, the customer will go to the one that is creating more Value, after taking into account the relationship and success. However, if you find a way to re-work the extra spoilage you may create more Value.

Customer Success Association suggests that their goal is to Create Value.

Customer obsession is much more than customer satisfaction or customer happiness. The philosophy is about doing what is right for the customer first, then working backwards. Moreover, a firm belief in customer obsession focuses the enterprise on being customer focused and less competitor focused.

Customer service is a function of operating a business, while customer obsession requires a complete shift in the way we think about our customer relationships.

Hugh Blaine states in seven principles of Transformational Leadership:

FB = (FE + FC + ME)

A flourishing business (FB) comes from flourishing employees (FE), flourishing customers (FC) and memorable experiences (ME).

Value creation as a concept goes beyond Customer Value. Value is customer defined and therefore you have to get into the hearts and minds of customers as suggested by Mohanbir Sawhney in Fundamentals of Customer Value.

As Drucker noted, "What is Value for the customer ... is anything but obvious." Quantifying Value is difficult because we don't understand customers, customers don't understand themselves and we don't speak the same language that customers speak. The first hurdle in quantifying Value is that we don't understand customers as well as we should. Consider how Mattel failed to understand the Japanese market for its Barbie dolls. Mattel was at a loss to understand why its world-famous doll wasn't an instant hit in Japan.

After much qualitative research, Mattel discovered that Barbie's legs were too long, and her chest too large – physical attributes young Japanese girls couldn't relate to. To appeal to Japanese sense of beauty and aesthetics, Mattel changed Barbie's dimensions and made the doll's eyes brown instead of blue.

The second barrier in quantifying Value is that customers don't always understand their own motives and cannot always articulate their needs. Consider the inexplicable popularity of sport utility vehicles (SUVs). Customers claim that they prefer SUVs over cars because SUVs are safer and handle better in difficult conditions. But Dr Clotaire Rapaille, a psychologist who studies this suggests SUVs are not safer and are fuel guzzlers, but it is the desire to have something bigger, fuelled by the reptilian brain that causes people to go for SUVs.

In the opening of his book, *7 Secrets of Marketing*, Dr Rapaille says, "Cultures, like individuals, have an unconscious. This unconscious is active in each of us, making us do things we might not be aware of." This collective cultural unconscious can be further defined as a pool of shared imprinting experiences that unconsciously pre-organise and influence the behaviour of a culture.

Expensive smart phones are yet another example. They may feel more reliable (not true), made by Apple, and a desire to belong to, and be ahead of, the curve may cause you to buy the phone.

Context has three important dimensions: the end user, the end-use situation and the environment. Customer assessments of Value will be a function of who they are, what they want to do, and the environment that they live and work within.

We have to think functional, economical and emotional Value. Value is a mindset, not a process alone.

Focus on Value creation. Forget your methodology, forget what you do technically, and live, breathe and do everything you can to understand your customer.

Some aspects of Customer Value are shown below.

> VDL suggests you understand why Customers buy, what attributes are important. Is cost more important than benefits or are benefits more important? Are you better than the competition?

Customer Value Attribute Tree and Relative Importance of Attributes[26]

Value consists of Benefits and Costs in an attribute tree shown below. The relative importance or weights of Benefits is X% and that of Costs is Y%. X+Y (the relative importance of Benefits and Cost) adds up to 100%. Sometimes readers get confused, because we said Value = Benefits − Cost. Benefits are what the customer perceives as benefits, whereas X is the relative importance in percentage of Benefits in the Value importance equation. Likewise for Cost, its relative importance in Value is Y%. So, the relative importance of cost and benefit add up to 100% (not the actual perception of cost and benefit. The customer still uses B-C to determine whether he got Value or not!)

> Value has Benefits and Cost as its main components.
> Their relative importance adds up to 100%.

The benefits the customer derives from the product, the service, the image of the product, emotional and psychological factors in the purchase, from the people (or employees, dealers, service agencies) of the company or the retailer. Benefits could include other items such as convenience, relationship or association with the company etc. Experience is built into each of these items, and the perception of the customer is based on many factors including experience, emotions, trust etc.

---

[26] Much of this is from Mahajan, 2018, How Creating Customer Value can make you a great executive, BEP and Mahajan, 2011, Total Customer Value Management.

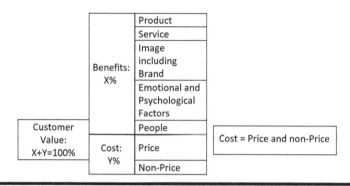

Figure 8.14   Customer Value Breaks up into Benefits and Cost

Why do I call emotions a benefit? For example, your emotional connect to a product or brand is a benefit you derive (familiarity, liking, experience), and if the company selling the product knew about this, they could influence it. And how you are emotionally feeling and feeling towards the purchase influences the Value you perceive.

The Cost is the other parameter that the customer looks at. Cost is also a perception and breaks up into **price** and **non-price** terms. Price terms include the price itself, discounts, interest costs, maintenance or running costs etc.

Very often, you do not know the precise price of a product or a service. Take a bundled telephone service: you may not know the price of the individual components of the offering, or when a phone is part of the deal, how do you price the service?

The non-price terms include price justification, ease of purchase, emotions, time and energy expended to buy or use the product and so forth. Many times, the non-price terms are more important in the buying decision than the price terms. An example is the purchase of greeting cards. Many of us do not buy greeting cards, as the non-price cost of

> Value is not cost or price. It is not the benefits you get. It is the worth of what you buy versus other alternatives.

buying (planning to buy, going to the store, parking, buying, mailing and returning home) is too high. As an aside, if your greeting card's competitor is a net-based offering, it may attract you to use the service contextually, when you suddenly feel like sending a card. The Value created may be so much higher than buying a physical card at that point in time.

You will notice also that the relative importance of the benefits and the cost add up to 100%. In Figure 8.14, the benefits have an importance of X% and the cost an importance of Y%. X+Y add up to 100%.

Benefits: A+B+C+D+E=100%	Product: A%
	Service: B%
	Image: C%
	Emotional and Psychological Factors: D%
	People: E%

Figure 8.15 Sub-Attributes Importance of Benefits

So, the benefits could be 20% and the cost 80%. Or the benefits could be 70% and the cost 30%. These numbers are derived from the market research and are not numbers given by the customer. These percentage numbers are determined from the research data through statistical analysis which will be described later.

Sub-Attributes of Benefits

Likewise, in Figure 8.15, we can see that sub-attributes of benefits, each one having an importance percentage shown as A% or B% and so on.

Very often, when there is not much to choose from between competing products, the product importance (A% in this case) could be as low as 5%. (This is often the case with commodities like fertiliser, cement etc.) On the other hand, if your product is well differentiated this number could be 50% or higher. It is important to note that having a great brand may not mean your product itself is well differentiated. Note that if there is no interaction with the people of the company or the retailer, the people could be of little importance, and could be left out of the attribute tree.

Components of Sub-Attributes

The product could be broken down into sub-attributes like the product itself, the product features, and the ease of use, the instructions, the packaging and the looks. You could add other attributes while removing the ones that are not of consequence.

> The relative importance of all the sub attributes of benefits add up to 100%.

The service could include the ease of service, the service response, the speed of service, proper and complete servicing, and the service people and their behaviour.

An example of how the sub-attributes break down into their components is shown in Figure 8.16 for image. We could have drawn similar trees for product, service, etc.

Sometimes, the brand of a product like cheese could be Philadelphia Cream Cheese and the company name Kraft. Both have an importance to the customer.

I tend to use the attribute image rather than using brand as the primary attribute, because image is all inclusive. Sometimes the company brand is more important and sometimes the product brand is significant, or the company and the product brand can be similar.

> Image includes the Brand and other factors.

You can see how many factors make up the image. In a study of a power company we found that the image was 50% of the benefits in Figure 2.2 (shown as C %) and the product, A% was only 20% of the importance.

In one study with a power company, the trust in the company, its efforts on sustainability and containing costs were about 75% of the image (I%+L%+M %) shown in Figure 8.16.

> Collaboration moves at the speed of trust...Chris Thompson

One can impact the brand through attractology (see section on Attractology), coolness etc.

Coolness is that mysterious quality that is difficult to describe. It keeps changing and is also a perception. It includes autonomy (being different, not conforming), authenticity (true to its mission or purpose), attitude (confidence and self-assurance) and association (belonging).

An example of autonomy or being different is Apple saying "Think Different" and Adidas saying "Celebrate Originality".

Luxury brands, and brands with followings must appear to be authentic and true to their purpose. These provide positive products and experiences.

Nike is an example of coolness.

	Brand of the Product G%
	Company name or Brand H%
	Trust in the company I%
Image G+H+I+J+K+L=100%	Association/relationship with the company J%
	The product enhances my image K%
	Sustainability/environmental focus of the company L%
	Efforts of the company to reduce prices M%

Figure 8.16   Sub-Attributes of Image

Brand Value

Brand is a perception that customers and the market have of your company or its products. Over time the perception can become closer to reality. Sometimes it can be better than reality and sometimes worse. But in the end the brand is an impression in our minds.

The brand adds Value to the company or the product. Generally, in the Value creation sense we tend to use the word image to include the brand. Image generally includes the brand of the product, the brand of the company and the brand of the people (executives, front-line and those people the customer comes in contact with).

Customer Value and Knowledge

Service Dominant Logic says knowledge is what is exchanged in service. Knowledge is an important part of benefits and business and should be looked at such. In Value creation knowledge is an important aspect. Some will say Value is knowledge also, and knowledge is an important component of Value creation.

Value and Manufacturing

Manufacturing has always been considered from an economic and cost perspective. Value Dominant Logic suggests that manufacturing be considered from a Value creation perspective.

For years, we have witnessed a big focus on economies of scale. Many of us were brought up on this concept. The longer the run size, the more money we could make. This, however, had the impact of building larger inventories, and the wait time for customers could be high. In fact, a Customer Value study with a very large steel company showed their customers were unhappy because precise times for the availability of construction steel products could not be given by the sales people, because these were controlled by manufacturing based on run sizes etc. This resulted in unhappy customers, because their projects were impacted.

Furniture companies, for example, moved away from economies of scale to flexible manufacturing where their specialised machines could produce in lot sizes of one or five depending on the machine design.

In today's age, manufacturing is undergoing sea changes. Apart from more efficient robot-manned plants, we are seeing 3D systems allowing for distributed manufacturing rather than distributing products.

Take the energy sector; they are now losing touch with connected homes. Suppliers like Google Nest can play a significant role in providing power and heating because they control the connected home, off grid (using micro-generation using the conventional grid for emergencies and peaks); mobile and virtual battery operated cars (with energy use off-grid, and the automobile becomes a mobile grid); data rich (using IoT and data to produce real time and useful data on energy consumption, needs, usage, the best source for energy etc.); and scaled down (where the manufacture is smaller, user companies start to produce their own energy [site based production]).

Innovation could be based on trend spotting. Innovation works best when people have a sense of ownership and a desire to belong and control their destiny such as in a kibbutz, as the early immigrants did. True innovators do not need to be incentivised, they just innovate because that is the way they are. A Value-creating mindset makes innovation easier.

Countries like Germany and Japan have the opportunity to re-invent their manufacturing by using internet and big data. Think of the internet of manufacturing. This requires merging big data with manufacturing technologies such as robotics. Once we learn to use the data, a revolution will happen and Create Value. The data has to be tracked and analysed. Big companies such as Siemens, SAP, General Electric and Amazon.com are working on this.

Much of the advantages of centralised large-scale energy production would disappear. Flexibility, agility and lean seem to become more important.

Mahajan's Principles of Flexibility

The First Principle of Flexibility and Mindset: Flexible managers are needed to create truly flexible organisations and systems.

The Second Principle of Flexibility and Mindset: You cannot effectively design or work on flexible systems, innovation and creativity unless you have a **Value creation** mindset and your mindset is flexible.

The Third Principle of Flexibility and Mindset: The unfettered quest for flexibility can destroy Value.

The Fourth Principle of Mindset Flexibility: Degree of flexibility varies with people, and depends on attitude, mindset and circumstances.

The Fifth Principle of Flexibility and Mindset: Flexibility requires management of dilemmas.

Value to Others: Society, Government and Shareholders

Glencore[27] In 2014, began to develop tools to improve and systematise their understanding of their socio-economic contributions. These tools helped them

---

[27] http://www.glencore.com/sustainability/society/creating-Value-for-society/

improve their management of contributions to their host regions. They create employment, increase tax payments, and we participate in the local society.

Arcelor Mittal says natural products; social and human contribution can be quantified in dollars and cents as investment.

Value Creation in Society

The discussion above can be related to Value creation in society. VDL suggests that Value has to be created in society in different ways by increasing the Value for the members of the society (Figure 8.17).

Thus, the overall Value comes from improvements to the society as a whole, such as general cleanliness in poor countries. This also improves the lot of the individual, such as reducing health hazards, which also is a societal improvement. There is a cost impact including reduction/involvement of people effort. In the VDL approach, competing societal projects can be prioritised. This could be the government's point of view. They have to allocate funds and choose projects that will give society the best results. How will citizens be impacted? What will create the most Value and for whom? Governments also have to think about externality. Will it impact that segment which was not meant to be impacted?

Society improvement could result in fewer people coming to government office, consequent reduction of people's time and travel, pollution and fewer officials needed. It could be the promotion of good (Fisk, 2009). It could be ease of operation and fewer mistakes and reduction of the possibility of corruption by having cleaner, faster, efficient and transparent transactions. It is the good in ourselves and the good in those we seek to interact with.

From an individual citizen's point of view (particularly those at the bottom of the pyramid), it could be I am in control and can transact 24/7. I do not have to

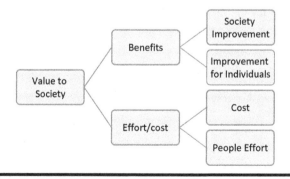

Figure 8.17   Value Creation in Society. (Author's Own)

visit an office and deal with bureaucrats, all of which are Value adding. Maybe I pay less for the service (costs could be monetary, psychological or physical).

It also could be a company that provides service to society which reverberates with its customers, and who can relate to this, and may prefer the company because of the Value it creates from the values it has.

Caring is a key aspect of Value and its creation and particularly sharing and caring at the Bottom of the Pyramid has crucial significance to society.

Value creation in society goes to poverty alleviation and work on the Bottom of the Pyramid, Transformative Service Research, sustainability. It goes to teaching and practicing Value creation. Teaching how to Create Value for yourself and your ecosystem and to recognise Value waiting to happen.

Repeating what we said in Chapter 1, Integrated Value is becoming more important as businesses are now starting to develop a wider role in society for businesses.

This goes beyond philanthropy and CSR, and also takes into account incorporating values, environment, conscious capitalism, happiness, sustainable business and the wider concept of shared Value.

Wayne Visser's definition: Integrated Value is the simultaneous building of multiple "non-financial" capitals (notably infrastructural, technological, social, ecological and human capital) through synergistic innovation across the nexus economy (including the resilience, exponential, access, circular and wellbeing economies) that result in net-positive effects, thus making our world more secure, smart, shared, sustainable and satisfying.

Measurement of Integrated Value

We have to measure:

> Value created for Employees
> Value created for Customers
> Value created for Partners
> Value created for Suppliers
> Value created for Society
> Value created for Shareholders

The question is whether to measure this directly or indirectly? Value added for employees and for Customers can be easily measured directly, and also for partners and suppliers.

Value created for society as seen by the customer can be measured but may not be very accurate, however it is a starting point.

Value created for shareholders has to be taken as a common measurement system bereft of extraordinary income and expenses and non-recurring expenses.

Correlations[28] of each of these to the shareholder Value are a first step and have to be refined by future researchers.

Such measurements can, in the future, determine shared Value.

Value Creation vs. Value Extraction: Making vs. Taking

Cesar Hidalgo[29] of MIT asks what Value is about. And how do we measure Value? Traditionally, the way of measuring Value has not been through measures of Value, but actually through measures of appropriation: measures of the amount of money that you can appropriate through that business, not the Value that it generates in society. We're starting to see this difference.

Google is an example. Google also offers, for free, searches for billions of people on a daily basis. It's the number one site on the Web, and it's generating an enormous amount of Value: providing access to information. But it's appropriating very little of that Value.

Hidalgo adds, Facebook's IPO was 100 billion, but it sells much less (10–15 billion dollars). What that shows you is that Facebook is providing this service to all these people, and all of these people are using this service, so Facebook is generating a large amount of Value. But its ability to appropriate from that Value is very little. Facebook can only appropriate a very small amount. If it were a traditional business with a billion customers, probably it would be able to appropriate more Value than in this type of business.

In this article, Hidalgo debates Customer Value creation (and Value creation in general) versus Value extraction. Too many people believe they are creating Value whereas they are extracting Value. The global financial crisis of 2008 makes us rethink the modern capitalist system which is far too speculative: It rewards takers over true makers or wealth creators. It allows the growth of finance, and greater rewards for speculative exchange of financial assets versus investment that leads to new physical assets and job creation.

In the recently completed First Global Conference on Creating Value at Leicester UK, organised by DMU and me, Ashok Ashta – MD & CEO – NMB-Minebea India, and an attendee wrote: "I personally enjoyed the blend with the practical as instantiated by the practitioner/academic presentations. If there is one line that will remain embedded in thought, and that I will perhaps reuse is, 'students looking to work in financial institutions, are aspiring to work in criminal organisations!'"

Debates about unsustainable growth are increasing calling for reforms and rethinking of the financial system. We need the financial system to re-focus on

---

[28] With permission of Wayne Visser, https://www.huffingtonpost.com/entry/integrated-value-what-it-is-what-its-not-and-why_us_59cffdc3e4b0f58902e5ccbf

[29] With permission from Cesar Hidalgo, https://www.edge.org/conversation/cesar_hidalgo-what-is-value-what-is-money

the long term, and sustainable development rather than quarterly returns, and gaining exorbitant executive pay. This includes proper governance and thinking about the future of us, and our planet.

Mariana Mazzucato in her book, *The Value of Everything* argues that critics of the current financial system remain powerless – in their ability to bring about real reform of the economic system – until they become firmly grounded in a discussion about the processes by which economic Value is created. It is not enough to argue for less Value extraction and more Value creation. First, "Value," a term that once lay at the heart of economic thinking, must be revived and better understood.

> Value has gone from being at the core of economic theory, tied to the dynamics of production (the division of labour, changing costs of production), to a subjective category tied to the 'preferences' of economic agents. Many ills, such as stagnant real wages, are interpreted in terms of the 'choices' that particular agents in the system make, for example unemployment is seen as related to the choice that workers make between working and leisure.

By losing our ability to recognise the difference between Value creation and Value extraction, Mariana argues, we have made it easier for some to call themselves Value creators and in the process extract Value, like the financial services companies.

Thus, GDP and corporate annual reports must reflect the quality of life indicators, happiness, caring etc. versus just financial gains.

Value extractors in finance and other sectors of the economy get more emboldened. Here, the crucial questions – which kinds of activities add Value to the economy and which simply extract Value for the sellers – are never asked. In the current way of thinking, financial trading, rapacious lending, funding property price bubbles are all Value added by definition.

When price determines Value, and if there is a deal to be done, then there is Value. Therefore, a pharmaceutical company can sell a drug at a hundred or a thousand times more than it costs to produce, there is no problem: The market has determined the Value and the price.

The same goes for chief executives who earn 340 times more than the average worker (the actual ratio in 2015 for companies in the S&P 500). The market has decided the Value of their services – there is nothing more to be said.

Mariana continues, the conventional discourse devalues and frightens actual and would-be Value creators outside the private business sector. It's not easy to feel good about yourself when you are constantly being told you're rubbish and/or part of the problem. That's often the situation for people working in the public sector, whether these are nurses, civil servants or teachers.

Mazzucato adds that when Apple, or whichever private company, makes billions of dollars for shareholders and many millions for top executives, you probably won't think that these gains actually come largely from leveraging the work done by others – whether these be government agencies, not-for-profit institutions or achievements fought for by civil society organisations including trade unions that have been critical for fighting for workers' training programmes.

All of which serves only to subtract Value from the economy and make for a less attractive future for almost everyone. Not having a clear view of the collective Value creation process, the public sector is thus "captured" – entranced by stories about wealth creation which have led to regressive tax policies that increase inequality.

This is not only true for the environment where picking up the mess of pollution will definitely increase GDP (due to the cleaning services paid for) while a cleaner environment won't necessarily (indeed if it leads to less "things" produced it could decrease GDP), but also as we saw to the world of finance where the distinction between financial services that feed industry's need for long-term credit versus those financial services that simply feed other parts of the financial sector are not distinguished. You can think of other examples: poor road construction leading to increased repairs builds GDP. M&A fees add to GDP. The middleman is making more than the producer.

Mariana makes the point strongly that finance is not pivotal for Value creation. Instead it has led to greater inequality, and to Value extraction. To her point she states that the wealth of the 62 very richest individuals increased 45% in five years (2010 – 2015), whereas the wealth of the bottom half in the world fell by 38%.

So, think of becoming a Value maker, a Value creator and not just a Value extractor, the role of many when they are in management. Maybe this is the time for you to consider your role. Are you going to be a blind follower? Can you do some things at your level? Examples of what you can do at your level, is to be transparent, caring for your employees and society, not accepting dishonesty from above. You can start to provide an island of "goodness" in your department, and if many do this, the message will be heard at the top. We call this the bottom-up approach, versus the top-down system we live in. Stop extracting Value.

Shareholder Value

There is a mistaken notion that focusing on profits will increase profits. It turns out creating Value does this. An analogy is that focusing on love increase love, rather than by creating more Value for the loved one.

> ...Shareholder value is the dumbest idea in the world. Jack Welch, former CEO, GE.

The inordinate focus on profits and shareholder wealth has caused a downturn in wealth creation. In particular, a major focus on quarterly profits has led to short termism and diminished Value.

The average lifespan of a company listed in the S&P 500 index of leading US companies has decreased by more than 50 years in the last century, from 67 years in the 1920s to just 15 years today, according to Professor Richard Foster from Yale University.

Today's rate of change "is at a faster pace than ever," he says.

Professor Foster estimates that by 2020, more than three-quarters of the S&P 500 will be companies that we have not heard of yet.[30]

For instance, there is no real proof that age makes a company any more profitable than younger companies. On the contrary, evidence from the stock market actually suggests that age could be a hindrance.

Of the 74 or so companies that have stayed in the S&P 500 for more than 40 years, only a dozen or so have managed to beat the average, according to a study by consultancy McKinsey.

In fact, if the S&P 500 were made up of only the companies that were part of the index in 1957, overall performance would have been some 20% worse.

Eric Orts, a Professor of Legal Studies and Business Ethics at Wharton, writes in his book (*Business Persons: A Legal Theory of the Firm*[31]), that executives Create Value for the shareholder. He mentions the concept of principal agents and that management is sometimes perceived as principal agents of shareholders. He discusses people coming together and forming teams to Create Value for the shareholder. Dwelling on corporate fraud, especially with respect to some accounting issues, partly has to do with (I quote) "incentives that are created by asking managers to only manage [with regard to] short-term shareholder Value. The theory is … that managers should manage [in a way that increases] shareholder Value." At one time creating "fraud" was a role of managers/accountants to Create Value for the company, but that is changing. And if we accept that people Create Value, then employees become important as do business partners for whom Value is to be created.

Paraphrasing Professor Orts, management has to create wealth for everybody, not just shareholders. Wealth does not just mean money, but also could be social wealth or other improvements. In fact, the State of Delaware allows corporations to state their purpose of not only making money but also of

---

[30] http://www.bbc.com/news/business-16611040

[31] Eric Orts: Business Persons, a Legal Theory of the Firm, presents a new legal theory of the firm, he provides an overview of the nature and purpose of business firms, contributes to current debates on the regulation of business firms.

having a social objective, such as improving the environment or alleviating poverty.

Therefore, managers have to look at the long term and not miss opportunities. Shareholders Create Value by understanding that retained earnings are the major source of growth and corporate well-being, and therefore should eschew short-term motives. He gives examples of Google who have successfully built companies on avoiding short-term thinking.

This is the Value Dominant Logic viewpoint.

Attractology

"The law of attraction is this: You don't attract what you want, you attract what you are." According to American philosopher and author Dr Wayne Dyer. This is important in creating Value in business, to increase awareness and sales.

The science of attraction and seduction, Attractology, isn't just the science of looking good, but of having personality traits that make you magnetic. This has nothing to do with attracting people of the opposite sex, but for businesses it means attracting customers.

Businesses have to understand how the law of attraction changes for them; you don't attract customers by telling them what you are. You attract customers by appearing how you are perceived. 'You,' of course, includes you, your products and your services.

Reality vs. Perception

According to Rory Sutherland,[32] one of the great mistakes of economics is that it fails to understand that "what something is, whether it's retirement, unemployment, cost, is a function, not only of its amount, but also its meaning."

The same product can mean different things to different people, and there is no such thing as objective product Value, at least when it comes to actually selling products (there are objective costs associated with making the product, of course).

Therefore, we have this huge opportunity to influence how people feel – how they perceive our product's Value – as well as the opportunity to optimise the customer.

---

[32] https://www.ted.com/talks/rory_sutherland_perspective_is_everything/transcript?
language=en

Value Chains and Maps

Value creation maps (part of Value chain thinking) are nothing but those items that can Create Value and lead to increased Customer Value Added (patents, brand, customer relationship, people, image, products and, of course, costs which are price and non-price).

Value Maps[33]

The Value Map is generally a plot of benefits versus costs. What it tells you is how a unit of cost impacts benefits or vice versa. It allows you to visually see your competitive position in the marketplace versus your competitors. With this kind of a map, we are able to track or predict your strategic moves to improve your competitive position. A typical Value map is shown in Figure 8.18.

In the Value map in Figure 8.18, you are shown three segments of the business, an economy product or service, like a low-end or economy car, an average one, or a high end or premium product or service. Irrespective of what type of product you are selling (economy, average or premium) to win, you must always create more Value than competition.

The Value map is plotted from the competitive profiles we discussed in the previous chapter. A key line is the benefit for price line (or the fair Value line). Any product or service close to this line is fairly priced. The farther you move

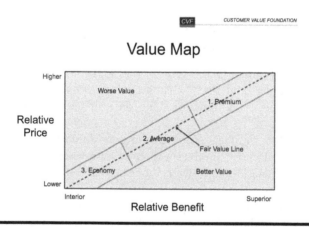

Figure 8.18   Value Map Showing Porter's Positioning of Companies, Premium, Average and Economy

---

[33] From Mahajan, 2018 How Creating Customer Value can make you a great executive, BEP, and Mahajan, 2011, Total Customer Value Management.

from this line and below it, you will Create Value. When you move above the line you will be reducing or destroying Value you create versus fair Value.

Here the company AA is creating high Value for its customers. They are creating even more Value for AA (members). AA (members) is AA customers who are enrolled in a membership program. Huge Value is being created for them. You can see this from seeing their position on the Value map and the distance from the fair Value line. None of you are in the business of giving away Value and reducing profits. So, we move the AA (members) Value upwards into a higher price zone or find ways to reduce our costs (by providing lower benefit).

Figure 8.19 focuses on increasing the Value to the Company or the profit. Starting with AA members, we notice an immense Customer Value is being created for them (see the distance from the fair Value line [the only line on the

> *Value Maps show your competitive positioning with the fair Value line.*

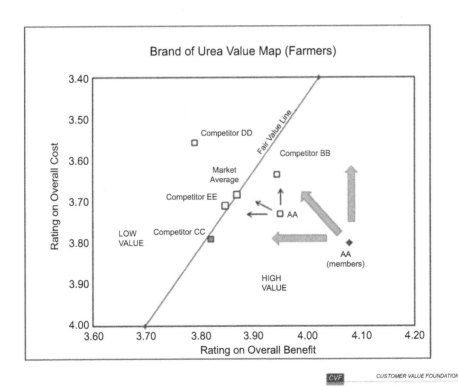

Figure 8.19   Showing How You Can Decrease Value…Do Not Give Away Value

chart]). We can increase the price or cost (shown by the vertical grey arrow going up), reduce the benefits (grey arrow going to the left), or both (grey arrow going diagonally towards the fair Value line). One could increase revenues by charging a membership fee (increasing price). A very low price or cost would also attract more members or Customers.

A better way is to increase price for AA's customers (members and non-members) or reduce the benefits (such as sales credit, or free delivery). You can see the position of AA (members) with reduced benefit and higher price or cost. Yet, AA (members) are receiving more Value than competitors are creating, albeit less than before price or cost were increased or benefit were reduced.

All these will increase the revenue to the company and its profit. It is better to ensure we continue to be in the high Value zone and add somewhat more Value than competitors.

These strategies have worked to increase Value to the company.

Discussion

Thus, you can see the Value of Customer Value Added study and scores. It tells you about your customer loyalty and retention, and what you have to do to improve loyalty. With the Value maps you can plot your competitive position versus competition using the fair Value line, and you can then build a strategy to provide optimum Value (not too much, not too little), and increase/decrease Value to the customer thereby increasing profits.

Value maps help you share profits equitably with customers and other stakeholders.

Benefits of Value Creation[34]

Value creation is the next big management practice.

Getting your entire ecosystem to resonate with you and your company ensures business leadership, longevity and long-term success. Value creation helps you and your executives to do this at little cost, improving your Customer Value index score so that your Customers can reward you with loyalty and market share!

Using customer power and ratings ensure disruptive and continued success. Value creation changes mindsets of people (employees and Customers) for conquering the future. The brand is being replaced by the informal customer score on the net. The Value Creation Index score will reflect customer sentiment and your future.

Recognising the role of an executive (and the company, which is made up of people) is to Create Value (and prevent destruction of Value) for himself, his employees, his partners and society and thereby create long-term and sustainable shareholder wealth.

---

[34] From Mahajan, 2018 How Creating Customer Value can make you a great executive, BEP, and Mahajan, 2011, Total Customer Value Management.

For the Company

Improved performance from Executives (see above).

Instituting the Value creation culture will ensure Value creation for customers precedes extraction of Value from them for the company.

Refocuses management thinking on creating Value for the employees, customers, partners in delivery and supply chains, unions and their people, society which in turn grows shareholder wealth.

The company will think of new products and services that Create Value for the customer, hopefully disruptively.

Value will be created for the company; it will get longevity and long-term success, and increased ROI. Value-creating companies will get a higher customer Value Index and become more desirable to your customers and non-customers (your competitors customers and customers not in your segment) see chart below, Figure 8.20.

Value Creation positively impacts your Stakeholders

Employees and Executives
- Becoming educated on the latest management ideas of Value Creation leading to Self Improvement and to superior performance and Value Creation for other employees, the Department and the Company and avoiding Value Destruction

Customers
- Increase Value to Customers, increasing loyalty, market share, and the customer Asset. Create Value for the customer before you extract Value

Partners
- Creating Value for your Partners (Supply and Delivery Chain and Unions) will increase Value for you, as they become more loyal to you and go the extra mile to benefit you

CEO
- Value Creation is a strategic and practical guide for CEO success and leadership style: refocuses on important work and not just on urgent work. Shows the CEO how focusing on Value Creation is a natural business practice, does not add to costs but to success and profits. Decision making can be made by understanding what creates more Value, and helps in managing dilemmas

Society
- Creating Value for Society and having Values that resonate with the customer will make you a preferred employer and company of choice for the customer, and they will reward you with more business and/or higher prices. Values Create Value

Company
- Value will be created for the company, it will get longevity and long term success, and increased ROI. Value creating companies will get a higher Customer Value Index, and become more desirable to your customers and non-customers

Shareholder
- Shareholder wealth will increase in the short and long term. Their company will be more respected and profits and share price will go up. A 1% increase in customer Value will increase share price 4.6%

Figure 8.20   How Value Creation Impacts Your Stakeholders

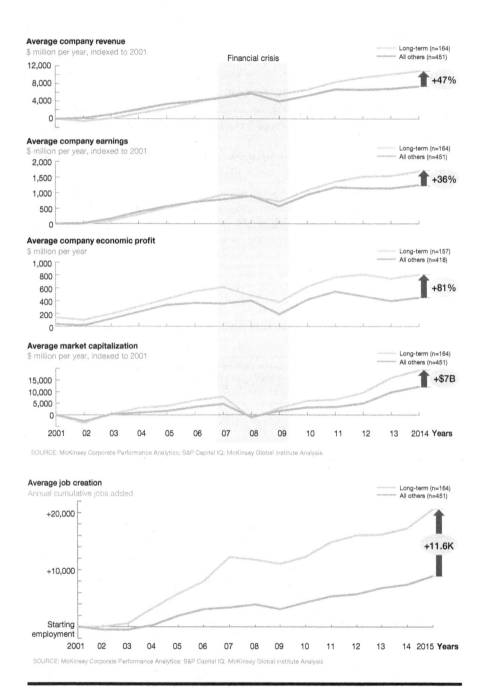

Figure 8.21   Long-Term Thinking Creates Better Result Than Short-Term Thinking

Mckinsey[35] in a recent article proves through research that companies that practice long-term thinking outperform companies that rely on short-term tactics, see Figure 8.21. Long-term thinking companies provide superior performance for revenue and earnings, investment, market capitalisation and job creation.

Benefits Corporation

Recognising this, Italy and Colombia have legislated Benefits Corporations to positive impact on society, workers, the community and the environment in addition to profit as its legally defined goals. Thirty-three States in the US have legislated such corporations. The purpose of a benefit corporation is to create general public benefit, which is defined as a material positive impact on society and the environment, i.e. maximum positive externalities and minimum negative.

A good start based on Value creation thinking.

Figure 8.22 shows an integrated view of Value creation by a company to its stakeholders.

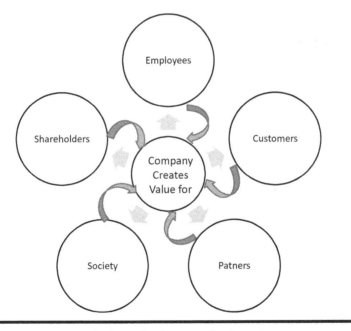

Figure 8.22   An Integrated View of Value Creation by a Company.

---

[35] https://www.mckinsey.com/global-themes/long-term-capitalism/where-companies-with-a-long-term-view-outperform-their-peers?cid=other-eml-ttn-mgi-mgi-oth-1712 with permission from Mckinsey.

How VDL Applies to Business

VDL and all its principles apply to business. Use these principles and what you have learnt. You will see that Value drives you, your business and your thinking. If you embrace Value as a driver, you will be ahead of competition and become winners. All eight principles of VDL are important to businesses.

Businesses can use VDl and Customer Value principles, measure Value and Create Value. VDL can help in looking outside the business ecosystems, in looking at opportunities, Value waiting to happen, solving dilemmas, changing the rules of the game, preventing and causing disruption. All these have been discussed.

Chapter 9

Value Dissipated, Discarded, Used

How VDL Applies

Value Dominant Logic remains germane when Value starts to dissipate or gets reduced or discarded or indeed is destroyed. People, businesses and society have to pay heed to this, notice or become aware of such possibilities to avoid Value dissipation or destruction. This is one way of staying ahead of disruption. If your thought process is positive and not just defensive, you can become a potential disruptor.

Remember, Value creation is an unfolding, continuous process, and according to SDL, there is no endpoint.

Value dissipation is a case of people or systems getting used to a single Value creating stream, or a major Value-creating system. When the Value-creating stream starts to dry up or the system no longer creates as much Value as it did before, it is natural to be depressed, or saddened. However, this is also a chance to re-invent yourself and re-build yourself to gain new or increased Value.

This is an interesting topic because, just like Value waiting to happen, we sometimes can discard Value because of our perception or our inability to see the Value. As an example, creativity's Value is based on what people perceive as new. If you do not see the newness, you may have no Value for the creativity. A very simple example is that you, as an agent, are given a brilliant book in an alien language, and you may discard the book and the Value it has, or the author has, just because you cannot understand the language, instead of sending it on to someone who can.

This is common, because critics, historians and journalists all report what they see based on their perception and state of mind, and can re-name, re-evaluate or report perceptually rather than factually.

Very often, I find people saying it is not worth meeting so and so or visiting this place, because they have already decided there is no Value in the person or otherwise.

I am not making a judgment on whether this is right or wrong. I just want readers to be aware of this, particularly as new technology, new ideas come their way and their pre-conceived ideas makes them discard these ideas as valueless or of having low Value (just because it does not appeal to our pre-conceived notions). An example is a client of mine that rejected a financial partnership offer from Biocon, and later rued their rejection as Biocon did phenomenally well. A case of pre-conceived ideas.

Value can also be dissipated or lessened. For example, when children leave the nest, the Value of parents may be reduced. The Value demand and needs and perceptions of both parents and children change and evolve.

Arnold Schwarzenegger posted a photo of him sleeping on the street under his famous bronze statue, and sadly wrote "how times have changed." His Value was reduced, according to him and he was not given a room in a hotel that had promised him when he was governor of California "at any moment you can come and have a room reserved for you." When Arnold stepped down as governor and went to the hotel, the administration refused to give him a room arguing that he should pay for it, since rooms were in great demand.

Everyone is your "friend" when you are important and valuable, but when you are not your Value is dissipated. Like my old slide rule that served me well when there were no calculators. Technology made the Value of the slide rule obsolete.

In the Human World, People Retire and Their Value Is Dissipated. They Have to Re-Activate or Re-Work Their Value

Examples

The general's wife is an example of someone who has difficulty to re-adjust after her husband's retirement (some adjust very well, while others cannot) as they have been recipients of Value

> VDL wants you to be ready for change, so that you do not feel Value is being destroyed.

(or good) from the underlings and society who look up to them, and they had gotten used to being the ones who gave orders.

A discarded suit loses its Value, but if picked up by someone in a charity shop and worn by someone who is homeless, it creates Value for that person.

Retirement or being fired or becoming redundant is another case of potential Value dissipation.

Your company can be disrupted because you did not plan for the future or had not thought about the future.

How Value Is Created or Destroyed?

Value is not destroyed, really. Your way of life changes and you feel that you are useless. Your well-being is impacted. You feel Value is being destroyed.

You can actually pre-empt this by planning and starting a new life when your old routine is changing. You need to come to grips with the change, and while enjoying the past memories, do not dwell on what you are missing.

Changing circumstances or environment can enhance or diminish Value in our eyes. We have to be conscious of this. So, customers may leave us as newer products, methods, services etc. come into play. Businesses and people have to be aware of this and have a periscope to see Value dissipation starting.

Why Is This Important?

Because in the fast-changing world, people and technologies are going to obsolescence faster, Value can dissipate. People have to learn to adjust and indeed overcome change. This is an area of great research potential for Value creation. A VDL mindset helps you anticipate, manage and cope.

This is the time for individuals and companies, societies and governments to start a plan to prevent or pre-empt Value disruption or decrease. We have to learn to cope with this.

Society, governments and businesses have to give serious thought to Value and Value obsolescence and its impact on people

Lessons

Change is inevitable, and the rate of change or transformation is increasing. Thus, Value could dissipate and we have to plan to prevent this if we consider the Value to be important.

Value may not be destroyed but its perception could be reduced or there are newer items that tend to create more Value than the older ones and hence Value of the older system may seem to diminish.

Value Dissipated and VDL

The first principle of VDL suggests that creation of Value is natural and necessary, but Value can also be dissipated or re-emerge.

The third principle states that you have to Create Value for others and they perceive the Value that is being created (and dissipated). And the seventh principle states you must create more Value than is being destroyed. VDL suggests how to face any dissipation of Value.

Chapter 10

Value Re-emerging

VDL is all about Value creation and destruction and sometimes about resurgence or re-emergence of Value.

There are so many examples of companies re-building themselves and re-emerging. There are people who do this.[1] Examples will be given later in this chapter.

Often, we see that Value dies or reduces by a fair amount. James Michener left $20mm for the Michener Center at the University of Texas, but few of the Michener Fellows have read his books and been thrilled by *Poland* or awed by *Hawaii* or shared his joy at finishing his novel in *The Novel*.

His Value exists with old-timers like me. His Value has diminished except to the Fellows at the Michener Center who are paid and enjoy his endowment.

Enid Blyton is forgotten and has been taken over by Rowling and her Harry Potter: Value faded and Value growing. So is P. G. Wodehouse who was read hugely 70 years ago.

Sometimes Value fades but re-emerges just as Winston Churchill did or Indira Gandhi did.

What causes this? Is it a case of need or no need, and re-need? Is it being at the right place at the right time?

The lesson to be learnt is not to give up hope and strive to Create Value in the prospect of coming back or re-succeeding. Keep thinking of how to Create Value.

Michener is an example of creating Value even after his death, but some part of the great Value has faded.

---

[1] https://www.cnbc.com/2015/12/22/four-iconic-brands-that-reinvented-themselves.html

Eisenhower was an also-ran officer at the start of the Second World War but emerged to be a creator of Value and even a greater President. As the Supreme Commander of the Allies, he was self-effacing enough not to be a threat to the other generals and allowed them to Create Value in their own way under an overall plan. He re-emerged during the Second World War as a genius. Eisenhower suggested the Eisenhower matrix where he differentiated between urgent and important tasks. Others have used this to decide between should-do and must-do jobs.

Douglas McArthur and his famous "I shall return" line from 1942 when he was forced to flee the Philippines, and then returned 31 months later to say, "I have returned," to create Value for the Allies.

The point is Value does not always die for ever. It can be revived.

Rebuild yourself, rebuild your portfolio and your being valuable and you can be a person of Value again.

> Value can be reduced or increased for you in different circumstances. VDL helps you go through the highs and the lows. VDL becomes a way of life.

I had a boss who created Value for others and created Value creators. He created Value for suppliers by the art of reverse negotiation, by giving something that the supplier valued (like a long-term contract, or concessions, in return for loyalty.)[2] Most of the future leaders in the company had worked with him or for him. At one time four of us worked for him. Two became chairmen of multi-billion dollar enterprises. The third became an entrepreneur building a niche business in a commodity ridden space, into a billion-dollar enterprise in a few years. He was able to command a price and long-term contracts for his innovative products. The fourth was me, who became a Value creation evangelist!

Other Examples Include

Old Spice was considered an old-fashioned brand when P&G rejuvenated itself for younger people with a new "weird" campaign. Old Spice grew to 28% market share and became number one in the market. It started the "The Man Your Man Could Smell Like" ads.

The current campaign, "Make a Smellmitment," has been viewed more than 31 million times on YouTube in the first six months after its debut. The brand currently has upward of 500 million YouTube subscribers.

Old Spice found a way of rejuvenating itself and becoming a Value creator.

---

[2] https://www.linkedin.com/pulse/supplier-strikes-back-gautam-mahajan/

Kelley's Blue Book for old cars got stymied by internet-based car pricing guides. Kelley's re-built itself by proving its relevance for antique and old cars to millennials. It has almost 30 million page views of its internet avatar.

KFC made its name on chicken (but boned chicken like drumsticks). As market share declined, they learnt that younger people did not prefer boned chicken but chicken sandwiches, nuggets etc. Millennials prefer more snacky meals than three full meals; KFC learnt from this and now have an evolving menu policy to provide more Value. In addition, instead of emphasising chicken days, they are becoming relevant by latching on to Mother's Day etc.

YP could help you create a full strategy on and offline and is the largest player in the field. YP is the new name for the Yellow Pages, yet another iconic brand. "We are there to be an advisor and a consultant and to put a full program together. That can include the print Yellow Pages, but that also includes everywhere a customer needs to be."

Did you know that Nokia used to sell rubber boots and that Shell used to sell seashells?

They reinvented themselves to build cell phones and become an oil giant, respectively.

Shell for example used to import decorated shells in ships otherwise arriving empty from the East, and then built this into a bigger import/export business such as rice, basil and copper from Japan and the East.

When the oil boom started, Shell built the first oil tanker, and traversed the Suez Canal in 1897. They became the Shell transport and trading company. They merged with royal Dutch petroleum to compete with Standard Oil. A great example of re-invention.

Nokia re-invented itself to become the world's number one cell phone company and lost all that when smartphones came in.

IBM in 1984 was the number one PC maker and exited all manufacturing to re-invent itself into an innovator and service provider.

Wipro, the Indian giant software company started as a producer of edible oils and then soaps. They entered IT in 1980, and now the bulk of their revenues come from IT though they are in lighting and traditional businesses.

Lego, Apple, McDonald's, Netflix and Amazon are also examples of Value creators who re-invented themselves.

We have just as many examples of those that destroyed themselves: Enron through poor values, Kodak because of a focus on the here and now and not on the future, Nokia giving up its pre-eminent position in cell phones.

Will retail stores see a Value resurgence, or humans prevail over AI?

Many failures happened because of an inordinate focus on short-term results, and the pursuit of profit, rather than the pursuit of Value creation (though many corporates think of this as profits or shareholder wealth). Conscious Capitalism and others are forcing companies to look at the long-term perspective and to look at creating Value for the entire ecosystem and sustainability.

You can see how Value is created or destroyed. Executives have to learn to use this and Create Value:

1. Have a set of values.
2. Build a culture of looking at the future and grow the self-esteem of executives who use the 6As: awareness (include curiosity), ability, attitude, agility, anticipation and ambidextrousness (read multidextrousness). This requires a mindset change.
3. Look for long-term results. Do not give up hope.
4. Be aware of the future and the unknown, think like a disruptor, avoid disruption.
5. Go from functional thinking to Value creation thinking.

Some of these changes are strategic; some are opportunistic, some as a result of a disruption or a jarring shock.

Keep relevant, change if you see opportunities, grab the Value, re-invent yourself, and either disrupt before competitors do or use the disruption to your advantage to be Value creators. Discontinuous thinking is required. A risk taking, indeed a big risk-taking ability is required.

Kaizen[3] in Japanese is continuous improvement that is the power of accumulated small changes, rather than Western revolutionary change. This is more operational than strategic. Kaizen thinking now includes readings from the Ambidextrous Organisation[4] where they talk about companies exploiting the present and exploring the future. This is creating Value from now and from the future.

The message of VDL is that Value can re-emerge; it can improve after having dissipated. Your VDL mindset will help.

Lessons

These include having a set of values, building a culture of the 6As, look for long-term results and do not give up hope. Value can re-emerge.

Value Re-Emerging and VDL

The first principle of VDL suggests Value creation is necessary for sustained human flourishing. It also suggests going beyond the classic business/social ecosystem. It can

---

[3] Kaizen: The Key to Japan's ... While the articles by Hammer and Imai clearly illustrate the fundamentals of Kaizen.
[4] The Ambidextrous Organization, O'Reilly, C. A., III. & Tuchman, M. L. (2016). HBR, April 2014 Lead and disrupt: How to solve the innovator's dilemma. Stanford Business Press.

be latent Value or Value waiting to happen, which when perceived could provide the basis for greater Value. The fifth principle suggests that you should leverage your potential, learning and creativity. The seventh principle suggests that you must ensure your Value creation is greater than the destructive forces.

Value Definitions

Why do I put this section under Value re-emerging? Consultants and academics in their desire to differentiate themselves bring out new terms for old terms. This in a sense is Value re-emerging.

Price Justification: This is now called Value Proposition but is no different from price justification.

Waterfall of Needs: This is now called the Customer Journey, which I have renamed as the Value journey.

Customer Experience: A beefed up version of customer satisfaction; (Were you satisfied with the experience?).

Customer Success: whose aim is to Create Value.

Value Constellations: This is another way of describing Value Chains. But Value Constellations are non-linear and describe Value captured from a network of multiple points.

By changing the names, people have re-energised the segment.

Where Do We Go from Here?

You have to Create Value as an individual; as a family; as a leader; as an executive; as a company; as a society; as an educationist. Examples have been shown to you. Now think about how you can inculcate a Value creation mindset and how you can Create Value and avoid destruction of Value. Our municipal corporation just dug holes for trees on the footpath. The earth was put on the road, and not next to the hole. A clear example of Value destruction. The diggers and their bosses just did their job of digging holes, with no other thought especially of road safety. With a Value creation mindset (training for these people may have been necessary), this would not have happened. You too must become curious and aware of what is around you, have a great attitude, be agile, anticipatory, able and ambidextrous.

The world is yours. Create Value and see the impact on you and your business. Make it the mantra for running your business and living your life.

Think of how you can Create Value waiting to happen. Think how you can go beyond functional thinking and ask how you can Create Value for the entire ecosystem. Make Value resurge if you are losing out or being disrupted. You will make a difference.

This book in its central theme of VDL has discussed why Value is important in different fields, and why it is a dominant logic. The eight VDL principles are discussed. It has portrayed how Value is created/destroyed in various ecosystems. It tells you to inculcate a Value creation mindset, and that to create true Value for yourself you have to Create Value for others, which includes your employees, partners, customers, society and shareholders. The book discusses Value creation versus Value extraction. It will lead to more Chief Value Creation Officers to encompass Chief Happiness Officers, Chief Customer Officers (Chief Customer Value Creators), Chief Employee Value Creators, and the like.

Just pick and choose what helps you in this book. Each chapter can give you ideas for how to become a Value creator or how to Create Value.

Be a success by creating Value. You can. Good luck!

Index

Page numbers in italics refer to figures; page numbers in bold refer to material in tables and text boxes. VDL = Value Dominant Logic.